D1507488

Performance-Based Medicine

Creating the High Performance Network to Optimize Managed Care Relationships

Performance-Based Medicine

Creating the High Performance Network to Optimize Managed Care Relationships

William J. De Marco, MA, CMC

CRC Press
Taylor & Francis Group
Boca Raton   London   New York

CRC Press is an imprint of the
Taylor & Francis Group, an **informa** business

A PRODUCTIVITY PRESS BOOK

CRC Press
Taylor & Francis Group
6000 Broken Sound Parkway NW, Suite 300
Boca Raton, FL 33487-2742

© 2012 by Taylor & Francis Group, LLC
CRC Press is an imprint of Taylor & Francis Group, an Informa business

No claim to original U.S. Government works

Printed in the United States of America on acid-free paper
Version Date: 20111019

International Standard Book Number: 978-1-4398-1288-4 (Hardback)

Visit the Taylor & Francis Web site at
http://www.taylorandfrancis.com

and the CRC Press Web site at
http://www.crcpress.com

This book represents so many of my teachers and advisors that it is difficult to name all of them as the evolution of thought from my time at Share Health Plan to the present day seems to be a building process. The health reform process proves that what was old is new, and I am grateful to all whose patience and willingness to offer me the opportunity of a lifetime allowed me to devote my life to the improvement of care and its management. It has made my career in health care a dynamic and challenging cause—and I am not done yet!!

To my team here at De Marco & Associates, Warren Surveys, Pendulum Health Care, you are the stable force to be able to build on and I appreciate each day with you.

Most of all, to my wife, Sonny, who stood by me, conducted tours of Share Clinic on weekend open houses, giving her an inside view of what the HMO revolution was about, supported the rough-and-tumble tribulations of building the businesses, and debated the thicker issues of ethics and morality in care delivery and policy while still being my best friend and mother to our son, I offer my undying admiration for her inspiration and saintly patience.

And to our son, Alexander Harrison De Marco, daughter-in-law Rose Catherine De Marco, and grandson Dominic William De Marco, you have renewed my spirit for public service and the values passed on to me by my father and mother. May you also strive for your dreams and achieve greatness without fear and overcome all obstacles with perseverance and prayer.

William John De Marco, M.A., CMC, KHS

Contents

Preface

The interesting thing about performance-based contracting is that as this movement picked up steam in the United States, it also picked up steam abroad. International comparisons of cost and quality astounded most Americans who had been told that the U.S. system is the best care system in the world. In fact, we rank 33rd in quality and number one in cost. Are we getting value? Is there a global shift toward some form of managed care? Are there fundamental changes used during the original transition to managed care that can be used to disrupt the current status quo and therefore improve care and reduce costs? Some of these issues are localized to the region or even the county in which providers work, and some issues are global and are easily transferable to local, regional, and national goals. It certainly goes without saying that all of these issues are thought-provoking and must be addressed now.

One leading debate has to do with information technology. This issue surfaced at the World Economic Forum in January and February, 2009. Kaiser Permanente Chairman and CEO George Halvorson played a leading role in the health care discussions. Halvorson, as chair of the Governors' Meetings for Healthcare, was responsible for presiding over a series of health-related meetings and then presenting a summary to the full body at the World Economic Forum, which started on Wednesday, January 28, and concluded Sunday, February 1, 2009. The theme was "Shaping the Post-Crisis World." Commonly referred to as "Davos," the World Economic Forum brings together 2,500 of the world's leading government, corporate, and community leaders and economists to discuss the challenges the world faces in the years ahead. The forum is organized into Governors' Meetings by industry, with full sessions in which information from those meetings is shared.

Kaiser Permanente's participation at the World Economic Forum came at an auspicious time. U.S. President Barack Obama has advanced health care reform as a key area of focus for his administration. In particular, President Obama's focus on electronic health records aligns with Kaiser Permanente's leadership in health information technology.

KP HealthConnect™ is the world's largest civilian electronic health record. KP HealthConnect has replaced most paper medical records in Kaiser Permanente's 421 medical offices. Kaiser Permanente's 14,000 physicians and 100,000 nurses use the system to care for the organization's 8.6 million members. More than 2 million Kaiser Permanente members use the organization's personal health record, My Health Manager, to schedule appointments, view lab results, communicate via secure e-mail with their physicians, and complete other important tasks.*

Mr. Halvorson offered his thoughts about how data has reshaped Kaiser operations and how many of the original assumptions in terms of leading patients to healing and post-illness evaluation have been changed by looking at data to see whether in fact the comparative effectiveness of treatment protocols could be justified in terms of resources and time. He encouraged other countries to look at their current industries, especially manufacturing, where parts and services are bought from vendors, according to competitor bidding and oftentimes rigid specifications, for production and delivery. He then asked them to look at health care to see whether this business method of purchasing, specifications, and using supply chain management had been addressed, and the answer is no on all counts.

In his book *Health Reform Now,*† Halvorson further explains that businesses that hire vendor integrators (VI) to assemble the key service components of the health care system and define performance guidelines for their purchase will not only help arrive at a better price but will provide a better idea of what demand their workers have in the marketplace that is not being well met by current or proposed services. This offers a chance for collaboration between buyer and seller to have the providers arrange for a new or better service than is currently offered and an opportunity for the purchaser to usher in a new competitor to offer better services in radiology, primary care, orthopedics or neurosurgery, etc. These VIs go further in capturing the attention of individual patients who can now electronically connect with a resource to help navigate patients through the system of coverage and services to optimize use of their health insurance without creating waste with incorrect tests and diagnoses or inconsistencies in obtaining prescriptions and in pay solutions.

This means that the infrastructure needs to connect outside the building of the provider and the employer as well as inside to better coordinate the care at the patient level using electronic appointments, e-prescribing, case management, and disease management follow-up and, finally, establishing an individual

---

* Kaiser Permanente Annual Report, 2009.
† George C. Halvorson, *Health Care Reform Now!: A Prescription for Change* (San Francisco: Jossey-Bass, 2007).

patient plan using local and regional resources to better manage self-care and take personal responsibility for wellness.

This personal responsibility has been long sought after by doctors and politicians as well as employers and insurance companies to try and remove the burden of cost and responsibility and place it onto the shoulders of the consumer. This wellness or health promotion approach has fallen on employers' deaf ears, who think there must be a better way to cut premium costs immediately versus adding costs through weight loss or smoking cessation clinics.

Part of the issue here is the buyers' unwillingness to actually invest in their human capital. Some of this is a matter of patients' beliefs that if they get sick it is covered in full. This risk goes back to the employer and the physician and places the insurer in the middle.

Systems thinker David Senge discusses this in the *Fifth Discipline* as overreliance on the intervener, thereby making the patient guiltless in the transaction.* He or she will blame the doctor for anything that may go wrong with his or her health. Compliance with prescribed methods of treatment is often missing, either because the patient does not clearly understand the issues and misses the points so critical to recovery or simply chooses not to try because he or she believes that the doctors will always fix him or her and the employer will always pay. We will expand upon this later in the book, because systems thinking is the difference between really identifying the problem versus just treating the symptom.

This cycle of care and financing is most likely at the core of many ills today, ills that should have been cured through early detection and awareness of one's own responsibility in the matter.

Disrupting this mindset is a new way of thinking about the business model of medicine of the past. Hospitals and physicians think that the goals of the delivery system are to produce more volume and higher price per patient to make up for the losses experienced due to federal reimbursement cutbacks, reductions in Medicare, reduced fee schedules or capitation from private payers, or, as we continue to find, higher administrative costs for salaried staff, malpractice insurance, practice systems, overhead and upkeep, all of which drive more and more dollars out of the practice. In addition, dollars are driven into the hands of increasing numbers of middle men, all trying to build networks and conduct utilization reviews after the services are provided or simply attempting to reprice and withhold payment due to rules that are unclear in the provider payer agreement.

---

* Peter M. Senge, *The Fifth Discipline* (New York: Currency Doubleday, 1990).

Many of these expenses are paid for with dollars that are reimbursed, but many are not. Many practices are seeing larger cracks in their financial stability as more expenses rise.

Private industry has been disrupting itself for decades, moving from workers to robots, to lean engineering, to outsourcing and insourcing the work needing to be done. In the new model, technology permits more exchange of specifications; standardized transactions are changing work processes; and posttransaction research is being conducted to continue with processes and improve outcomes.

Federal statutes and local regulations combined with cultural trends and social mores change how industry maneuvers and manipulates itself. For example, when fuel standards were changed for trucks versus cars, crossovers and SUVs were created. They were not trucks, although their frames and chassis were built like a truck; instead, they were designated as something new that was not included in the fuel efficiency regulations. People purchased these as oversized station wagons. Private industry knew what they wanted and how to reorganize and change their process points to compete in yet another market area that was not officially a traditional car, truck, or van market. The ability to perfect the processes and results through a series of engineering and human capital changes allowed the vision of what they wanted to actually occur.

Envision the perfect diagnostic-related group (DRG) of acute care and outpatient care being executed in the emergency room (ER), the surgical suite, or the therapy department. What does it look like? How much does it cost? Can we replicate this over and over and still get consistently above-average results?

We have clients who get the Medicare allowable for cataract removal and actually make a margin on all Medicare patients, whereas others cry and complain that Medicare is paying too little so they refuse to do the procedure for Medicare patients. All of this will lead us to the disruption of reimbursement staged over time by Medicare to first modify payment rules of what is allowed and billable to a Resource-Based Value System (RBRVS) that is guided by a conversion factor that varies from area to area. (This RBRVS is a fee schedule with a not-to-exceed number that has been in place since 1987.)

The next reimbursement reform may occur in adjusting this formula, but what seems to really be driving reform is the patient suddenly being exposed to these high-deductible plans where a hernia could be an out-of-pocket event. This makes patients ask, "What did I get for that out-of-pocket cost?" "What will happen the next time I go in?" "Are drugs covered?" "What if I get an infection and have to go to the ER?" "Will I need therapy or radiation?"

All of this is billed in today's marketplace as separate, but as Medicare has already started to prove, building and comparing episodes of care tied to an illness will be a tremendous transition definer to begin to level out reimbursement based on patient needs. As long as the diagnosis is correct, the outcome in terms of inpatient, outpatient, and therapy services should be on budget.

If providers can innovate the process to do all that is needed at less than the budget established, this margin of savings could be harvested by the provider. Right now, this savings goes back to the third-party insurance company or Medicare.

What we will cover in the following pages is how you, as a hospital, health maintenance organization (HMO), physician group, or employer can arrive at an optimized reimbursement cost and coverage access decision that will be attractive to consumers yet fulfill the need for a working margin. And we will help show where quality fits in to all of this. We, as an industry, have done a poor job so far of presenting and selling the case for quality to payers as well as consumers. We may think that we are providing the best care and the top benchmark of medicine, until someone actually views us from the outside and starts looking at the gaps between practice styles and readmissions due to preventable infection rates, and the small but ongoing argument of what is consistently good care versus substandard care.

Most successful quality initiatives begin with leadership, whether in executive management or leading physicians or employers/payers. Seasoned decision makers understand that the vision of what needs to be done must be clear in addition to being able to take stock of the current situation of rules, regulations, resources, staffing, and environmental issues. However, after a couple of victories lost and delays along the way, the luster may tarnish and we may feel that the vision and plans should change. Why? Because we forgot about the reality of where we really are and that to get to the next step requires a solid foundation of the here and now. Once we understand where we are now, building the path between where we are and where we want to be is a transition that must be made.

What we will cover in the following pages will help leaders build a today reality and a tomorrow vision and help them understand the tools available in beginning the initial transitional planning for their organizations.

What we cannot do is check your own honest appraisal of reality. You and your team will need to be oh so honest and say, "Yes, it's a mess, but let's build on what we do have versus continuing to fool ourselves about this concrete reality we breathe daily." Reality changes and this gives all organizations, large and small, an opportunity to compete on strength and core values in a shifting marketplace. Now is the time to determine whether your organization will survive as a status quo operation or will get ahead of the relevant changes and differentiate itself in the market with innovative products, services, and capabilities.

Many organizations will wait to have all the rules and regulations in place and then spend the rest of their existence attempting to beat the rules by manipulating reimbursement or putting on a façade of innovation with little or no substance. Other organizations have built their own plan and vision and hired the biostatisticians, the medical management staff, and the high-level managed care, performance executives, and clinical leadership to create a model that custom fits their market in order to be seamless in their core services, thus giving them an opportunity to invest in innovation and future services long before the competition gets there. Differentiation is a tool to get to innovation by creating a market versus reacting to the market.

Introduction

The introduction of heath reform measures and the promise of a new delivery and financing system have many health plan and provider executives concerned. As always, change is going to take time, and getting prepared will be a principal topic of local budget discussions as final legislation is passed.

We do believe that there will be reform steps in 2011 that will permanently change the landscape of providers by forcing them to not only change codes and charges but also make the sincere effort to create lean engineering of services and elimination of waste. By measuring the gains from removing this waste, providers and health plans may be able to share the harvest of these savings and redeploy these dollars into their respective organizations. At least this is a fundamental promise of the pay-for-performance system integration.

Health plans and insurance companies who have taken to the performance systems quickly to try and tier physicians and hospitals by services believe that they have made a concentrated effort to refer cases to the most qualified and efficient doctors and hospitals. And they have seen considerable success. In doing this, these health plans and insurance companies have created member incentives to use the highest quality providers, have integrated medical management, and, in some cases, have provided incentives for physicians to improve quality and outcomes through shared savings.

It is estimated that if Medicare did these same things today throughout the nation, there would be $400 billion in savings created over 10 years.* This would be enough to pay half of the trillion dollars being discussed to cover not only Medicare but also uninsured and commercial small business enrollees into a public plan. In other words, we do have the money for health reform. We are already spending it but not wisely.

In this transition process to performance-based contracting, many mistakes were made and will continue to be made as we all try to learn and relearn the

---

* *Federal Health Care Cost Containment How in Practice Can This Be Done*, working paper, (Minneapolis: UnitedHealthcare Group, May 2009).

fundamentals of care management and coordination. Together these efforts can improve health status and reduce costs. Without a focused effort of collaboration among patients, payers, and providers, we have a chaotic non-system, badly fragmented, overly expensive, and in some cases dangerous to the patient.

This condemning remark usually draws a response of disbelief from most Americans, who believe that we do have a better care system than anywhere else in the world. That may have been true long ago, but our results, the number of lives lost to preventable illnesses, the cost per procedure, improvement in health status, and the rising number of uninsured tell us that the current system is overly expensive and not equitable for all.

We do not proclaim that pay-for-performance or performance-based contracting will save the day. Unfortunately, our system is so complicated and infected with incremental reforms of past rules that we will need more than pay for performance to improve.

However, unless we get at the key connection between payment and improving the delivery system, we will continue to see money thrown at a delivery system that has insatiable demand.

Dr. Uwe Reinhardt, Princeton professor of economics, points out that our current economic issues of care cost increases are not going to be solved by benefit changes or insurance company premium financing techniques. Rather, much of what an employer pays and an employee pays has become market driven by not only a local economy but rather an international economy where product cost, input of wages, and benefits vary from governments that subsidize their workers benefits versus those that do not.

> Corporations are not human beings. They are legal structures binding together a group of human beings around a common purpose defined in the corporation's charter. These groups of human beings can be categorized into (1) employees, (2) owners (shareholders), and (3) customers. It follows that when a corporation is taxed, it must of necessity pass on that tax to one or the other subgroups of human beings associated with the corporation, or all of them. Now, if the corporation faces a price-elastic demand for its products and must compete with corporations that may not pay the same level of profit taxes, then the corporation will find it difficult to pass on the profit tax to customers in the form of higher prices. Similarly, if the firm's current and potential future owners (shareholders) can easily invest their funds elsewhere in the global capital market (e.g., in developing countries with low-cost labor), then the ability of the corporation to shift the profit tax back to owners in the form of a lower rate of return on capital invested in the corporation is limited as well.

This suggests that labor, the less mobile group of human beings, may well have to absorb the bulk of the profit tax in the form of lower take-home pay.*

It is further misunderstood that employees/patients (now consumers) are less likely to choose the correct physicians or hospital service for a specific malady because they are more concerned that if they do not see the doctor covered by their respective insurance, it will not be paid. Again, an economic decision, not a decision based on a doctor's competency, quality, or outcomes, is made.

Many provider networks became national in scope to accommodate national employers' needs. The distinction in terms of quality and capability was not the big issue here either; rather, the number of doctors and locations in the network was the goal. We now see as time has passed that many of these decisions concerning large, all-encompassing networks were good for the insurance company to gather enrollees and premium revenue but did little to advance the case for quality or quality improvement.

A physician with 10 or 15 patients tied to an insurance company will not make major behavioral changes when asked to by that insurance company, whereas physicians with 50% or more of their practice tied up with that same insurance company will make these changes to their behavior to retain this business, even at discounted rates. In other words, the broader the network, the less likely one doctor would be seeing a dominant proportion of patients that would signal that changing behavior is in his or her best interest.

In this discussion, the concept of behavioral change may mean a minor modification of assuring consistency of process (i.e., statins administered to patient after first heart attack, eye examination of diabetics and other measures that the physician probably follows, just not consistently). In other cases it may be a major change in script writing, a change in better documentation, or doctors who do not move level 2 visits to level 5 visits on half their patients to be able to bill at a higher rate for the time they see a patient.

So, in effect, larger networks that could offer multiple sites do not necessarily save health plans, insurance companies, or employers money because discounted physicians' behaviors are oftentimes changed, but that change is in a direction toward ordering more tests and more procedures on patients as a way to make up lost income by creating more revenue for each patient seen. This may only benefit the patient marginally at best or not at all.

---

* Uwe Reinhardt, Ph.D., Princeton University lecture notes January 2008.

So where is this middle point of care and cost, and how can the doctor and the patient be incentivized to use the correct amount of care at the optimum cost?

There is a floor and a ceiling in most fee schedules but no real incentive to be consistent in actually getting the patient better. In fact, the incentives in our production-based income program now firmly in place in health care encourage us to do more and more production of care.

But why not?

If a physician restrains himself for the sake of cost containment, is he not reducing his own income? Where do those savings go?

In short, superior performance and substandard performance in medicine pay the same. Innovation to improve care is not at all rewarded, and the ongoing discussion between cognitive care and handholding by primary care versus the more procedurally driven care from specialty care continues to drive a wedge between what should be a seamless network of referrals and services.

A reconstruction of the fee schedule system and payment arrangement that truly affected the industry came to pass in the 1990s. When seeking this same set of balances, Dr. William Hasio of Harvard University was asked to develop a resource-based, relative value system of payment for primary and specialty care. Using a multifaceted scoring process that took into consideration complexity, geography, practice costs, and other components, the relative value equation was then adjusted against a conversion factor that converted the cost now paid by Medicare for these patients into a fee schedule that would be adjusted annually depending upon the dollars actually used in the physicians' component of Medicare.

This sounds more complicated than it actually was. When explaining this system to office managers, they were mortified to learn that I had taught my 7-year-old son how to do the equation for a family practice level 1 office call. Most physicians perform a handful of the same procedures daily, so once calculated, billed, and accepted by Medicare, the change was done.

Now we have this large budget of physician services being paid out by Medicare and then apportioned across the nation depending upon multiple adjustments to a classic economic formula. The conversion factors were adjusted to accommodate more dollars for primary care, with the expectation that primary care physicians would do less referral to specialty care if they were paid to actually do the cognitive work of diagnosis. Accommodations for age of physicians and other areas of both patient and physician populations were made with an expectation that this change in reimbursement would help support behavioral changes and make the primary and specialty care continuity more transparent and realistic versus the process of dumping Medicare enrollees onto specialists because primary care doctors could not afford to see them due to low reimbursement.

Chapter 1

Integration and HMOs: How Did We Get This So Wrong?

From the very beginning of the discussions about integration, the examples used were provider-owned entities such as Kaiser, Health Partners, Intermountain, and other health maintenance organizations (HMOs), and all were seen as seamless enterprises able to control price and volume because the owners were actually involved in the production of the product. In effect, HMOs were the very first integrated systems tying together the delivery and financing of care. This binds the patient both in terms of clinical care and affordability, knowing that the insurance plan would always offer the benefits *and* a place to receive those benefits.

This guarantee or covenant of caring is what built HMOs in the early 1970s and drew in thousands of consumers who trusted their physicians and their health plan.

This is totally separate from the current situation where the largest HMOs are not HMOs at all but rather insurance companies who finance care after an accident or illness has occurred. These insurance companies saw HMOs as a product line with preventive services covered and no deductible.

A product with no means to control volume or quality of medical services was produced. This, instead of improving care realigns discounted payment to push down providers' incomes unless providers follow a dizzying array of rules. Many of these rules became so blatant that, in a successful lawsuit against United Health Plans in Chicago, the plaintiff physician proved that he was acting on orders from United, and the judge ruled that this was no longer a contractual relationship but rather one of employee/employer. United Health was accused of practicing medicine. Many suits before and after have tempered the relationship between plan and provider to distance this relationship, but in few cases did the provider network actually understand that if they organized independent of the insurance company they could not only control and negotiate quality standards but also put some of the savings back in their own pocket versus giving it all to the insurance companies.

This provider organization goes by many names, going back to *accountable health organizations* (AHOs), now *accountable care organizations* when we were talking about managed competition. A new entity called *provider sponsored organizations* (PSOs) was promoted to create a way to integrate payment and quality measurement. As plans became larger, hospitals formed increasingly larger cartels to try to bring reimbursement up to a higher level or the HMO would be forced to lose the contract and have no providers and, therefore, no enrollees in a given territory. Many of these cartels, Physician Hospital Organizations (PHOs), and provider networks were subject to antitrust investigation for price fixing and attempting to conspire to force providers to accept terms and conditions that were not beneficial to the community or to the plan.

In all of these variations of integrated systems and integrated delivery networks (IDNs), the thought of somehow creating a structure with negotiating power became the single-minded goal versus actually improving care and rearranging process and outcome.

By removing waste from the system of uncoordinated care and nonfunctional silos of administrative costs, the services could be offered at a lesser price. By reducing the unnecessary services of both inpatient and outpatient care while still assuring that necessary care would be available, providers *and* payers *and* patients would save money and get great care more rapidly.

This goes back to the original HMO concept. The HMO became the reorganizer of services and overlaid some of it specifications and performance measures on top of the traditional payer provider agreements.

Provider-sponsored plans had a natural advantage as we said earlier, because their goal was to remove waste and increase quality. By doing this, the provider and the HMO they owned could sell the benefit plan at a lesser premium than a competing insurance plan. In addition, the original, or as I will call it, the Classic HMO, was organized to then offer more benefits with these savings. Initial savings from covering physical exams and early periodic treatment for infants all paid for the extra benefits offered.

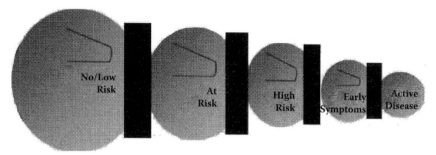

Health is a continuous variable, according to George Isham, MD, Health Partners Medical Director and Chief Health Officer. A person is not simply healthy or sick; there are various degrees of health. The Partners for Better Health program tries to move members along the disease/health continuum, toward lower risk and greater health through prevention.

Figure 1.1 The disease–health continuum. (From George C. Halverson and George J. Isham. *Epidemic of Care: A Call for Safer, Better, and More Accountable Health Care.* **San Francisco: Jossey-Bass, 2003.)**

In effect, prevention cost the plans nothing as long as they could use this patient health status information as a foundation for the case management and coordination of care. This allowed each patient to have an early warning system as they moved from high risk to chronic disease. Everything that the plan could do to prevent this potential high-risk patient to stay out of the high-risk category had to be done (see Figure 1.1). Otherwise, premiums started to climb and soon the high-risk and chronically ill patient population would force the plan out of business because the only remaining patients in the plan had expensive illnesses and it would price itself out of the market.

It all comes down to three large issues that have led us to performance based contracting. They are reimbursement, coordination, and performance.

Reimbursement

The traditional medical practice and hospital makes more money by generating more services for which they can bill. This "production" mentality of creating more and more sophisticated services with admittedly better acuity and precision added to the cost of care. When a fixed priced payment system was introduced, physicians and hospitals both fought it because they did not understand that higher income was usually followed by greater expense. An example follows:

Community-Acquired Pneumonia Story from Intermountain Health System in Salt Lake City, Utah

The community-acquired pneumonia (CAP) Protocol (Figure 1.2) revolved around saving money and saving lives by having physicians get antibiotics to patients quicker. As the proportion of compliant physicians improved, the implementation created positive outcomes, to which the hospital's CEO said, "Show it to me in my budget."

Figure 1.3 shows the real truth, and that is that as complication rates fell the net income from revenue fell.

In simple terms, the complicated patients being seen with respiratory problems and needing to be put on a ventilator and billed as Diagnostic Related Group (DRG) 475 were slowly moving backwards into DRG 89 because they were being caught early and getting antibiotics and being sent home. The problem was that Intermountain was reimbursed $16,400 for DRG 475 for something that generally cost them $15,600. DRG 89, however, cost Intermountain $5,200 to provide but Medicare only reimbursed $4,800. So you can see Intermountain was replacing procedures with a net income gain of $800.00 with procedures that have a $400.00 income loss.

A discussion of these phenomena was presented in the *New York Times* by Reed Abelson some years back. It said that, "We as hospitals and physicians are

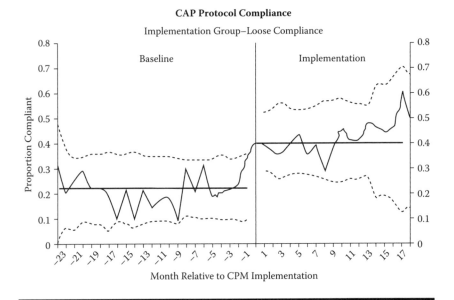

CAP Protocol Compliance

Implementation Group–Loose Compliance

Month Relative to CPM Implementation

Figure 1.2 CAP protocol compliance.

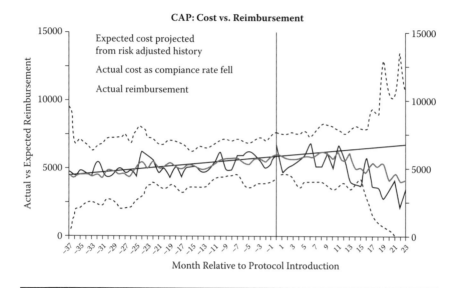

Figure 1.3   CAP: Cost versus reimbursement.

actually rewarded to keep people sick versus get them well because there is more money in keeping them sick."*

This, Dr. Brent James, medical director of Intermountain Health System, believes, was the trigger that started the entire pay for performance movement. Government and private payers are using this argument with employers and patients to prove that the system has problems and will not reform itself.

Well, what can be done?

Figure 1.4 shows how different methods to lower costs affect payment. Reducing units, cases, etc., all can cut costs, but they also cut net income in many cases.

Figure 1.4 also shows the Intermountain experience as 80% of the payments come to them under discount or case rate.

What it says in Figure 1.4 is that the payers are making a large margin on these services because they are not being managed. The more we reengineer our hospitals to be more efficient and effective, the more savings are created for the insurer.

The conclusion one reaches is that the only way that providers are going to survive in the future is to create a carefully structured, shared-risk arrangement with payers or own the payer themselves. That is, if we let insurance companies run the numbers and tell us where our losses are, we are opening the piggy bank of net profit and cash flow to organizations who could create a problem for us.

---

* Reed Abelson, While the U.S. Spends Heavily on Health Care: A Study Faults the Quality, *New York Times*, July 17, 2008.

Improvement to Cost Structure	Payment Mechanism			
	Discounted FFS	Per Case	Per Diem	Shared Risk
Decrease Cost per Unit	↑	↑	↑	↑
Decrease # Units per case				
Decrease other units per case	↓	↑	↑	↑
Decrease LOS (# of days)	↓	↑	↓	↑

Figure 1.4   Impact on net income.

This explains why many integrated systems and hospital-owned HMOs fail. Hospitals need to have data on a product line basis to survive. Not every product line does well because as complications arise so do expenses. These expenses all have an impact on net revenue when connecting them to reimbursement.

Margins between cost and charges were narrower, which required more volume. When that volume was not present the temptation was to increase complex services even though there was not a good clinical rationale to use it.

Many hospitals and physicians continue to fight words like *capitation* and *fixed fee schedules*. They see these as barring them from income to repay their investment in equipment, staff, and training for these sophisticated procedures. This misses the mark as to how performance-based contracting is changing things with a focus on managed care companies and employers seeking to contract for best-in-class services in a given community versus merely contracting with a hospital. Because hospitals have become accustomed to using loss leader services to bring in volume and then cross-subsidizing departments and services to balance their books, the new vision is that each of these services will need to be captured by specialty and department and then negotiated as an Episode Treatment Group (ETG) or Episode Resource Grouping (ERG).

Reimbursement is a key changing factor because of the emphasis on performance and is a critical part of actually developing a high-performance integrated system.

Coordination

Under the new rubric of value-based purchasing, hospitals, physicians, and health plans have new but familiar demands being placed upon them by private and public employers.

Value-based purchasing terminology and conceptual underpinnings come from Professor Walt McClure's prudent buyer program, an early attempt to have employers seek a value chain relationship between care delivery, quality, and cost.

The concept of value-based health care purchasing is that buyers should hold providers of health care accountable for both cost and quality of care.* Value-based purchasing brings together information on the quality of health care, including patient outcomes and health status, with data on the dollar outlays going toward health. It focuses on managing the use of the health care system to reduce inappropriate care and to identify and reward the best-performing providers. This strategy can be contrasted with more limited efforts to negotiate price discounts, which reduce costs but do little to ensure that quality of care is improved.

The key elements of value-based purchasing include the following:

- Contracts spelling out the responsibilities of employers as purchasers with selected insurance, managed care, and hospital and physician groups as suppliers
- Information to support the management of purchasing activities
- Quality management to drive continuous improvements in the process of health care purchasing and in the delivery of health care services
- Incentives to encourage and reward desired practices by providers and consumers
- Education to help employees become better heath care consumers

In a system based on value-based purchasing, employers and other purchasers gather and analyze information on the costs and quality of various competing providers and health plans. They contract selectively with plans or provider organizations based on demonstrated performance or, at the least, proposed approaches for improving performance. Ideally, quality information becomes a factor in the setting of plan prices, and employee contributions vary with each plan's "score," which reflects a combination of quality and cost indicators. In this manner, the best-performing plans and providers are rewarded with greater volume of enrollees or patients.

Performance

Several employer coalitions including those found in Indiana, Colorado, and St. Louis, are tracking and reporting actual versus benchmark performance

---

* Value Based Purchasing as defined by the White House Executive Order, signed by President George Bush, August 8, 2007 and reported by HHS Secretary Leavitt.

on an increasing large sum of patient claims data. They, as purchasers, are beginning to experience the value of consistently above-average execution of care protocols and follow-up. This, along with prevention, health promotion of healthy lifestyles, and the ability to drill down on more and more risk-adjusted data, has made these purchasers able to measure and replicate value in the care continuum.

We are really at the beginning of this data-driven decision making, and for many providers this is an opportunity to negotiate performance guidelines that are simple and follow current patterns of practice. Before this gets very sophisticated and before purchasers suddenly demand elaborate reporting and penalties, it is clear that providers would gain quite a bit of ground and trust from purchasers by stating their current quality goals and projects that are in place, and begin sharing data between purchasers.

Purchasers generally have not only local provider information but also provider information on the competition. Employers and health plans are beginning to compare process outcomes using one or more scales from The Agency for Health Quality and Review (AHQR) or basic Health Employer Data Information Set (HEDIS) reporting.

AHQR has volumes of free tools and reporting guidelines for local communities to set their baselines to begin the process of improvement. National standards can be used for default areas where there is not enough data for a single specialty, but for other procedures and specialties this organization is a vault of useful data. HEDIS is actually the worksheet to get to National Committee on Quality Assurance (NCQA) approval. It is the data that most HMOs and insurance companies and Third Party Administrators (TPAs) use to report utilization to their respective employer clients. Providers who are not aware of this miss a great opportunity to improve communications around process controls and improvement and again regain some level of trust. By following the HMO reporting process, providers finally will begin to see how health plans and insurers are arriving at performance scores. As we said earlier, these scores tie to payment category but soon will dictate whether your provider entity is even able to participate in a high-performance preferred panel. This becomes a market share issue as well as a payment issue, and our experience has proven that payers make mistakes in reporting provider utilization but because the provider is not there to review and correct the error with their own data, the mistake goes unchecked and can cost money, time, and aggravation.

The next chapter will discuss in more depth the performance aspects that go into measurement. Benchmarks, not benefits, are what purchasers are interested in learning about. Employers and even Medicare have all tried to redesign benefits to angle coverage away from the benefit plan in hopes of shaving a few dollars of utilization off the bottom line. These reductions have not always been as successful because the provider that is being used is often the wrong provider or a lower tier provider with less capability in a given discipline or procedure.

Spending more on health care and/or Medicare as a fraction of household income, which is shown in federal budgets, or gross domestic product, is not necessarily inappropriate, because health and health care are normal goods that most people will voluntarily spend more on as income rises.

But a growing body of evidence makes clear that Americans in general are getting or perceive that they are getting relatively little value per dollar of spending for their health care and/or from the Medicare program. Thus, we are spending far more than we need to for what we are getting. Our overall health system's inefficiency is one of the main reasons that 16% of our population has no health insurance at all, and the opportunity cost of the federal government paying its current share of that inefficiency threatens other social priorities over time. It is estimated that over $400 billion in Medicare overpayments and wasteful payments is spent annually. Hence, the urgent need to reduce this low value spending—while creating a value purchasing infrastructure to reduce cost growth in the long run. This is increasingly widely understood.

Chapter 2

Performance Measurement: A Science with No Followers

In other industries, performance-based contracting has been the touchstone for successful response to bidding and procurement going back to the 1940s when World War II produced frantic activity to produce services and goods for the military. As the standards and specifications for everything from helmets to tanks came down from Washington, D.C., government contractors bid on price and quality. This created the platform for a very complicated series of projects surrounding the refinement of specifications based upon feedback from the field as to what was or was not working. This was originally part of the intelligence gathering process that grew to become operations research. It also became a focal point in the engineering sequence as to *why* select specifications were used. This feedback loop was fed back to contractors and reflected in the specifications for the next version of products. Thus, the specific issue of connecting one version of a product to the next was encountered. (Examples: electrical outlets changed, but lighting fixtures did not; a need to upgrade ammunition to reduce cost was met by one contractor, but the development of the rifle was not changed.)

Finally, the entire focus of warfare conditions changed from the snowbound combat of central Europe to the jungle conditions in Korea and Vietnam, and along with these environmental changes in the theaters of operation, internal bidding between specialized low-cost producers of products and innovations began to occur both in terms of field-tested products and in terms of more sophisticated operations research to look at ways to skillfully communicate specifications of the future to several contractors simultaneously. This allowed battle-tested products and methods used to employ these products to be critiqued by the engineers so they could begin to apply new engineering techniques to produce a better solution for the military.

To this day, if you walk into a large defense contractor like Honeywell, customers like Boeing have offices right in the facility so that as specifications change and multiple client needs change, subcontractors see how all the fixtures and outlets connect.

Part of this was, and for most companies still is, research and development and operations management. Much of this as well was simply a survey and response testing of the contractor's curiosity and creativity in being able to deliver on not just a better product but also a better method to use the product successfully in combat or civilian circumstances.

This brought innovation from both the user and the producer of the product. For example, combat uniforms worn today in Desert Storm and Afghanistan are drastically different than what was used in World War II, New Hebrides, or even Vietnam, in both durability and functionality. Today, soldiers are able to carry personal telecommunications devices and upgraded pistols and ammunition, and they wear bullet-stopping armor and goggles for sand storms—all standard issue equipment for the infantry. The use of Global Positioning Satellite (GPS) locators and laser-guided missiles is commonplace today but these were new developments in the Korean conflict era.

These same contractor and purchaser processes were (and still are) used in the manufacturing, automotive, steel, and plastic extrusion industries, from custom-fit needs of a wide group of purchasers and fabricators to nuts and screws and alternative fasteners. Each time parts per thousand were purchased, manufacturers and purchasers counted the rejects—sometimes 5% and sometimes 30%. And somewhere between these percentages a line had to be drawn to clearly indicate what was considered good (acceptable) and bad (unacceptable).

Early on, Edward Deming, Joseph Juran, and others began looking at what were passing grades of good to bad, ranking quality based upon number of defects. The United States first rejected this thought process, so Deming's books were sold overseas. The Japanese, for one, thought this was truly how Americans had built such a prosperous nation, so they first adopted the measurement and performance concept and then engineered various means to reduce rejects by tightening the process design and manufacture. Without too much trouble, the Japanese rebuilt their entire steel manufacturing process around an improved Bessemer process using new technology and up-to-date process points rigidly controlled by charts and a culture whose loyalty was nationalized shortly after

World War II. In the words of Professor Lester Thurow, "the Japanese rebuilt their postwar economy to create new productivity standards and profitable products because they had to."*

Despite successes in the production and costs areas of manufacturing, energy, banking, and other market segments, the health care industry has been slow to respond. We will go into several reasons and examples as to why in the course of this book but, in general, health care's lack of standardization in performance in what was good and what was bad care was missing. For the same price, one could be seen by a good doctor or a bad doctor.

Another reason for this slow response by health care was lack of data. It follows that without guidelines and standards, data is useless, and separating waste from good medicine continued to vary.

Finally, the lack of standardization and data reporting was compounded by the unusual position health care held in most households of being a free or almost free service for which their employer paid. The user or patient was insulated from the economics and could go to a high-priced facility or doctor, and the difference was never felt by the user. The doctor would normally get paid billed charges, or billed charges with a discount, and the employer would shake his head, wondering why costs were rising at a rapid rate. And I want to make this point very clear—it is not that costs are going up that makes Blue Chip companies see red; it is the fact that it is going up so rapidly with little or no explanation as to why. After several thousand employer meetings and interviews with clients, we see that the rising cost is not as important to them as to how fast it is rising. Employers ask, "Please, just tell me what it will be next year and I can budget for it and pass it along in the cost of my product."

So there is no follow-up for performance indicators as long as employers buy benefits that either overemphasize the use of services by offering Cadillac coverage that requires little to be paid by the employee or underemphasize the use of services through exclusions and $5,000 deductibles that create a barrier to receiving needed services. As long as employers can add these costs into goods and services and as long as patients/users are willing to be bystanders in the transaction without seeking out best practices or best outcomes, there is no real emphasis on performance.

However, this is changing. Over the last 5 years, global economics has put a price cap on what companies can charge for their products, so Cadillac benefit plans are being replaced or negotiated away. Consumers are seeing their own money go for drugs and office visits that were heretofore free to them and doctors are being inspected and turned upside down with reporting and compliance rules that require several full-time staff just to track down payments.

---

* Lester Thurow, *The Future of Capitalism* (New York: Penguin Books, 1977).

So what are we doing for performance-based contracting in medicine? How will it work and how will it change? And how will using it improve this system?

The early gurus in health quality would all say that their teacher and mentor is Don Berwick, M.D. Dr. Berwick is undoubtedly the original leader in the quality movement in medicine, helping doctors see that more care is just as bad as less care. Statistics are revealing how patients are becoming sicker with drug-induced diabetes, and we are seeing chronic care and multiple tests changing the course of lives of patients that should have recovered but somehow got sicker or even died, often of a disease or infection other than the one for which they were admitted.

In early 1974, Dr. Berwick began a lonely quest to revolutionize medicine, using quality standards and some engineering principles from Deming and Donabedian. He created the Institute for Healthcare Improvement (IHI), an independent, not-for-profit organization helping to lead the improvement of health care throughout the world. Founded in 1991 and based in Cambridge, Massachusetts, IHI works to accelerate improvement by building the will to change, cultivating promising concepts for improving patient care, and helping health care systems put those ideas into action.

Moving along the IHI timeline (http://about/documents/IHITimeline dec10.www.ihi.org.pdf) inspired additional studies to begin looking at the comparisons of use of health care services by geographic location. Dr. John Wennberg of Dartmouth made a national impact on medical practice and policy through his study of the very wide variations in treatment and outcome for such procedures as prostate treatment. He demonstrated watchful waiting versus surgery every time the diagnosis is confirmed—stating that it should be a patient's choice. This is because the guarantee of health after prostate removal cannot be made and in many cases the patient is better off waiting until the diseased prostate is an absolute threat to his life or the health of other organs. His work and the work of his graduate students on mapping care outcomes by state, county, and, in some case, census track, offers insight into just how different M.D.s are trained school by school and also how difficult it is to understand the words *standards of care*.

"Huge inefficiencies in the U.S. health care system are hamstringing the nation's ability to expand access to care," according to a new analysis of Medicare spending by researchers of the Dartmouth Atlas Project (Figure 2.1), published February 26, 2009, in the *New England Journal of Medicine*.* Many experts

---

* E.S. Fisher, J.P. Bynum, J.S. Skinner, Healthcare "Slowing the Growth of Health Care Costs – Lessons from Regional Variation," *New England Journal of Medicine*, February 26, 2009.

Inconsistent Treatment

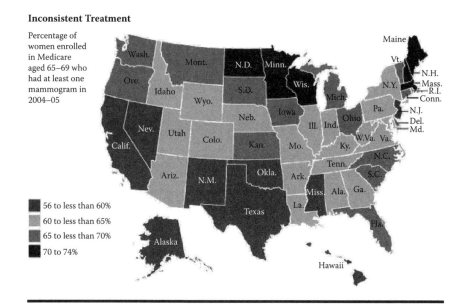

Percentage of women enrolled in Medicare aged 65–69 who had at least one mammogram in 2004–05

■ 56 to less than 60%
▨ 60 to less than 65%
▨ 65 to less than 70%
■ 70 to 74%

Figure 2.1   Percentage of women enrolled in Medicare aged 65–69 who had at least one mammogram in 2004–2005. (From Robert Wood Johnson Foundation and the Dartmouth Atlas Project. www.dartmouthatlas.org.)

have blamed the growth in spending on advances in medical technology. But the differences in growth rates across regions show that advancing technology is only part of the explanation. Patients in high-cost regions have access to the same technology as those in low-cost regions, and those in low-cost regions are not deprived of needed care. On the contrary, the researchers note that care is often better in low-cost areas. The authors argue that the differences in growth are largely due to discretionary decisions by physicians that are influenced by the local availability of hospital beds, imaging centers, and other resources and a payment system that rewards growth and higher utilization.

For example, Figure 2.2 shows per capita Medicare spending from 1992 through 2006 in five U.S. hospital-referral regions. Overall Medicare spending, adjusted for general price inflation, rose by 3.5% annually. But there was considerable variation among regions. Per capita, inflation-adjusted spending in Miami grew at an annual rate of 5.0%, compared with just 2.3% in Salem, Oregon, and 2.4% in San Francisco. In dollar terms, the growth in per capita Medicare expenditures between 1992 and 2006 in Miami ($8,085) was nearly equal to the level of 2006 expenditures in San Francisco ($8,331). A total of 26 hospital-referral regions (including Dallas) had more rapid spending growth than Miami, and 18 regions (including San Diego) had slower growth than Salem.

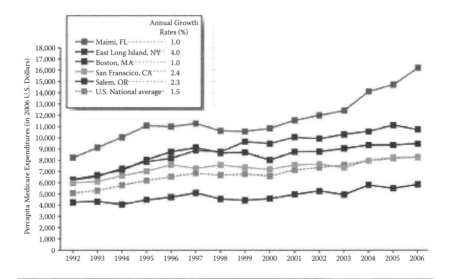

Figure 2.2 **Annual growth rates of per capita Medicare spending in five U.S. hospital-referral regions, 1992–2006. Data are in 2006 dollars and were adjusted with the use of the gross domestic product implicit price deflator (From the *Economic Report of the President*, 2008. http://www.gpoaccess. gov/eop/index.html). For age, sex, and race. (Data from the Dartmouth Atlas Project.)**

Over time, the recognition that perhaps the quality of care in the United States was so variable that standardization was going to be impossible was discussed by Medicare and other payers.

In the slow process of collecting Medicare claims and outcomes data from Medicare Advantage Health Plans, these demonstration projects were considered on the cutting edge. Meanwhile, the Institute of Medicine Projects on Chasm of Care began to point the way to a series of serious problems that affected both managed care and non-managed care populations in the areas of consistency of care and deviations for recommended quality measures. It also compared the U.S. system to those abroad and factually stated that the current course of reimbursement without recognition of outcome was truly without any precedent in any other country. Further, it certainly was not consistent with other industries in America where vendors were required to meet or exceed measures of performance and standards of practice before being allowed to deliver services to their clients—in this case, patients.

In 1996, the Institute of Medicine (IOM) launched a concerted, ongoing effort focused on assessing and improving the nation's quality of care, which is now in its third phase. This phase built on an intensive review of the literature conducted by RAND to understand the scope of this issue.* A framework was established that defined the nature of the problem as one of overuse, misuse, and underuse of health care services.† More specifically, the report *Ensuring Quality Cancer Care* (1999) documented the wide gulf that exists between ideal and current practice.‡

Furthering Measurement and Informed Purchasing

The IOM report, *Leadership by Example: Coordinating Government Roles in Improving Health Care Quality* (2002), encouraged the federal government to take full advantage of its influential position as purchaser, regulator, and provider of health care services to determine quality for the health care sector. The vision for each of these distinct federal roles is very much in concert with ideas laid out in the Quality Chasm report.§

Other efforts in this area include *Envisioning the National Healthcare Quality Report* (2001)¶ and *Guidance for the National Healthcare Disparities Report* (2002),** both of which were developed in accordance with a theme to not only point out the shortcomings of the delivery system but to assist in formulating basic principles for changing and improving this system of care. We have discussed this in many of our presentations and are always surprised to find out how many hospital executives and physicians have *not* read these reports even though they are the daily diet of most employers, employer coalitions, and insurance companies. This perhaps best explains a chasm between some health care executives not knowing as much about the problem areas as do the government and purchasers of their services.

So, again, the audience seems to be turning its back on the basis for performance reengineering. The gap continues to widen as many published reports

---

* Committee on Quality of Health Care in America, *Crossing the Quality Chasm: A New Health System for the 21st Century* (National Academies Press, 2001).

† Ibid.

‡ Maria Hewitt, Joseph V. Simone. *Ensuring Quality Cancer Care* (National Academies Press; 1999).

§ Janet M. Corrigan, Jill Eden, and Barbara M. Smith, Editors. *Leadership by Example: Coordinating Government Roles in Improving Health Care Quality* (Washington, D.C.: National Academies Press, 2003).

¶ Margarita P. Hurtado, Elaine K. Swift, Janet M. Corrigan, Editors, *Envisioning the National Healthcare Quality Report – 2001* Committee on the National Quality Report on Health Care Delivery, Board of Health Care Services (Washington, D.C.: Institute of Medicine, 2001).

** Elaine K. Swift, Editor, Guidance for the National Healthcare Disparities Report, Committee on Guidance for Designing a National Healthcare Disparities Report (Washington, D.C.: National Academies Press, 2002).

on measures indicate that hospital care standards are diminishing while costs continue to rise.

Probably the most publicized issue on performance measurement and its application was a demo conducted several years ago with Premier Hospital Systems and the government's Medicare population. This went beyond the formation of measures as the government borrowed measures used by several existing agencies and organizations to remain consistent with some practice and acute care tracking already in place. However, it went to the next level of actually changing reimbursement. We will talk further about reimbursement in the next chapter.

Getting back to quality measures, if we accept this body of reports and research, we can adopt the definition of *quality* and link this into performance to say: "The degree to which health services for individuals and populations increase the likelihood of desired health outcomes that are consistent with current professional knowledge."

As we speak, the entire wealth of this knowledge, along with government and provider data from the demonstration projects now in their fourth year, all point to a more detailed system of measurement, specific point values, and scoring based on quality and cost. This area of value-based purchasing is being promoted to employers as a means to require more quality and safety data being reported by their carriers and managed care companies, which are then offered to their employees. This is the statement of qualification to bid discussed earlier. On the hospital and physician side, it requires that data be forthcoming for specific procedures. The value-based purchasing recommendations by Medicare, the Physician Quality Review System (PQRS), and other practice-level reporting requirements all help the government to centralize a database on practices and patterns. This also enables doctors and hospitals to earn extra dollars and a pay-for-information program before wading into a true pay-for-performance system of care. To achieve these scores, health plan providers and employers need to be able to work together to identify gaps in the care process. These gaps can represent small consumer satisfaction issues like wait times for appointments but can also uncover large gaps in patient care such as not offering a statin after a heart attack, taking magnetic resonance images before X-rays for back and leg pain, and not identifying *Helicobacter pylori* with a simple viral test before prescribing a drug for ulcers—all ways to better coordinate care through prevention and or building the capability for a precise diagnosis.

Coordinating primary to specialty referrals and necessary in-hospital stays are all things employers and insurance companies are familiar with, but they often lack the data or the medical expertise for proper follow-up. Anticipating a patient's therapy needs and following up on an admission or even preventing an admission through home care and outpatient therapy are all avenues to help save utilization and bring down premium costs. Offering this coordination of services has always been considered "backed in" to the product, but we have discovered through the Institute of Medicine studies that there is a large chasm between good and bad care, as Figure 2.2 shows. And this chasm is widening as annual analysis shows that the number of lower quartile hospitals have a greater death rate than the top quartile hospitals in just about every measure. It is further estimated that if all hospitals practiced with the same level of performance as the top quartile of hospitals nationally, not only would disease management and quality be performed more efficiently but costs and waste would be taken out of the system to the point that savings could pay for health care coverage for every man, woman, and child.

Chapter 3

Reimbursement: From Fee for Service to Risk Adjusters

One of the missing elements for providers and managed care is how to carry the guidelines and performance measures into reality.

As we discussed in the previous chapter, there is a long-term quest for quality indicators tied to a point evaluation process that eventually leads to how providers are reimbursed. To get the data to determine that the care being rendered is actually as good if not better than average, providers need to share data with the health plans/payers to create a baseline for measurement. If not, they will suffer the consequence of failed pay-for-performance (P4P) plans elsewhere when national or contrived guidelines are implemented in a community that may not have all the resources or expertise to accurately determine these same proficiency standards.

The government discovered that when trying to collect basic information in their Physician Quality Reporting System (PQRS) program, formerly called PQRI until January 1, 2011, they had much greater participation when they paid doctors for using "G" codes instead of just asking for them voluntarily. This has also been true in commercial managed care circles where paid claims data told most of the story about utilization and practice patterns, but many of the more chronic illness scenarios needed medical chart review to verify that the multiple causes of an episode of care were fed into a single receptacle of data and

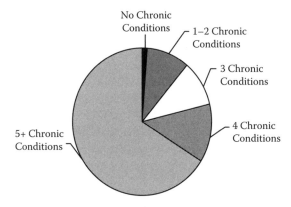

Figure 3.1 Percentage of Medicare spending by number of chronic conditions. (From George C. Halvorson, *Health Care Will Not Reform Itself.* Boca Raton, FL: CRC Press, 2009, p. 31.)

then merged with patient population databases to determine what, if anything, needed to change in the treatment guidelines and whether they were doing a good job at linking the conditions and costs into this data point.

Figure 3.1 shows that spending for a patient with one chronic condition is only a few times the average cost of patients with no chronic conditions, but spending is 25 times greater with five or more chronic conditions.

This flaw in the current system creates opportunities for distorted data and creates openings for fraud and abuse of billing. Linking payment to uncoordinated care will not change anything, but linking payment to coordinated care shows managed care companies, insurance companies, and others the value of a grouped inpatient and outpatient episode of care that brings in pharmacy, therapy costs, and other critical care costs to match up with the diagnosis. They compare this to other patients with similar illnesses and comorbidities, same age groups, and gender, to determine what the expected outcome will be for this care, this diagnosis, and this group of patients and, therefore, what the cost should be for this disease grouping.

When comparing the actual budget for services against the projected budget of services, we find gaps. Sometimes these gaps are due to a fee schedule payout at a higher or lower rate and sometimes we find gaps in under- and overtreatment. As we pointed out earlier, variations in geography and practice style may account for large gaps in care outcome and costs. However, the missing link continues to be between efficacy and the payment. Without these areas linked, the health care delivery system and the insurance system cannot change in a meaningful and measurable way.

So, let's talk about reimbursement. We have always assumed that everyone knows about Medicare and its payment origins, but we find in our client work that this is often a step we need to go back and review.

Where Does the Money Come from for Public Reimbursement of Medicare Claims?

■ Medicare financing and future projections: Medicare Parts A, B, and D (beginning in 2006) are financed differently. Payroll taxes paid by workers and employers finance the majority of Part A (the Hospital Insurance [HI] Trust Fund). The Part B Supplementary Medical Insurance (SMI) Trust Fund is financed by a combination of beneficiary premiums (24%) and general tax revenues (most of the remainder).

■ General revenue makes up roughly three quarters of revenues for Part B and (beginning in 2006) Part D.

■ In total, Medicare revenue in FY2007 came mostly from general revenue (41%), payroll taxes (40%), and beneficiary premiums (11%). According to the Medicare Board of Trustees' 2006 intermediate assumptions, total Part A spending is expected to exceed income in 2012, and the HI Trust Fund reserves are projected to be exhausted by 2020. Spending for Part B services, however, are now rising faster than spending for Part A services.*

■ The aging of the Baby Boom generation, a reduction in the ratio of workers to beneficiaries, and other demographic and economic factors will likely play a role in the debate over additional changes in Medicare's financing in the coming years. With the aging of the population and expected increases in overall health care costs, Medicare spending is projected to grow at a rate significantly higher than that of the overall economy.

■ Between 2000 and 2030, Medicare's share of the gross domestic product is estimated to triple from 2.3 to 6.8%. The addition of the prescription drug benefit in 2006 accounts for about one third of the increase.

Global Implications of Rising Costs: Why Raising Fees Is No Longer an Option

Why is this so important to understand? The answer goes beyond our national concerns. It now threatens the global economy within which most industries operate.

Maggie Maher, author of *Profit Driven Medicine*, points out in her notes from an interview with Peter Orszag, then-director of Office of Management

---

* General Accounting Office (GAO) Annual Report on Medicare 2009.

and Budget (OMB) and now advisor to the White House on health care economics, "It is not credit famine, the long-term price of energy, competition from China, the loss of jobs overseas, or even a surfeit of Chrysler SUVs. It is," Orszag declared in October 2008, "the nation's looming fiscal gap—*which is driven primarily by rising health care costs.*" "Healthcare inflation cannot be ignored," Orszag added, because "If we fail to put the nation on a sounder fiscal course, we will ultimately reach a point where investors [will] lose confidence and no longer be as willing to purchase Treasury debt at anything but exorbitant interest rates."*

Today, investors outside the United States hold $2.74 trillion of treasuries, or 52% of the $5.22 trillion in debt that the United States has issued. But now foreign buying of our treasuries is falling. And, as Orszag has explained elsewhere, if we have to pay "exorbitant interest rates" to persuade foreign investors to continue buying our treasuries, "over time, foreign investors would claim larger and larger shares of the nation's output and fewer resources would be available for domestic consumption."† Put simply, our standard of living would fall.

Moreover, unlike spending to repair bridges, strengthen schools, or protect the environment, *Orszag suggests that the "excess" growth in health care spending is not adding to the wealth—or the health—of the nation.* "The gains from higher spending are not clear," the Congressional Budget Office noted recently. "Substantial evidence exists that more expensive care does not always mean higher-quality care."‡

Orszag made it clear. "Rising health care costs and their consequences for Medicare and Medicaid constitute the nation's central fiscal challenge." There is so much "excess" in our health care system that, Orszag observes, "there are opportunities to reduce costs without impairing health outcomes overall."§ Less costly care does not mean lower quality care. We can provide good, comprehensive care for everyone.

So, as reimbursement goes to cost and cost goes to reimbursement, we see that a necessary change is inevitable to either continue to see reduced fee schedules to physicians and hospitals or develop an alternative to cutting fees and try to achieve more and better care with an existing fee schedule or a fee schedule plus a performance payment.

---

* Maggie Mahar, *The Truth about Spiraling Health Care Prices in the U.S., Part II* Interview with Peter Orszag, Congressional Budget Office Director, November 3, 2008 from the blog, www.healthbeatblog.org.

† Ibid.

‡ Ibid.

§ Ibid.

Reimbursement changes according to performance: whereas superior performance is rewarded with better fees and market share, substandard performance can represent a takeaway of dollars and potentially of market share.

More than a Trend

In reviewing the data from Premier as well as the Integrated Healthcare Association (IHA) information, it is of interest to point out that as the lower tier or quartile of performers examines the differences between their organization and those in the top tier, there is a decided change in the physician and/or hospital organization to begin moving toward the higher performance standard. This is without discussion of income or investment in infrastructure but is more a move toward recognition that the health care provider is, in fact, a top-tier provider.

In terms of employers, we are finding that the use of tiering today is limited with only about 5% of employers using it. However, some 44% are now considering it based upon an employee benefit survey conducted by Wyatt.*

On August 17, 2009, *The Wall Street Journal* pointed out that pay for performance was integral to the entire health care reform process. In addition, the Medicaid public programs are involved with pay for performance in several states. It is estimated some 25% of Medicaid programs are now using pay for performance.

As these changes occur, more sophisticated data capture reporting, and analysis requirements are demanded by pay for performance. This is consistent with both the Bridges to Excellence and Leapfrog programs that want to reward and emphasize more use of information technology. It also points out the opportunity for providers to develop their own dashboard for decision making into the future.[†]

We believe that this will continue and is a permanent change that will keep happening.

The Current Status of P4P

We estimate that there are approximately 300 programs of varying levels of success now in process or implemented in the United States. We will discuss international pay-for-performance efforts in future chapters.

---

* Wyatt Annual Report to Employees, 2009.
† www.leapfroggroup.org.

Approximately one third of these programs are targeted to hospitals, specifically the Leapfrog program. But many of these organizations indicate that they have chosen a handful of guidelines with which to start. In other words, to try to launch a pay-for-performance program for all areas has been set aside by almost all organizations in an attempt to gradually build upon successes in managing those "gaps" between actual and projected utilization and cost.

As would be expected, there are great variations in organizations that are sponsoring these programs. Some include provider enterprises as well as investor groups. We also have vendor organizations that are starting to sponsor many of these pay-for-performance programs. Several employer coalitions are moving forward in obtaining the proper measurement systems and metrics and developing reward systems in conjunction with their vendors or with provider organizations within their community. We believe that this collaborative approach offers the greatest opportunity for change in any region or single marketplace.

We believe that the Centers for Medicare and Medicaid Services (CMS) organization will continue to be a major market driver in developing new programs and even reimbursement calculations for the pay-for-performance system as well as for gain sharing.

As the increase for demands for both quality and value point to more discussion about efficiency and effectiveness, we envision a number of measures will be modified and/or eliminated over the coming years. Physicians and hospitals will find a better way to measure and report on improved metrics and long-term savings.

At the present time, all P4P programs are measuring process points (i.e., the ability to change the process of delivering care or administrative services versus evidence based outcomes), and as more data is required, there will be more discussion on evidence-based outcomes.

What we find overall is that as physicians and hospitals envision their participation in the pay-for-performance arena, information technology will be enhanced at the practice, hospital, and perhaps even employer and insurance levels. More "meaningful use" legislation will dictate that these types of reporting, analysis, and billing systems must be designed on an open architecture basis versus the current tradition of developing closed architecture data receptacles.

As one can imagine, the concept of developing performance measures and quality outcomes eventually leads providers, payers, and consumers to begin looking at performance in an entirely new light. Pendulum Healthcare and De Marco and Associates have underscored the use of performance-based contracting (PBC) for the last 10 years and have invented this concept out of our experience in developing health plans. This would provide additional tools and services that would enable both the consumer and the provider to judge their overall effectiveness in care management. What we find is that performance-based contracting includes pay for performance but also an ongoing quality improvement process. The quality improvement process means that a feedback loop comes to the providers and to the payers in an attempt to modify or improve upon measurements on an ongoing basis.

This is why we use the word *guideline* more than *standard*. The use of the word standard assumes that it is a static measurement and will not change in the future. As we all know, quality will change as time goes on and new technology, new procedures, and new payment opportunities arise.

In addition to quality improvement, we see a role for disease management. Disease management continues to broaden itself beyond the telephonic review of patients on a case-by-case basis to really become more of a system involving the front end of the delivery system, where patients are brought into the system, diagnosed, identified in terms of data and health status, through to the far end of the system as patients are discharged from the inpatient sector or are followed as a result of a primary to specialty care referral for a chronic illness.

Also, the use of informatics at a more sophisticated level will be the outcome of a successful performance-based contracting strategy. It is interesting to note that in presenting alongside of the Premier Hospital president in Philadelphia some years ago, we were asked what kind of data system is ideal for pay for performance. The initial Premier program actually used simple Excel spreadsheets to first start capturing data from different departments as part of a gap analysis to eventually design their own system. Many of these tools are available on www.Premierinc.com. Examples can be seen in terms of quality reporting from the Agency for Health Research and Quality (AHRQ).

In addition to informatics, private payer issues need to be taken into consideration. Once hospitals or physicians begin this process, it will become clear that they need to have an understanding of who their customers are. That is, most information in provider billing circles is collected against four buckets. They are Blue Cross/Blue Shield, self-pay, Medicare, and Medicaid. This is not adequate for pay for performance, especially when working with payers of varying benefits, patient populations, and overall costs. What private payers are looking for is hospitals and physicians who are, in conjunction with an insurer or directly with an employer, able to identify specific quality attributes for their institution or outpatient service programs. Private payers have a dizzying array of options— from large, self-funded groups to small employers who are desperately trying to find ways to develop a better understanding of where their employees should go for care.

This leads us to the discussion of tiering and the fact that top-tier, second-tier, and perhaps third-tier providers are eventually designed as part of the benefit program provided by private payers or managed care companies to provide incentives for their enrollees to use the best provider possible for a specific benefit or disease.

Private payer needs are reflected in many of the new managed care contracts. These contracts are essentially provider management organizations in most areas. With the exception of provider-sponsored plans, where the providers have ownership and control over the production of medical services, most insurance companies are mere financing mechanisms. Managed care enterprises are keeping score of the utilization as well as the quality of providers that are attached to their various products and services sold to private payers. As managed care continues to lead this pay-for-performance-based contracting strategy, it is important to note that the new products managed care companies have will continue to force physicians and hospitals to use new info-tech and new product definitions that will eventually change the way provider organizations contract with managed care enterprises.

This brings us to the central focus of managed care and its medical management component and pay for performance and its medical management component. As employers mature in their understanding of and buying benchmarks and not just benefits, they are starting to develop specifications for medical management, In addition, employers are starting to follow the value based purchasing requirements set forth by CMS for both hospitals and various payers.

Although as we speak to the enforcement of these specifications and even the intent of the request for proposals from managed care and/or providers, its response has been limited. We see this as being something that will, over time, require more attention by both providers and payers as consumers begin asking more questions about where the top-performing physicians and hospital services reside.

We therefore must start to look at performance-based contracting as the next step in pay for performance. Performance-based contracting is similar to pay for performance in its basic concepts. However, rather than focusing exclusively on a handful of managed care contracts, performance-based contracting requires that the entire organization begin to use this performance data within the hospital or physician organization to make decisions on improving processes and also creating new efficiencies through the use of technology or improved clinical skill.

Payment in exchange for this superior effort can be harvested through select contracts with managed care organizations; however, Medicare, Medicaid, private payers, and small business coalitions are all moving in the direction of performance pay. This means that 80–90% of the income for your physician, hospital, or provider enterprise could come from a contract based on performance over the coming years.

Managed care companies continue to refine their abilities to extract information on a patient, provider, and geographic/location specific basis. What this means is that as a hospital emerges as a top performer for obstetrics/gynecology or for cancer, there may be a preferred contract with savings introduced to that particular facility, whereas another facility across town may have the best services for heart or for orthopedics and may receive a preferred contract for these. This gives the health plan an opportunity to create centers of excellence directly tied to performance and requires the physicians and hospitals to develop not only a single department but an external support network of transitional services for management, therapy, prescription drugs, ongoing specialty referrals, and other therapies that may not be part of their current work.

Envision, if you will, these virtual network organizations as specialty independent practice associations (IPAs) comprised of both professional and support services. These accountable health organizations (AHOs) have been discussed for two decades as a potential opportunity for payers and providers to work together in developing an improved outcome for specific diagnoses, and now the reform bill has created the incentive for accountable care organizations (ACOs) to share in savings with Medicare through the Medicare Shared Savings Program.

The challenge for hospitals and physicians will be to selectively identify *International Classification of Diseases* (10th edition; ICD-10) codes and other services that will fit into this grouping of services to be delivered to patients based upon specific diagnosis and health status of the patient. This means that cross-subsidizing departments by specialty for inpatient and outpatient services may no longer be possible. Each ledger will need to be a stand-alone ledger with volume and pricing that enables this AHO/ACO to operate in conjunction with both payers and providers in a given community.

How Much Reimbursement Does It Take to Change Behavior?

One of the problems with estimating savings and pay levels has been the amount of money set aside in the performance range pool. A 2% payment, as under some models, may be a large dollar amount for a hospital whose entire margin may be 2% but represents a smaller sum to practicing primary care doctors. Specialty care will first consider what the patient volume is and this number will be calculated against it. Medicare has had some successes because Medicare payments often represent 30–40% of a specialty physician's bottom line, but other private payers, who may have only 10–12% of the payment flow to a specialty practice would have a hard time establishing a reason to change behavior.

This can also mean that specialists would need to be grouped either physically or virtually through a medical home or group without walls concept and have their baseline and performance standards organized by their own Management Services Organization (MSO) or the health plan's billing and payment resources. Making a group incentive has proven to be more effective than a single physician pay-for-performance incentive.

Primary care has also been elusive in its participation, partly because each health plan has had separate and, in some areas, conflicting data points that were required to be paid, whereas other, smaller practices had so few patients from payers that an incentive of less than 10% was questioned as being worth changing behavior.

Will Gain Sharing and P4P Together Represent Enough Dollars to Shift the Behavior of Specialists?

An area that has been of interest to specialists is how to connect the pay-for-performance negotiated rates to a gain-sharing formula with the hospital. This means a savings to the hospitals for following physician-developed guidelines for surgery process improvement and outcomes. A direct monetary reward is paid by CMS in addition to the pay-for-performance reward offered by the health plan. Examples would include readmission rate reductions, an especially sensitive area, with "never events" being enforced by Medicare and many larger private payers.

Gain sharing has several added dimensions to it, not the least of which is the legal issues that require both a standard of care and carefully managed use of some equipment and drugs. According to the law firm of McDermott, Will, & Emery* "The Centers for Medicare and Medicaid Services (CMS) recognizes that P4P and gainsharing programs can be beneficial to providers, payers and beneficiaries. In order to encourage the development of performance improvement and cost savings programs, the proposed 2009 Medicare Physician Fee Schedule (PFS) regulation, 73 FR 38502, creates an exception to the Stark Law specifically tailored to these programs.

CMS proposes an exception that covers "incentive payment" and "shared savings" programs. Incentive payment programs are programs such as P4P and quality-based purchasing programs that create financial incentives for physicians to improve the quality of patient care. Shared savings programs are programs such as gain-sharing programs that provide financial incentives to physicians to reduce the cost of patient care in the form of a share of such savings. In the proposed FY2009 Inpatient Prospective Payment System (IPPS) rule, CMS

---

* McDermott, Will, & Emery, press release June 2009.

solicited comments regarding an exception to the Stark Law that would cover gain-sharing arrangements. CMS now believes that it needs to provide a broader exception that covers additional types of incentive programs.

The exception included in the proposed PFS closely resembles the model of gain-sharing programs originally developed by Goodroe Consulting and approved by the Office of Inspector General (OIG) in a series of advisory opinions addressing Civil Monetary Penalty (CMP) and anti-kickback concerns. The OIG advisory opinions concluded that the gain-sharing arrangements violated both the CMP and (assuming the requisite intent) the anti-kickback statutes but that the OIG would not impose sanctions on the programs because they included specific safeguards that would limit the risk of abuses that the statutes are intended to prevent. The primary difference between the proposed rule and the OIG-approved programs is that the proposed rule covers both P4P (as "incentive payment programs") and gain-sharing arrangements (as "shared savings programs"). CMS proposes a single set of requirements that covers both types of programs because CMS believes that many programs are likely to include both quality and cost measures. However, CMS recognizes that the different types of programs present different risks of program and patient abuse.*

The history of this concept and the discussion of the Goodroe Consulting exemption can be found at the OIG website or Goodroe Consulting website but basically necessitates a formal billing by hospitals and written contracts between participating physicians and the hospitals or a third-party entity set up as the "scorekeeper" in these transactions. What is not clear are the Stark rules on kickbacks, and we refer providers and health plans to seek their legal counsel on this or to search the McDermott, Will, & Emery website for the July 10, 2008, memo at http://www.mwe.com.†

Primary Care and the Medical Home? A Good Organizational Model of Performance-Based Contracting?

We continue to see primary care provider (PCP) groups forming into actual bricks-and-mortar medical homes but also see the evolution of virtual networks surrounding specific disease groupings. Some of these may have large followings of senior populations and may, therefore, associate with multispecialty networks of geriatric services.

---

* McDermott, Will & Emery, press release June 2009.
† *CMS Includes Additional Stark Proposals in IPPS Proposed Rule*, McDermott, Will & Emery website, www.mwe.com, April 25, 2008; *Proposed Stark Exceptions Covers Pay-for-Performance & Gainsharing Programs*, McDermott, Will & Emery website, www.mwe.com, July 10, 2008.

The first such medical home emerged as a pediatric network offering services from surgical care to infant and newborn counseling. Payment to a medical home for all these services can be done on a global basis by service grouping and diagnosis or can be done on a subcapitated basis as primary care in a larger grouping.

Chapter 4

Early Pay for Performance

The early pay-for-performance (P4P) agreements—Mount Sinai 1977, Health Ways 1978, and CIGNA 1980, along with Medicare's early 2006 demo projections—all had flaws, as do the current Leapfrog and Bridges concepts.

Pay for performance was actually used by health maintenance organizations (HMOs) and some hospitals as early as the mid-1970s when the expansion of capitation created an opportunity for doctors and hospitals to benefit financially by improving effectiveness of care and taking unneeded costs out of the system. Early pay-for-performance discussions centered around financial rewards as well as recognition for nonclinical improvement.

The experiment at Mount Sinai Hospital in Los Angeles began in 1979.* There was a problem with referrals and documentation between primary and specialty care. Incomplete notes from referring primary care providers (PCPs) forced duplicate testing. This, in turn created additional costs to be forced into the system to make up for this poor documentation. In an effort to set a standard and use this gap as a learning opportunity, specialty physicians rated the primary care referral on completeness, usability, insights, and other clarifying points found on the written referral. This rating earned points for the physician. In a "turnabout is fair play" effort to keep things balanced, PCPs then rated the specialist referral back to the PCP once the episode or diagnosis was confirmed.

---

* Joel Levinson, MD, addressing the Group Health Association of America meeting, June 3, 1979, Palm Springs, CA.

The specialist also earned points that were accumulated quarterly and exchanged for payment based upon estimated savings. This was then paid by the medical center out of their global capitation from the HMOs.

In 1981, CIGNA, owner of several medical groups in Arizona, created a pilot project in their Phoenix Medical Group. They wanted to study the efficiency of wait times as well as document the proficiency of getting the right diagnosis the first time out. The medical director and the insurance company (who was paying extra for misdiagnoses, readmissions, and customer loss because of wait times) were both concerned with these issues. Point values were assigned based upon the importance of the issue, and dollars were set aside for those groups or departments that made improvements. This shows that group reward of a specialty may work better for the insurance company versus individual rewards. The reason, according to the medical director, is that insurance companies can seem intrusive when the guidelines are missing. The group must establish the guidelines through trial and error and get all of the group to adhere to their findings through peer pressure, "which is more effective than money or recognition in changing behavior." Their experience was that physicians were not willing to "leave it alone" once they had a baseline and wanted to constantly tinker with ways to upgrade their performance. In so doing, they could create an additional reward for themselves and "scale this performance to volume." In other words, as average length of stay dropped, there was a risk of readmissions. To make sure that this did not happen, protocols for recovery and discharge were critical. Despite the fact that volume of admissions did go up as a function of more enrollees joining the program, the key performance indicators of admission criteria and discharges remained constant, so the CIGNA premium development assumptions were consistent with this constantly improving best practice.

One of the first government-sponsored pay-for-performance program demos was the Premier Hospitals project. Premier has been at the forefront of P4P since 2003, when they teamed with the Centers for Medicare and Medicaid Services (CMS) to create the Hospital Quality Incentive Demonstration (HQID), a first of its kind initiative to determine whether financial incentives are effective at improving the quality of inpatient hospital care. More than 260 hospitals voluntarily participated in the project, which has been extended for an additional 3 years (through 2009).

Results from the first 2 years of the HQID show that even modest incentives yielded improved quality of care, as hospitals have consistently improved performance. Overall quality (based on delivery of 30 nationally standardized care measures) rose 11.8% among participants in the first 2 years.

Hospitals participating in CMS, Premier Healthcare Alliance's HQID, and value-based purchasing (VBP) project raised their overall quality by an average of 17.2% over 4 years. This was based on their delivery of more than 30 nationally standardized and widely accepted care measures to patients in five clinical areas.

These improvements saved the lives of an estimated 4,700 heart attack patients in 4 years, according to a Premier analysis of mortality rates at hospitals participating in the project. The more than 1.5 million patients treated in five clinical areas at the 230 participating hospitals also received approximately 500,000 additional recommended evidence-based clinical quality measures, such as smoking cessation, discharge instructions, and pneumococcal vaccination, during that same time frame.

Additional research by Premier using the Hospital Compare data set showed that, by March 2008, HQID participants scored on average 6.9 percentage points higher (94.64% compared to 87.36%) than nonparticipants on 19 performance measures used by Hospital Compare, the government's scorecard for hospital quality.

CMS extended the project for 3 additional years through September 2009 to test the effectiveness of new incentive models and ways to improve patient care. Beginning with Year 4 results, participants are eligible to receive the following awards:

1. Attainment Award—Hospitals that attain or exceed the median level composite quality score (CQS) benchmark from two years prior will receive an incentive payment.
2. Top Performer Award—The top 20% of hospitals in each clinical area will receive an additional incentive payment. This group will receive the Attainment Award as well.
3. Improvement Award—Hospitals that attain median level performance and are among the top 20% of hospitals with the largest percentage quality improvements in each clinical area will receive an additional incentive payment.

The new payment model has been shown to promote increased quality improvements in the project. Thirteen hospitals moved from the bottom to the top 20% of hospitals in one or more clinical areas, improving quality scores by an average of 28.1 percentage points over 4 years.

Overall, under the project extension's new reimbursement model, CMS announced that it will award incentive payments of almost $12 million in Year 4 to 225 providers for top performance as well as top improvement and for reaching a level of attainment in the project's five clinical areas. Additionally, 1,258 awards were given to these top providers in the fourth year of the project, a fivefold increase from previous years. Through the project's first 4 years, CMS has awarded more than $36.5 million to top providers.

Decile Thresholds

Example: Year 1 Acute Myocardial Infarction Payment Scenario

A *decile threshold* is the CQS that defines the lower limit of the particular decile. Note that there is no "upper limit" for decile 1 or "lower limit" for decile 10. Each decile, by definition, contains 10% of the hospitals, so approximately the same number of hospitals is in each decile. This example shows the thresholds for Year 1 in the acute myocardial infarction (AMI) clinical focus area (see Table 4.1). Note that in the first 3 years of the project (Year 1, Year 2, and Year 3) hospitals in the first decile were awarded a 2% incentive bonus on their Medicare payments for patients in that clinical area. Hospitals in the second decile were awarded a 1% bonus. The thresholds for the ninth and tenth deciles are now established at these values, based on Year 1 data. Any hospital whose CQS in Year 3 falls below the ninth decile threshold (falling into the tenth decile as defined by Year 1) will receive a 2% penalty on their Medicare payments for patients in this clinical area. Hospitals whose CQS in Year 3 falls between the eighth and ninth decile threshold established in Year 1 will receive a 1% penalty (Figures 4.1 through 4.4).

Pay for Performance Has Created a New Industry

In addition to the Premier Hospital quality incentive demonstration sponsored by CMS, physician group practice (PGP) demonstrations were sponsored by CMS to encourage large, multispecialty group practices to manage care along the lines of performance measurements identified and set forth by CMS (see Appendix A).

This created several new programs by purchasers, specifically employers, one of which was the Leapfrog Group. This was formed in the year 2000, after the Institute of Medicine reports discussed earlier. Several lead U.S. corporations formed to improve safety, quality, value, and affordability of health care for their insured population. The name Leapfrog comes from four leaps that were required as broad goals of the program. These leaps are as follows:

1. Computer-based order entry to eliminate errors in dispensing drugs as well as to enhance document-coordinated care capabilities of physicians and hospital organizations.
2. Evidence-based hospital referrals—rather than a mere referral based on diagnosis, it was asked that evidence be used in the development of these measurements so that the medicine used to define the admission for an illness or disease could in fact be documented and thereby proven to be of value.

Table 4.1   FY2009 Candidate Measures for VBP Financial Incentive

Clinical Quality — Process-of-Care Measures		*Entered RHQDAPU*
Acute Myocardial Infarction (AMI)		
AMI-1	Aspirin at arrival[a]	11/2004
AMI-2	Aspirin prescribed at discharge[a]	11/2004
AMI-3	ACE inhibitor (ACE-I) or angiotensin receptor blocker (ARB) for left ventricular systolic dysfunction[a]	11/2004
AMI-4	Adult smoking cessation advice/counseling[a]	4/2005
AMI-5	Beta blocker prescribed at discharge[a]	11/2004
AMI-7a	Thrombolytic agent received within 30 minutes of hospital arrival	4/2005
AMI-8a	Primary percutaneous coronary intervention (PCI) received within 90 minutes of arrival	4/2005
Heart Failure (HF)		
HF-1	Discharge instructions	4/2005
HF-3	ACE inhibitor (ACE-I) or angiotensin receptor blocker (ARB) for left ventricular systolic dysfunction	11/2004
HF-4	Adult smoking cessation advice/counseling[a]	4/2005
Pneumonia (PN)		
PN-2	Pneumococcal vaccination status	11/2004
PN-3b	Blood culture performed in emergency department before first antibiotic received in hospital	4/2005
PN-4	Adult smoking cessation advice/counseling	4/2005
PN-6	Appropriate antibiotic selection	9/2005
PN-7	Influenza vaccination status	1/2006

(continued)

Table 4.1   FY2009 Candidate Measures for VBP Financial Incentive (continued)

Clinical Quality—Process-of-Care Measures		Entered RHQDAPU
Surgical Care Improvement/Surgical Infection Prevention (SCIP/SIP)		
SCIP-Inf-1	Prophylactic antibiotic received within 1 hour prior to surgical incision	9/2005
SCIP-Inf-3	Prophylactic antibiotics discontinued within 24 hours after surgery end time	9/2005
Clinical Quality—Outcome Measure		
	30-Day AMI mortality	6/2007
	30-Day HF mortality	6/2007
Patient-Centered Care Measures		
	HCAHPS	12/2007

[a] Denotes topped-out measure. All of the process-of-care measures with the exception of influenza vaccine and the prophylactic antibiotic selection measure were used in analysis that supported development of the proposed performance assessment model.

3. Intensive care unit staffing by specialists. Many of the employers had noticed that nonspecialists were staffing in the intensive care units (ICUs) and/or other allied health personnel, and there was an insistence that specialists be available in the ICU for patients in need of these types of services.
4. National Quality Forum (NQF) safe practices were to be required of all hospitals in the delivery of their care.

RHQDAPU = Reporting Hospital Quality Data for Annual Payment Update

These broad-based goals were specifications used for hospitals to be able to bid on either employer or, in some cases, health plan contracting for services. In many cases, employers delegated the responsibility to the health plan, insisting

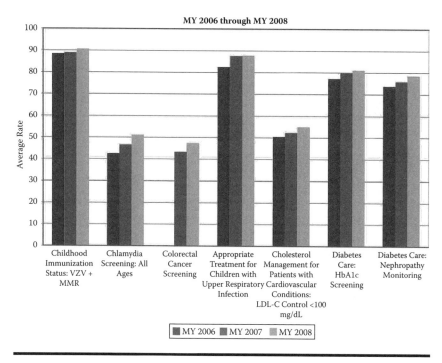

MY 2006 through MY 2008

Figure 4.1 Clinical quality measures: average rates by measure. (From Integrated Healthcare Association, Pay for Performance 2008. Results, Executive Summary. With permission.)

that all hospitals participating in the health plan follow the Leapfrog group criteria.

Finally, in 2005, Hospital Rewards Program was instituted by the Leapfrog Group. The goal was to monitor five clinical areas, patterned after the CMS Premier demo. Based on successful participation and attainment of these goals, certain dollars would be set aside for hospitals to compete based on quality.

Another organization that emerged, Bridges to Excellence, was tied to one of the data companies, MedStat. This is a multistate, multi-employer coalition that focuses more on the Institute of Medicine concepts and, through a set of principles, governed the concepts, including the reengineering of care processes to reduce mistakes, defects, and waste and to provide performance data for employers and the physicians to evaluate their overall process. Three programs, so far, have emerged from the Bridges to Excellence concept. One is Physician Office Link, the second is Diabetes Care Link, and the third is the Cardiac Care Link.

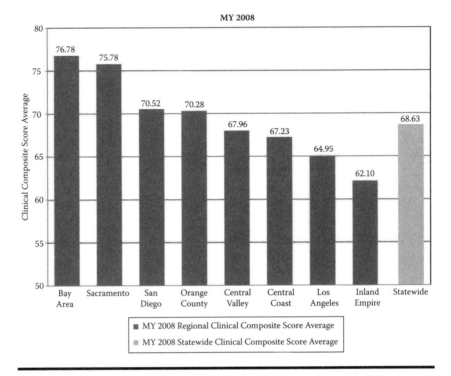

Figure 4.2 Clinical composite score averages by California region. (From Integrated Healthcare Association, Pay for Performance 2008 Results, Executive Summary. With permission.)

The reward system in Bridges to Excellence is focused more on the incorporation of information technology and outpatient services, whereas the Leapfrog Group is more focused on inpatient services.

Of all of the large-scale pay-for-performance programs, Integrated Healthcare Association (IHA) in California represents a series of purchasers, health plan medical directors, and physician group directors. This association was announced in 2002, and the clinical measures that were to be examined included mammography, immunizations, asthma, diabetes, and coronary artery disease. These areas were then linked to patient satisfaction, prevention, chronic care management, and information technology. The National Committee on Quality Assurance (NCQA) is the intermediary in order to aggregate the data. Approximately $54,000,000 was paid in bonuses in the year 2004. The IHA is a statewide leadership group consisting of eight health plans and 200 medical groups, representing 35,000 physicians who provide care for 11.5 million HMO members. The program has continued to expand and now includes the

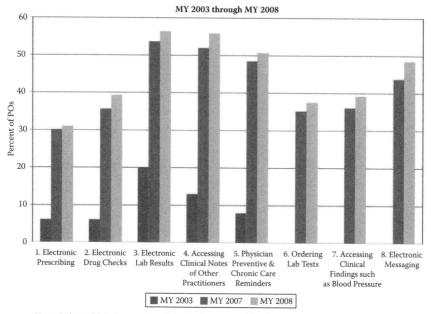

Note: Ordering lab tests, accessing clinical findings such as blood pressure, and electronic messaging activities were added after MY 2003.

Figure 4.3   IT-enabled systemness: percentages of physical organizations using point-of-care IT activities. *Note:* Ordering blood tests, accessing clinical findings such as blood pressure, and electronic messaging activities were added after MY 2003. (From Integrated Healthcare Association, Pay for Performance 2008 Results, Executive Summary. With permission.)

evaluation of medical technology, purchasing, reward of health care efficiency, and affordability.

According to the June 2009 annual report, IHA has experienced many successes. These include the creation of a single performance-based measure set and public report card, which was a major step forward. The use of aggregated data from multiple payers to score results significantly increased the measure, reliability, and trust of physicians. The IHA has created a collaborative environment between health plans and physician groups, which serves as a platform for other initiatives. The physician groups have accepted the challenge of performance measurement and have actively engaged in quality improvement efforts. Incremental quality improvements have been steadily realized, but breakthrough improvement has not been achieved. Dramatic regional and geographic variations in quality have surfaced; payments represented only a small percentage of compensation relative to other programs, which likely contributed

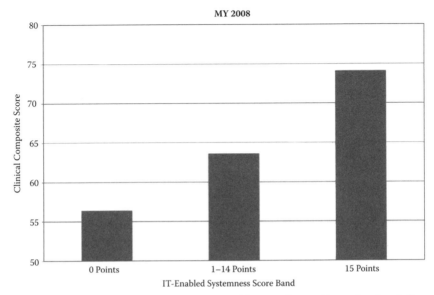

Note: Clinical composite score averages are calculated for POs with reportable rates for at least half of the clinical quality measures.

Figure 4.4 IT-enabled systemness: clinical composite scores distribution by IT-enabled systemness score band. *Note:* **clinical composite score averages are calculated for POs with reportable rates for at least half of the clinical quality measures. (From Integrated Healthcare Association, Pay for Performance 2008 Results, Executive Summary. With permission.)**

to the program performance; and, finally, wide variables in payments by health plans have raised concerns about "free riders" motivating plans with higher payments to reduce payment levels.

The P4P incentives have come in several forms, one of which is financial and the other public reporting to consumers as well as health plans in terms of top performers and the public recognition that goes with this. Of the many incentives, financial incentives continue to remain the most influential.

During the early formation of the program, several important principles were adopted. One key principle was agreement that all participating health plans would determine incentive payments based upon aggregate performance of physician groups, not performance of just the patients served by a single health plan. This principle leveraged the power of collaboration but other aspects of the "pay" in pay for performance remained unresolved. From the start of the program, the primary goal was an incentive payment that was large enough to drive breakthrough performance improvement while keeping pace with an

Table 4.2 Total Plan Payouts

2004	$38,000,000
2005	$54,000,000
2006	$55,000,000
2007	$65,000,000
2008	$52,000,000

Data from IHA report 2009.

expanding measurement set. However, the incentive amount and how it should be structured and funded remains one of the open issues even today.

In 2006, a 5-year strategic plan was developed that established important pay-related goals (Table 4.2). First of all, create a safe haven to advance consistent payment methodology. Secondly, have incentive payments reach 10% of compensation by the year 2010. A payment committee was formed in 2007 after resolving legal concerns over potential anti-trust issues, as will be described later in this book. However, little progress has been made toward achieving the 10% payment target. And, in fact, total incentive payments climbed in 2008. Payment issues remain a central and ongoing challenge for the program. They will likely require fundamental reform. This can be a contentious issue, but participating plans and physician groups are considering ways to restructure the program.

California physician groups receive most of their compensation for HMO enrollees in the form of professional services capitation. These payments are supplemented by the P4P incentive payments along with incentive payments for non-P4P measures related to medical and administrative efficiency.

To put these incentive payments in context, the P4P payouts of $65,000,000 in 2007, combined with additional non-P4P incentive payments of $89,000,000, created a total of $154,000,000 in incentive payments for the year 2007. The total incentive payments equaled about 2% of the total base compensation paid to physician organizations in 2007.

Physician groups received a higher or lower percentage of incentive payments based upon performance. Nonetheless, many stakeholders legitimately raised the need for much larger incentive opportunities to reward participating physician groups. Surveys by program evaluators indicate that physician groups believe that an incentive potential of at least 5% of total compensation is required to motivate any significant change.

The decrease in the total P4P incentive payment for 2008 was primarily the result of one health plan deciding to shift $8,000,000 of incentives previously allocated for the P4P measures to a non-P4P shared savings program. In shared savings programs, health plans share with physician groups the savings that have been generated by their superior work. This efficiency/gain sharing approach will be part of the P4P measurement starting in 2009–2010.

Public Recognition

Top performers are identified by calculating composite scores in each measurement domain, which are then weighted according to the recommended P4P payment weights. An overall performance composite score of each participating physician group is calculated in the top 20% of groups, with the highest overall composite score designated as top overall performer statewide. In 2007, for instance, P4P began recognizing physician group improvement to underscore the benefit of program participation beyond just the highest performers. The physician group in each of eight geographic regions that demonstrated the highest relative quality improvement over the previous year was designated an award winner.

The award for most improved was named posthumously for Ronald P. Bangasser, M.D., a family physician and previous vice chairman of the board of Beaver Medical Group. He also chaired the IHA P4P technical quality committee and served on numerous high-profile state and national committees. To determine the award winners, an improvement score is calculated for each physician group based on the percentage of relative improvement the group achieved in their overall composite score from the previous year to the current measurement year.

Public recognition awards for top-performing and most improved groups have been well received. Many groups use their awards to acknowledge the hard work of internal team members and highlight these awards in advertising and marketing materials.

More than a Trend

In reviewing the data from Premier as well as the IHA information, it is of interest to point out that as the lower tier or quartile of performers examines the differences between their organization and those in the top tier, there is a decided change in the physician and/or hospital organization to begin moving toward the higher performance standard. This is without discussion of income or investment in infrastructure but more a move toward recognition that the health care provider is, in fact, a top-tier provider.

In terms of employers, we are finding that the use of tiering today is limited. About 5% of employers are using it.

On August 17, 2009, *The Wall Street Journal** pointed out that pay for performance was integral to the entire health care reform process. In addition, the Medicaid public programs are involved with pay for performance in several states. It is estimated that some 25% of Medicaid programs are now using pay for performance.

As these changes occur, increasingly sophisticated data capture reporting and analysis requirements are demanded by pay for performance. This is consistent with the Bridges to Excellence and Leapfrog programs, both of which want to reward and emphasize more use of information technology. It also points out the opportunity for providers to develop their own dashboard for decision making in the future.

We believe that this use of technology will continue and is a permanent change for practices, but it is important to note that it will keep evolving over time. Just as hospitals are learning that many services now offered are unprofitable, practices are learning both in money and proficiency that certain procedures are not profitable.

We worked with a urologist who was a proficient and gifted surgeon but spent so much time doing routine exams and paperwork that he was not able to leverage that talent. He decided to go to all of the practitioners and emergency rooms who were referring patients and said he wanted to see patients who had a specific set of symptoms. He promised that he would see them within 24 hours and that he was trying to build a practice of surgery so some of the older doctors and PCPs would have a ready source of technical skill to refer to. In a very short period of time (6 months), he had shifted his practice to a full surgical practice, had negotiated a severity scale for payment with several larger health plans, and had seen his income per patient rise 400%. This allowed him to further invest in outpatient surgical equipment to become a urology Ambulatory Surgery Clinic (ASC). He brought in an assistant and when he was overrun began networking with other surgeons. He eventually developed a regional network and formed a specialty independent practice association (IPA) that gave him even more clout. His next step was to sign contracts with several pharmaceutical companies to do outcomes research and conduct trials of patients in the network. The result of this paid work for pharmaceutical companies was additional revenue streams and the ability to support his claim that they had a high-quality, high-performance network with superior outcomes over anyone out of network in the region.

In another instance, our analysis of a medical staff pointed to a very dangerous series of bad outcomes for an obstetrician/gynecologist (OB/GYN).

---

* Jane Zhang, "Medicare Tests Pay for Performance," *Wall Street Journal*, 8/17/09.

His statistics on gynecology were good because he had the ability and desire to see elderly women and also do excellent prenatal and postnatal care. But in the delivery room, under pressure in life-and-death situations, he oftentimes made bad judgment calls or had to be rescued by another surgeon. These "near misses" cost the hospital reimbursement from denied claims that could be attributed to negligent care and often made the malpractice carrier shudder and raise rates. It was suggested that maybe he could focus away from deliveries and instead focus on a geriatric marketplace or assist in other related services that did not require surgical stress. He tried this for a while but was angry with the hospital and our study, until he took a vacation and, using a personal coach, began to see a different career path of wealth management. He decided to leave the expensive practice and his partners bought him out. The practice became his first client, and now this physician runs the practice division of an international wealth management company making even more money than an OB/GYN and enjoying much less stress. He now attributes this life change to making him a better father and saving his marriage, plus he is now working as a counselor to doctors with disabilities ranging from AIDS to alcoholism.

The Current Status of P4P

We estimate that there are approximately 300 programs of varying levels of success now in process or implemented in the United States. (We will discuss international pay-for-performance efforts in future chapters.)

Approximately one third of these programs are targeted to hospitals, specifically the Leapfrog program. But many of these programs indicate that they have chosen a handful of guidelines with which to start. In other words, to try to launch a pay-for-performance program for all areas has been set aside by organizations in an attempt to gradually build upon successes in managing those gaps between actual and projected utilization and cost.

As would be expected, there are great variations in organizations that are sponsoring these programs. Some include provider enterprises as well as investor groups. We also have vendor organizations that are starting to sponsor many of these pay-for-performance programs whereby several employer coalitions are moving forward in obtaining the proper measurement systems and metrics to develop reward systems in conjunction with their vendors or with provider organizations within their community. We believe that this collaborative approach offers the greatest opportunity for change in any region or single marketplace.

We also believe that the CMS organization will continue to be a major market driver in developing new programs and even reimbursement calculations for the pay-for-performance system as well as in gain sharing.

As the increase for demands for both quality and value point to more discussion about efficiency and effectiveness, we envision that a number of measures will be modified and/or eliminated over the coming years. Physicians and hospitals will find a better way to measure and report on improved metrics and long-term savings.

At the present time, all P4P programs are measuring process points (i.e., the ability to change the process of delivering care or administrative services versus evidence-based outcomes). As more data is required, there will be more discussion on evidence-based outcomes.

What we find overall is that as physicians and hospitals envision their participation in the pay-for-performance arena, information technology will be enhanced at the practice, hospital, and perhaps even employer and insurance levels. More meaningful use legislation will dictate that these types of reporting, analysis, and billing systems must be designed on an open architecture basis versus the current tradition of developing closed architecture data receptacles.

These early trends in pay for performance have proven that physicians will respond to guidelines based upon medical evidence and that technology can be used successfully to ease the transition in terms of documentation and reporting. Although some studies are still tentative in proclaiming savings, most of the studies to date have been able to document improvements in quality and process.

These are reasons to pursue improvements to get at the ultimate goal of being able to consistently improve outcomes.

Chapter 5

Performance Language and Practice

Where Health Care Delivery and Information Technology Intersect

One of the most significant changes in health care management in the past 10 years has been an increasing reliance upon information technology to assist us in making the delivery system more manageable and accountable. Newt Gingrich likes to speak about the differences between health care information technology and banking technology. He asks why, when he sees a physician, must he come up with the insurance information, demographic information, and symptoms he talked to the doctor about yesterday and when it comes time for an X-ray or lab test, it takes weeks to get the results back for the doctor to review. By comparison, he can fly to London, go to an ATM, and insert his card and in 8 seconds the card's demographics, requests, and verification are all read and documented and he has his money.*

Banking and finance became involved with technology and electronic transactions in the early 1960s, when data processing through a centralized data center was all the rage. Many of us recall the air-conditioned, well-lit, glass-enclosed space where processing was done, and we remember the expansion of IBM, UNIVAC, CONTROL DATA, and Honeywell. And many of us also recall

---

* Neut Gringrich lecture to American Health Insurance Plans, Annual Meeting, Washington, D.C., January 2007.

early attempts to barcode transactions and transmit data from bank to bank, thereby allowing mass batching and account reconciliation, similar to what we attempt to do today as we auto-adjudicate claims and outsource various aspects of revenue reconciliations and billing. The banking center I worked for in the early 1970s reconciled transactions for 12 regional banks from Minnesota to Montana daily and balanced the books using transaction codes transmitted over the telephone coupled with connections to the central processing unit. This early version of outsourcing transaction data across multiple geographies never really made it into health care until the late 1980s.

Business Process Outsourcing is a $40-billion-a-year business in a rule-based environment, with millions of transactions occurring over fiber-optic cable between health plans, insurance companies, and banks every hour of the day. Much of this has become globalized and expressed in transactions per millions. Medical tourism has globalized many insurance companies' verification and eligibility practices. Insurers and health plans are as eager to have physicians enter the electronic medical record world as are patients, because it means more continuity between doctors and health plans as well as more rapid response on radiology and laboratory requests.

For many physicians and hospitals, however, there are barriers to entering this digital age; some of these are legitimate and some are not.

Surveys by the American Hospital Association, the federal government, and vendors continue to point out that though industry in general spends 5% or more of its annual budget on information technology, hospitals spend less than 2%.* We are still in the age of paper, slowly making transactions to the next version of software and hardware, but the industry of consumers, purchasers, and third-party organizations has already made the jump to web-based transaction processing, affording them the opportunity to manage inputs from inside and outside their own four walls.

The Solution Is within Our Four Walls

Many hospitals wanting to fine-tune the patient management process have focused almost exclusively on the inpatient care and hotel services offered on an institutional basis. Many of the patient-centered and care management processes almost never reach outside the walls of the institution. Yet in the age of performance in a digital reporting environment, the questions insurance companies and the government, on behalf of not only Medicare but also the quality agencies

---

* *Continued Progress, Hospital Use of Information Technology* (Chicago: American Hospital Association, June 2007).

affiliated with the state and federal government, are asking require more detailed data capture of the patient's initial diagnosis, rationale for that diagnosis, admission authorizations, input from primary care practitioner (PCP) to specialist to hospital to discharge planners and, then, to follow up with the patient after discharge to determine whether the actual care delivered was appropriate and, in fact, improved the patient's health status.

This is being done by comparing patients of similar age, complexity, and diagnosis against other patients with similar characteristics to come up with at least a norm of what protocol can relieve the suffering quickly and what it should cost to do this work. This is different than the past focus on cost inputs and diagnosis-related groups (DRG) outputs; it really is focusing on centering patient populations and benchmarks with health status improvement, a key marker of performance-based medicine.

Experts disagree on both benchmarks being used for health status improvement and, by reporting this data, hospitals tell me that they are concerned that they will suddenly be compared to other facilities with a more controlled (healthier) population and better resources to affect a positive end result, in which case they may be comparing apples and oranges. This puts hospitals at a competitive disadvantage, because a scoring of three and four stars often means the difference between adequate and substandard occupancy. Doctors are also looking at quality rankings among hospitals, insisting that they want to deal with four-star facilities only to ensure that they are "in the game" when pay for performance and bundled payments enter the market.

Three points become clear in this discussion:

1. Physicians, not hospitals, do the admitting for most cases except those that enter through the emergency room doors. This means that physicians and hospitals who will be ranked and analyzed by documented diagnosis by payers and the government and initial status of the patient should be working closely together, in terms of communication and authorization as well as electronically to document coding, notes and rationale, referral authorization, and recommended follow-up.
2. The hospital that purchases published data by outside companies who pleasantly award best practice statistics to the highest bidder needs to know that just the slightest shift in payer mix, that is, a dropped managed care agreement or an employer moving out of town, affects the statistics. Being the best heart center today and losing this award tomorrow creates a big question in the minds of managed care companies, employers, and consumers. No one hospital can be the best at everything, and with further disruption of referral patterns from storefront physicians and nurse

practitioners (NPs), patient-funded deductibles allowing out-of-network care, and competing volumes of statistics on the Internet, the science of patient loyalty is more linked to the "approved insurance network" chosen at work than by patient choice.

3. Hospitals and physicians waiting for managed care companies to start the pay-for-performance challenge may seem like a good idea. Why invest a lot of money in systems and training? However, we have seen many provider-sponsored plans, such as Intermountain, Tufts, and Health Partners Minnesota, seize and maintain the high ground by internally launching performance-based contracting and reporting available to consumers and employers.

Providers may say, "We have a loyal following of patients and doctors. We do not have to prove how good we are; we are doing fine." (We actually received a letter to this effect from a large Chicago hospital.) These are the famous last words of an organization in denial. As one physician CEO making his point in supporting change stated, "This stuff is not going away."

"This stuff" is now being published by employers and health plans as a means to show that they are being accountable to the needs of the members/beneficiaries/shareholders. It shows that they follow the government's plan to move to a value-based purchasing environment. In addition, databases run by government on a state-by-state basis are now becoming transparent, revealing best practice norms for a state. Pennsylvania, California, Minnesota, and Wisconsin are but a few of the states with excellent data repositories that are moving to include not just hospital statistics but also physician, nursing home, and related services and facilities for easy access by the health data research community as well as the consumers who have internet access.

This can be a blind spot for providers who think they have this data in a format that will be acceptable to payers. Upon looking at the specifications of health plans and employers in terms of delivery of select procedures to select patients and observing various safety standards recommended by employer advisors like Bridge to Excellence, providers quickly realize that they do not have this data, at least in a useable form, and that to produce incorrect data may be more harmful than not producing it at all.

Part of this issue is communication. That is, the criteria and data feeds that managed care and employers use are going to be different than what a clinical study or utilization review report on frequency and volume of services may show on a financial report.

For example, we had the opportunity to address 300 CFOs on this and related topics and we asked for a show of hands concerning how many were familiar with Health Employer Data Information Set (HEDIS) reporting.

Maybe only a dozen hands went up. When asked whether they were familiar with the Institute of Medicine project and the various reports regarding care gaps and improvement recommendations, even fewer hands went up. I am sure if I had asked about Joint Commission Accreditation of Hospital Organization (JCAHO) standards and Centers for Medicare & Medicaid Services (CMS) case mix adjustment reports, many hands would have gone up, but these are not the same criteria that purchasers use.

Consumer Assessment of Healthcare Providers and Systems (CHAPS) is yet another report used by purchasers to determine patient satisfaction with services. Many hospitals would benefit from the self-examination of what some patients thought of their services and the services of their admitting physicians.

These data are collected and reported to the National Committee on Quality Assurance (NCQA), a nongovernment reporting entity that grants certification to those health plans and insurers who can assure that they are in the top quartiles of quality and patient satisfaction. To earn this, a local health plan must submit to a rigorous and expensive process, but it offers a third-party endorsement of the plan's expertise in managing care and indirectly endorses the providers associated with that plan.

Changing providers and developing high-performance panels of only the top providers has merit, because employers who see this NCQA certification know that they can buy from an organization with confidence. It also is a watchdog, observing and monitoring every move. To earn and then lose this certification would be tantamount to a hospital being proclaimed as a top heart facility in an area one day and then losing it the next. It creates mistrust among employers, who ask, "What are these people doing with my money?"

Can We Get Our Terminology Correct First?

It struck me as odd that with all the MBA and MHA executive training and all the physician training on statistical methods and research proposals, we need to start many of our meetings with a discussion of fundamental measurement principles and definitions of what many of our words mean. It is almost as if the Tower of Babel were upon us. With all of our training and professing of wanting quality in health care, we really cannot even agree on a starting point, so the pay-for-performance and overall performance-based medicine initiatives were doomed to failure.

Once we did start using a set of defined characteristics to build momentum and energy toward a common goal, real progress was made. This is very similar to reading a blueprint and having a shared meaning and understanding of what the drawing and its symbols mean. Then it is easy to see the linkages for electricity and plumbing as well as building in safeguards for vents and stress points in the structure. Draftsmen make a living using the same symbols in increasingly creative and complex ways to address new needs for optimization of energy and building materials to eliminate waste. The blueprint represents the basis for the contractors to then bid out materials and time to implement the plan and build the structure.

Once again, the blueprint is not only instructive of the results but also what steps needed to be taken first, second, and then in a sequence as each contractor appears on the scene, first to build the foundation, then the shell, then the floors, walls, and the roofers do not show up until the frame is solid and the walls are in place. We found that many hospitals, physician groups, and especially payers were busy painting the kitchen trim while it was still on the truck. Most of this, as discussed earlier, was communication problems and not understanding the sequence of events because there was no shared understanding of the words, concepts, and symbols of what was to be done and especially *why*. Goals were missing or not communicated effectively.

So, let's start with the obvious. Providers are still asking how much it will cost to launch and manage a performance-based contracting process and how long before they will get a return on investment. The answer is not just an investment question but also a time question.

Short Term versus Long Term

When we purchased our first laptop computer in 1986 for an exorbitant $5,000, we thought the specifications and utility for that laptop would serve us for 10-plus years. The battery itself was 4 pounds, so it was more of a knee crusher than a laptop and it seemed very sturdy and reliable. Right now my Blackberry has the same capacity and probably more functionality than that purchase. These hand-held technologies change every 3 years, as do laptops.

What made me think that this was a long-term investment was the cost. Not a good definition. As we all know, the price for a fully loaded laptop today can be under $1,500.00, but *at the time* it was thought that no one would use more than a couple hundred megabytes. Who would have thought we would need to have a phone and projector and camera connected to do remote calling and processing? We thought *at the time* that every hotel would have a hook-up to the Internet so I could work on messages and letters and have a continuous connection allowing work to occur without interruption. This was an ideal vision that underscored the value of the purchase. But that value was impossible to measure.

Was purchasing this a short- or long-run decision? Most business people think in terms of one-year short run and 3-year long run. Smart, experienced business people know that reality often dictates one over the other. We hear, "It was a good idea at the time," quite often when technology is involved, but getting ahead to have the latest and greatest application and solution changes even in 2 years. We think this is part of the reason why software as service and outsourcing is starting to be considered as a viable means to link inside and outside the delivery system.

Efficiency

Inasmuch as we all believe that we understand efficiency, it is once again worth noting that there are several ways to define and therefore measure *efficiency*.

Maximum Output for a Fixed Budget

This is where managers determine from many inputs the greatest quantity of goods or services for a set amount of dollars. For example, we can take the number of nurse hours, physician hours, treatment spaces, and technology that yields that maximum number of annual visits to an emergency department for an annual budget of, let's say, $5 million. In this example, "efficiency is the highest output you can produce for a specific number of dollars."[*]

In the alternative, let us look at another way to get to the same goal.

Minimum Cost for a Fixed Output

This is where managers have already determined the best combination of inputs that produces a fixed quantity of a good or service at the least expensive cost. For example, again using an emergency room, what is the lowest annual budget to produce 50,000 annual visits? Viewing the definition of efficiency from this perspective we can say "efficiency is the minimum number of dollars needed to meet a pre-determined production goal."[†]

Now this looks very different in its results, but if you are trained in classic economic theory, or married to someone who is, you recognize this as the bottom of the U-shaped cost curves. Without getting into the mathematics and permutations of cost curves, our point is that one can follow the path of minimizing costs for a predetermined output or maximizing output for a predetermined budget, but

---

[*] Jeff Bauer and Mark Hagland, *Paradox and Imperatives in Healthcare* (New York: Productivity Press, 2007).
[†] Ibid.

if you have department heads who delegate such project analysis to managers who modify these into long-term strategies, this could be a trap.

It is a trap because many doctors, hospital executives, health plan executives, and mid-level managers will define efficiency as the greatest output for the least cost. The ability for the maximum (greatest output) and the minimum (least cost) to coexist in the same closed system is mathematically impossible! You can only maximize or minimize one variable, and in health care we have many cost and regulatory restraints that make these calculations even more complicated, so we need to shoot for cost minimization or output maximization for a fixed cost.

Efficiency can be any measure/production unit, department, or service line, but one has to make a decision to determine which way to define efficiency and then stick with it.

Another trap is the directors who tell department heads to produce more for less. This will always lead to inefficiency for several reasons. What management needs to do is focus on that *one thing* that can be improved and done well. For example, a single DRG, a single admission, discharge for a service line, etc. Start with an annual goal or budget as an output measure and "back into the numbers." Look at ways to minimize cost *or* maximize output, but stay within that goal or budget. Despite what accounting says, the answer is not always cost minimization. Management's role, then, is to focus on one path or the other and to do it and remain consistent. One may end up doing some calculations on a case-by-case basis, because not all variables are known, but there needs to be clarity on which path we are on.

Finally, another trap all organizations eventually wrestle with is the fact that efficiency in health care is a moving target. New technology, drugs, process measures, communications, or payments will affect how you do your measures and how you arrive at goals and budgets for various service lines. This will become more critical as we move away from traditional payment for production into a bundled payment atmosphere where there are rewards for improving population's health status both in terms of getting money above and beyond billed charges but also being able to reinvest this margin into better equipment, better staff coverage, and new technology.

All of these things are positives but will accelerate with change and the use of more guidelines for predictable care. Consultans think that this change process will be a positive challenge to management because it is self-creating, will force management to take a long-term view of things, and will reduce the distance between patient and provider as care coordination becomes more precise and measurable.

Why is effectiveness measurement important? Because it can identify wasted resources; that is, dollars that, when identified, can be reallocated to other areas of the health plan or hospital without any increase in prices.

"Efficiency decreases as waste increases or vice versa."[*]

Adjustment should also be made for opportunity costs, meaning that while all this waste was going on, other more positive and profitable activities could have been occurring or expanding.

To follow on with our example, suppose that the hospital conducts an efficiency study and determines that 50,000 visits in an emergency room (ER) can be obtained for $4 million. If the hospital is spending $5 million to produce these same 50,000 visits, $1 million is being wasted. Some of this may be overstaffing of nurses and doctors when the ER is not very busy, or it is the salaried clerks who do insurance verification and technicians who are drawn off other services on an as-needed basis.

We had a hospital administrator who did a time motion study to see how long it took to get drugs prescribed by the physician from the hospital pharmacy to the patient. In some cases it was days, and in most cases the drug went through 17 different pairs of hands. The error rate was high, correction costs were expensive, and the number of patients who came in with pneumonia and waited for an antibiotic for days only got sicker, with some having to be put on a ventilator. Dr. Bret James, medical director for Intermountain Health Plans, has shown that the hospital that loses the opportunity to administer an antibiotic within hours of a pneumonia admission hurts itself because the ventilator is operated at a loss, whereas the prescription drugs and a couple of days' observation is at a gain.[†] These change costs, plus all of the talent time and error correction time, is all waste, because they did not have to happen in an efficient system.

So it is easy to see that creating savings is not all cost cutting. It is captured through process reengineering and looking at gaps between present-day deliveries versus future deliveries.

Actuaries have estimated that one third of those patients now in the hospital do not need to be there. Approximately 40% are there due to a preventable disease; 40% are there for a disease that could be better treated on an outpatient basis with physical therapy, drugs, diet, or home health; and the remaining 20% are not healing as they should, either because of a misdiagnosis, a recurring set of symptoms, or because they are dying from a nosocomial infection (an infection they received after admission that has nothing to do with the primary diagnosis). It is estimated that, at a minimum, 12–18% could be saved through reallocation and process reengineering.

---

[*] Jeff Bauer and Mark Hagland, *Paradox and Imperatives in Healthcare* (New York: Productivity Press, 2007).

[†] Dr. Bret James, Medical Director, Intermountain Health Plans, Salt Lake City, Presentation at P4P Summit (Los Angeles, March 2009).

Translating this to a national scheme, how much health care could we produce for 17% of the gross national product (GNP)? We should be able to produce a lot more, and we should also be able to bend the cost curve by 5% GNP if the bottom performing hospitals were to just reach a plateau of average efficiency. According to the Agency for Health Quality and Research (AHQR), if all hospitals were to perform at the top-performing tier, the GNP cost reduction could be another 4–5%. Most importantly, by removing that much waste, over 1,000 lives per year would be saved.

Effectiveness

So now on to another word that is sometimes synonymous with efficiency but is totally different in its assumptions, definition, and measurement.

Effectiveness is a measure of the relative compliance with objective specifications of expected performance. That is, if a guideline is developed with specific protocols and procedures and it works (that is, it generates the desired result) 100% of the time, we would say that this guideline is 100% effective. In health care, we know that many factors enter into this measurement, not the least of which are current health status, age, and, often, unfortunately, economic status, which can be linked to insurance access.

In the manufacturing world, the number of defects can represent a definition of effective manufacturing process. Six Sigma and lean manufacturing are part of this, along with our ongoing search for total quality management.

What those of us with behavioral science backgrounds would say is that effectiveness also has to do with patient and physician expectations of the encounter. Effective products create consumer loyalty. I am on my tenth Volkswagen for my wife, son, and myself. Why? Because I am not a gear head who likes to tinker; instead, I expect reliable transportation, few defects, and efficient use of gasoline, because we all drive quite a bit for work and family. So, for me, the Volkswagen brand is a value. It represents both the effectiveness of dependability I expect and efficiency of resources used.

For trustees and board members of health plans, health systems, and medical networks, this effectiveness is an absolute, because to offer discount care that is substandard is of no value to employers or patients.

Grades and Effectiveness

Another point to bring out in this discussion is the situation where we receive a grade after the work has been completed. It was not planned or premeditated, it simply just happened. Our son, a Montessori method graduate, would receive test scores after he had been asked to learn something. The teacher would grade this and identify his shortcomings by showing the errors and reinforcing the teaching. He would again take the test and, of course, pass, showing a milestone of accumulated knowledge. In music theory class outside of Montessori, he was tested, and when he had several incorrect answers, he asked about what he needed to know and then asked to take the test again. The traditional teacher and several students were bewildered that he would ask to be graded after he knew the answers.

This speaks to the general idea of managed care companies holding information back from hospitals and report cards being delivered on performance specifications into which the doctor had no input. Releasing of data went with the old school of closed systems. Microsoft and Apple, Intel, Dell, and now the social networks, goals are to push information down into the organization so it could be used at several levels to create better work specifications and hopefully make improvements in work output and decision making. Many experts, including the current CMS Chairman Dr. Don Berwick (see Chapter 3), tell us that efficient and effective care will also require that we push care needs down into the organization and train or retrain technicians to be able to make decisions and follow pathways for 80% of the population with routine and predictable outcomes. This frees up the specialists and other "high-end" practitioners to deal with complexities of the 20% who would otherwise burn up 80% of the limited health services and resources as they wander through a maze of unnecessary tests and observations. So if we teach care guidelines and pathways as part of this transition to care value, we must be able to share payer and provider data in some way that is not punishment but rather an opportunity for discovery and focused improvement.

The government's recent health reform legislation has budgeted millions to research comparative effectiveness and reduction in error rate for such things as unnecessary readmissions and the development of many of these episodes' guidelines.

Risk Adjusters and Comparative Effectiveness

We think that risk adjusters and similar discussions have complicated what some want to be a straightforward, if–then–therefore relationship between care rendered and outcomes. When adjusting for risk of patient care, we see the mortality and morbidity factors come into play and this, in our experience, helps both practitioners and patients to custom design an outcome or, at a minimum, a pathway of process to achieve the next plateau of healing.

Most of what is prescribed by pathway protocols and general care delivery takes into consideration the unique health status of the patient and does not develop an isolated, fixed and rigid standard to be followed. We discourage the use of standards of care. There is no such thing unless all medical practice is static. The reality is the introduction of new surgical techniques, technology, and drugs and requires a floating guideline that can be met or exceeded depending upon the capability of the professional, his resources, and, finally, the patient expectation in terms of what is a realistic outcome today versus tomorrow. Care standards require thinking in terms of a logical connection of expectations that does not exist in modern medicine because there is both a process of elimination of the scientific method and, more importantly, other patients in the population who have a comparative anomaly that must be measured against today's patient, and we must ask: Are the standards flexible? Are the care pathways able to take health status into consideration? Can the standards actually be replicated in the facility designated in this delivery system, and can the care system actually report feedback on the changes in the health status, or will valuable data be lost in the transitional management of the patient for care to home care?

Hospitals, even small, 200-bed or fewer hospitals, stand to lose $1.3 million per year due to poor quality metrics. As both Medicare and private payers penalize inpatient and outpatient procedures as ineffective or inefficient waste, the quality argument will create the rationale for lost reimbursement, especially with chronic care patients.

Organizational Issues of Planning and Control

Many who have entered into quality improvement projects, such as Baylor in Dallas, Virginia Mason Clinic, and Everett Clinic in Washington state, have all reported that their quality improvement efforts do, in fact, return double and triple return on investment when considering the efficiency of patient throughput and the effectiveness of a designed premeditated outcome. Merging these two factors of care with technology monitoring and measurement against norms or specifications shows that results are not measured after the fact and that goal setting is essential to the planning process.

Control is vested with the practitioner's ability to be consistent in the process and outcomes, which requires documentation and a sensitivity to the health status and preexisting situation of the patient's health. Is there a care guideline?

Goals should be set high. For example, both process goals should be set at an above average level—80% statins to a cardiac patient as well as smoking cessation instruction to 80% of patients. These performance points are meant to be exceeded, and savings can be described in terms of potential lives without complications and a reduction of actual deaths by early intervention with guidance and prescriptions.

Health Partners Medical Director George Isham, M.D., states that the key is to identify the best guidelines for the best cases that have the greatest impact on the population served. That does not mean just cost reduction but true care improvement for the greatest number of people, using a straightforward guideline for the majority of patients presenting with a specific diagnosis.

The Twin Cities, often cited as an example for care delivery excellence, has aligned its outcomes data against normative specifications by combining deidentified data for four health plans. The health plans have invested in the development of the Institute for Care Systems Integration (see http://www.ICSI.com). The centralized database and outcome information are reviewed by physicians representing each of the four plans, and guidelines are agreed upon and therefore recommended to all physicians participating in one or more health plans in the area. This database is available to practitioners as well as consumers so they can develop a general expectation of what their doctor may recommend and also what will happen if they do not follow this recommendation. Staging it by severity level, the patient can see that perhaps not following the drug regimen recommended by the physician may involve the progression of a serious disease requiring more drugs and more interventions, including surgery. Failing to follow these phase 2 guidelines may increase the probability of long-term chronic illness and finally long-term hospitalization. Many patients who want to avoid serious complications have followed their doctor's orders and these compliant patients usually improve their health status in a measurable way.

Quality Data

We have been mystified by the acceptance of quality data reported in frequency of use and units of care but with no real comparison to normative data. This, as discussed above, is like being graded after the class but offers no real way to discover how or even why it could be better. The De Marco & Associates data company, and Pendulum HealthCare Development Corporation, started producing quality data by reporting data on utilization, severity adjusted as displayed in Figure 5.1 (local hospital comparisons). This has progressed to utilization and cost data, showing once again the value of the care delivered because without the cost element the quality means nothing.

Many years ago, U.S. consumers were told that Japan's prices were cheap but the quality was poor; that is, defects per thousand were very high. This meant that cheap was not good. With health care quality, without comparison to norms of performance for the current institution of regional norms, this is a blind acceptance of the unrealistic assumption that local performance is best

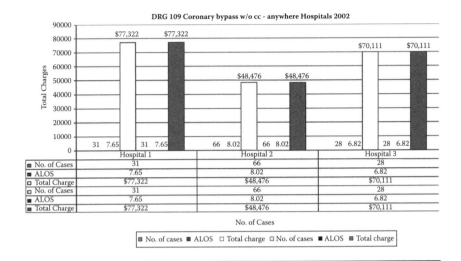

Figure 5.1   Comparison of DRG 109 Cost and Utilization Illustration.

performance. Most doctors we work with want to know what the number is. Is it an error rate of 10% or 39%?

This is the future of creating planned specifications in advance of delivery and concentrating on not just the high-cost procedures but rather those high-volume procedures that can affect the greatest number of patients.

Data shown in Tables 5.1 and 5.2 and Figure 5.2 (Pendulum Healthcare Development Corp. [PHDC] original reports and report cards) are the next generation of quality reporting with guidelines built into the care equation.

It is worth noting that the government's own expectation looks at a three- and four-star approach to quality. This is beginning to mesh with a three- and four-star quality measurement for Medicare Advantage health plans and, we suspect, will eventually be applied to accountable care organizations as they begin to stream beneficiaries away from the Medicare Advantage plans and back into traditional Medicare due to pricing subsidies being cut from the Medicare Advantage plans. We see this as very political at a time when the government should be pushing down its risk for better care management to these Medicare contractors. But, as discussed earlier in this book, the move for many large, for-profit insurance plans into the Medicare sector has made this a difficult issue for lawmakers. Explaining why these contractors are paid more than standard Medicare rates for their role in managing Medicare, and their profit margins continue to swell with high executive pay and perks, is very difficult indeed, and voters are thinking that this is unfair.

Table 5.1 Masked Employer Report

Population Profiling System—Employer Ranking Total Dollars Paid for Covered Individuals
Population Automotive Manufacturing > 100 Employees
Benchmark Raybesico Exhaust Products

	Provider					Population				Benchmark			
1	****	******	163	$1.643	$257,817	$236.334	$29,483	1.12*	079	$221.651	$45.166	1.21**	0.79
2	****	******	202	$1.529	$308,774	$296.345	$10,429	1.03	079	$277.451	$31.313	1.11*	0.79
3	2100554	Raybesico	204	$1.919	$391,417	$334.161	$7,255	1.02	101	$367.270	$34.147	1.10*	1.01
4	****	******	290	$2.100	$608,935	$606.443	$3,492	1.01	112	$663.062	$45.873	1.08	1.12
5	****	******	110	$1.919	$211,037	$207.943	$3,144	1.02	102	$193.337	$17.700	1.09	1.02
6	****	******	137	$2.285	$313,091	$334.455	-$21,355	0.94	131	$311.044	$2047	1.01	1.31
7	****	******	113	$1.432	$167,484	$199.923	-$32,439	0.84*	095	$185.928	$18.444	0.90*	0.95
Average per provider			174	$1.840	$324,085	$324.036	$0	1.00	100	$301.400	$22,636	1.07	1.07
Total for rema			1.219		$2.253605	$2.268.606	$0			$2.109.803	$153,802		
Average of patient				$1.861		$1.851	$0			$1.731	$1.30		

Table 5.2 Population Profiling System per Member per Month (PMPM) Average Dollars—Specialty: Family Practice

Provider Rank	PCP ID	PCP Name	Average No. of Members	Total Member Months	Actual PMPM ($)	Expected PMPM ($)	Difference ($)	Percentage Difference	Performance Index	Statistical Significance	Relative CCI [RCCI]
27	XXXX	**********	393	4,752	93.34	63.64	24.70	36	1.35	**	1.04
28	XXXX	**********	48	577	71.67	47.43	24.24	51	1.51		0.72
29	XXXX	**********	213	2,555	91.25	67.40	23.85	35	1.35	**	1.02
30	XXXX	**********	235	2,833	97.50	74.79	22.81	30	1.30	**	1.13
31	XXXX	**********	475	5,715	95.90	75.93	20.97	28	1.23	**	1.15
32	XXXX	**********	619	7,433	112.04	91.91	20.13	22	1.22	**	1.39
33	XXXX	**********	524	6,285	85.53	66.63	19.85	30	1.30	**	1.01
34	XXXX	**********	250	3,116	81.87	62.42	19.45	31	1.31	*	0.94
35	XXXX	**********	255	3,190	95.66	78.05	17.60	23	1.23		1.18
36	XXXX	**********	773	9,281	74.33	55.83	17.50	31	1.31	**	0.85
37	XXXX	**********	355	4,271	73.46	57.30	1618	28	1.28	**	0.87

38	0002	Brian Henry, M.D.	274	3,291	77.93	61.93	15.05	25	1.25	**	0.63
39	XXXX	**********	235	2,823	69.80	54.07	15.73	29	1.29	**	0.82
40	XXXX	**********	101	1,208	58.82	44.00	14.82	34	1.34	*	0.66
41	XXXX	**********	63	751	60.45	46.01	14.44	31	1.31		0.69
42	XXXX	**********	325	3,939	87.79	73.50	14.29	19	1.19	*	1.11
43	XXXX	**********	370	4,439	91.97	77.77	14.20	18	1.18	*	1.17
44	XXXX	**********	553	7,897	69.48	55.42	14.05	25	1.25	**	0.84
45	XXXX	**********	185	2,214	95.13	83.02	12.11	15	1.15		1.25

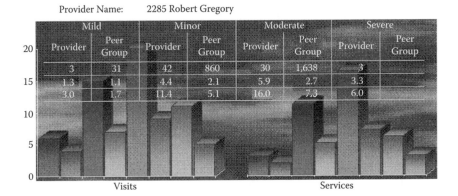

Figure 5.2 Population profiling system. Provider case load by complexity level.

This is an impossible thing to justify at a time when Medicare and all of health reform is desperate for dollars to pay for reform. In terms of data, large contractors have access to large volumes of data, but local players are limited. The size of the universe of statistical data will expand over time in order for us to move from process-oriented changes in the tasks purchasers and physicians do toward a more outcomes-oriented environment. But for now these cuts will impact all health plans and their opportunity to perform reliable measures in-house.

Outcomes Data

Outcomes data is slowly being collected by health plans and insurance companies. As mentioned above, state governments are slowly seeing the value of this data for both research and commercial application. Raw data, as is used by organizations such as Bridges to Excellence, has value in the contract of building a foundation of inpatient or outpatient care. As this association-based organizations, driven in many cases by vendors, align the inpatient and outpatient data to provide an episode of care, we can start actually tinkering with the process to arrive at an outcome that is consistent and reproducible. This is not a simple task, as seasoned physicians have used their own personal skills of inquiry and testing available in their regions to get solutions, whereas younger physicians are just now developing these skills. The seasoned physician challenges many of the outcomes-oriented protocols as being "cookbook medicine," yet with today's technology, we again see doctors yearn for very complex and mysterious diagnoses while delegating most routine care. This is especially true of surgeons, where a "surgical signature" can be identified. This signature may be wrought and memorized as the "right" thing to do by the surgeon, yet new technology is slowly adapted. For example, statins given to a patient after a first heart attack has been a care benchmark and guideline in many association and health plan protocols for almost 12 years. Yet many doctors will resist this despite evidence and countless studies because it is not what they were taught and therefore not what they will always recommend. In pay for performance, payment for this recommended treatment has moved the needle slightly, but analysis begs the question: Why don't physicians accept innovation? Well, the answer is slowly becoming clear. This tampers with their opinion that care has been rendered without statins for years, so why change now? Will it really help my patients? Analysis by our research teams can sometimes identify a surgical signature going back to the medical school the doctor went to and sometimes even the mentor who taught a particular procedure at that school.

The final distinction most doctors want to know is not just will this help my patient but also what evidence does the administrator or insurer present to support his claim.

Evidence-Based Outcomes Data

Many times doctors are told by pharmaceutical companies and managed care that a certain procedure or benchmark has proved to be positive for patients. The doctors are skeptical of the pharmaceutical companies, after listening to the railings of Harvard University professors in the medical school who finally admitted that their research and teachings incorporated certain drugs and brand name pharmaceutical companies because they pay the physicians to review outcomes data and research. Are the facts presented unbiased and created with the patient in mind, or is it a big pharma ad?

Mayo's outstanding proclamation regarding the effects of exposure to fenfluramine and phentermine in combination and to dexfenfluramine alone on heart valves was a lifesaving finding but probably an economic stab in the back to pharmaceutical companies who arranged to have this drug proven safe with research papers and evidence, yet the evidence was biased. As a result, a dangerous drug was taken from the market (http://www.ncbi.nlm.nih.gov/pubmed/10807073).

My favorite illustration comes from the Hollywood writers of the updated *Fugitive* movie where Harrison Ford is faced with exposing a complex plot by big pharma to endorse a heart medication that researchers knew was flawed yet were willing to kill any researcher who admitted its failings. Dramatic, yes, but it makes a point that doctors, like all of us, are asking real questions about the efficacy and actual research behind drugs recommended by pharmaceutical companies. Managed care has the same lack of credibility and many ask, "Is this a good protocol based upon evidence or an actuarial calculation to reduce costs and make the insurance company rich?" Good question. After years of doctors being told everything by research sources of questionable background, we see a slow acceptance of many protocols and guidelines set in motion without adequate study or investigation.

Our point here is that evidence-based guidelines and protocols have entered the vernacular of medicine as performance criteria for doctors to actually see the research and meta-analysis of the background of why this guideline may be better than what they are now using. When you see evidence-based outcomes, you know the tool to use. The medical protocols of the Specialty Society and American Medical Association (AMA) are being produced, and many of these associations have seen a day where a consistent application of what we know will work could be a way to reduce malpractice liability as well as reduce variations and cost of care deliveries for a specific population.

Lean Engineering

Welcome to the future of engineering and reengineering, where protocols and guidelines need to be reengineered to fit the best use of local resources. This, to us, makes the most sense because, though reform has been promised for decades, the best reform has been slowly emerging at the local level, incorporating not just physicians but also nurses, administrators, technicians, and, in some cases, health plans, who have great volumes of data and can measure the change of healthy status for patients in a test for new outcomes.

A variety of firms have popped up, but a favorite is an Irish company that only serves health care globally and can offer lean thinking to the industry here in the United States based on actual experience and evidence of care improvement. Leading Edge Group (http://www.leadingedgescm.com/healthcare/what-is-lean-healthcare) offers three key elements needed to be lean. They are as follows:

1. Eliminate waste through understanding the value to the patient and how to deliver that value.
2. Create an efficient and waste-free continuous-flow system built on pull vs. a "batch and queue" approach.
3. Continually pursue a perfect system.

Lean, in this framework, is intended to reduce the waste of reentering the same data on patient forms over and over, reduce time looking for charts, and reduce wait times for labs and X-rays that always require rescheduling of follow-up appointments, which in turn pushes back those patients who need the care, all because the management of documents and handoff of stored materials is overly time consuming.

Six Sigma

We can spend months on this concept because it does represent a step in the correct direction. It borrows directly from industrial engineering in describing defects per 1,000 units of something produced. The goal of zero defects is the vision, so total quality management and other famous labels apply, but we bring it up here with the intention of stating, perhaps, the obvious. By setting goals in place ahead of production, one can see progress toward goals. By reporting production and nothing else, there are no goals or understanding of what progress should be made.

Motorola was a large leader in six sigma. Measurement of variation is a goal, sometimes looking for what part of the process needs to be measured is a critical aspect to setting goals. Mike was information technology leader during the early Six Sigma process at Motorola and now assists our clients with trying to get at critical data features that relate to performance monitoring for Pendulum HealthCare Development Corporation. Six Sigma is also a registered trademark of Motorola and is an actual statistical process referring to defect levels that occur below 3.4 defects per million.

Learning Organizations

Learning organizations have been discussed since the early information technology days of research and development efforts at Microsoft and Intel created internal "skunk works" (Steve Jobs's reference to their research and development group think) to boldly go where no executive has gone and invent new ways of describing, grouping, and analyzing problem sets and solution theories that offer breakthrough thinking and breakthrough strategy. These early attempts at trying to predict the future with best- and worst-case scenarios seemed strategic and, in most cases, involved performance improvement and applications of the above principles. However, as the theory of the learning organization evolved, it pushed itself down into the organization to not only train and promote executives but also start grooming young directors and managers for future roles in the organization. This made for a differentiator in a way of speaking and built a brand based upon these thinkers and doers. Buck Rodgers, in *The IBM Way*, changes how we think about quotas and motivating sales forces. Clayton Christensen, in *The Innovator's Prescription,** describes an elaborate application of his earlier work in disremediation and finding a way for the little guy to be heard in the noisy marketplace. And Ichak Adizes, in several books, describes how to use positive conflict to bring about change and how to manage change at each stage of the life cycle of a company to make it more sustainable but to never be totally comfortable and satisfiedto stop moving forward.[†]

In *Built to Last*, authored by Stanford professors James Collins and Jerry Poras, they say, "If we had bet our lives on the continued success and adaptability of any single company over the past 50 to 100 years it would be 3M."[‡] This triggered an interview between then-CEO Desi De Simone and Marshall Loeb, *Fortune* reporter.[§] He asked De Simone what his secrets were in running a diverse global company with 66,000 products.

De Simone's advice:

1. Give folks time to follow their muse. He believes that by giving employees 15 hours a month to follow their own research projects this will encourage creativity. Accidents happen and things like Post-it Notes are created. The story goes this way. Art Fry wanted adhesive papers to mark the hymns in his hymnal at church. So he and his friend Spence Silver spent their creative research time on developing such a product. In 2009 sales of Post-its exceeded $100 million.
2. Create a culture of cooperation. It is inevitable that as you are working for 3M you will need to know something about another discipline. Meeting face to face or even by e-mail with experts in the company helps to coordinate resources and goals and may also create a breakthrough as more disciplines get together to create or build upon solutions. This discourages "turfiness" and though it sounds simple, few businesses actually use it.
3. Measure your results. 3M has 45 business units that produce products and services and continues to grow, but as new products and new divisions expand, it is tempting to rely on last year's victory. De Simone has raised the bar from 25% of revenue for new products to 35% revenue from new

---

* Clayton Christensen, *The Innovator's Prescription* (New York: McGraw Hill, 2009).
† Ichak Adizes, *Corporate Life Cycles* (Paramus, NJ: Prentiss Hall Press, 1989).
‡ Marshall Loeb, "Ten Commandments for Managing Creative People: With an environment that fosters innovative thinking, you can stumble onto a lot of lucky accidents. Just ask the CEO of 3M" *Fortune*, January 16, 1995.
§ Ibid.

products. This means that everyone has the chance and an obligation to contribute to these goals with new and fresh thinking.

4. Stay ahead of the customer. The most interesting products, De Simone says, are products that people need but cannot articulate that they need right now. For example, we have all seen the light reflective rails on highways for nighttime driving and safety. Customers said it was adequate but 3M techies said they were not satisfied. There were still too many accidents. So after a company-wide analysis of every light source imaginable, they invented a bulb that can throw light for 500 yards. This has worked extremely well and accidents are down.

5. Stage a lot of celebrations. The company continually rewards outstanding accomplishments with stock and bonuses. While peers cheer on their celebrated colleagues, honorees get a certificate. There is even an annual 3M Oscar night, where De Simone personally awards special honorees with considerable fanfare. Eminent inventors are inducted into the Carlton Society, a hall of fame for the many contributions the company staff has made.

6. Make the company innovative. In this light, De Simone says he hates to lay off people because it ruins the morale of all of the other would-be innovators. What decline of employees that has occurred is through attrition. He says that business cycles change, but that's no reason to get rid of people. "Even if we are stumbling we are still moving forward."*

7. Give your management assignments overseas. 3M's top 135 executives have spent a minimum of 3 years stationed overseas. He himself was in Brazil for 14 years before being promoted to corporate. He speaks five languages and brought $14 billion in sales while in Brazil. He believes that when you live outside of headquarters you have to be more resourceful, translate languages and legal rules to fit your situation, and, not unlike running a small business, you have to talk to the bank and be accountable to your surroundings.

8. Keep spending on R&D. 3M has increased its R&D spending each and every year of its existence.

9. Do not heed everything Wall Street tells you. "Back in the eighties," says De Simone, "when every analyst was complaining about how we should leverage our company more with borrowing, we would say, "We do not

---

* Marshall Loeb, "Ten Commandments for Managing Creative People: With an environment that fosters innovative thinking, you can stumble onto a lot of lucky accidents. Just ask the CEO of 3M" *Fortune*, January 16, 1995.

think that's a safe thing to do; we're conservative farmer types out here in the Midwest."*

10. When you have a cushion of cash it's easy to make R&D decisions. Can you imagine applying some of these concepts to your own learning organization? Bring people in from the small hospital chains to headquarters after they have learned how to address these issues on their own with limited resources. Encourage managers to focus on their own research. Imagine what we would come up with! We could stay ahead of the customer instead of merely responding to their needs, spend money on R&D instead of leveraging every dollar in buildings and equipment, and invest in those areas that can actually improve performance and coordination of care.

You may ask whether anyone is doing this, and the answer is yes. In *Management Lessons from Mayo Clinic*, Kent Seltman discusses the proud history of Mayo in traditions and medical care, the ability to protect this brand as a destination medical care facility for over 100 years, and the learning organization that builds in quality and invests in bringing the best talent and keeping it by creating logical rungs of leadership training and mobility with a huge and vastly complex organization. This is what integration was supposed to be: performance at its top level of competence and the organization uniting its departments and showing its ability to communicate to doctors and hospital staff together with clinicians. It is vital getting the message and the vision out there and not losing it to "turfiness" by merely responding to customer needs while competitors move ahead and actually lead their needs through carefully designed communication and patient satisfaction R&D.

Yes, it is happening, and we now have the tools and technology and even some models of care to research at Mayo, Cleveland, Baylor, and Intermountain Health, who are all discovering that the provider model of the future must be integrated at the data level to produce useful performance data. To capture this adequately, Medicare, HMOs, and large employers are moving toward a bundled payment goal to unite detailed patient encounter data with care guidelines and producing incentives for sharing dollar savings in exchange for improvements in efficiency and effectiveness.

Reengineering is the foundation of "what to do with analytics," a new science for health care that continues to offer the promise of better benchmarks based on evidence-based care.

---

* Leonard L. Berry and Kent Seltman, *Management Lessons from Mayo Clinic* (New York: McGraw Hill, 2008).

Chapter 6

Reengineering

In the early chapters we emphasized the fact that early industrial models of process redesign and improvement were seldom applied to specific health care enterprises because there seemed to be so many considerations for each illness that the ability to reliably include all the appropriate factors was impossible. This was due to a lack of data, a lack of precision in engineering steps of the current process, and, frankly, a lack of interest by health care practitioners and executives who had no real clinical or financial incentive to improve care. Therefore, care management, up until the early 1960s, was really more a matter of individual efforts and crusades than any concerted effort by larger organizations.

Early Guidelines

My friend George Isham, M.D., Medical Director of Health Partners, and editor of the Institute of Medicine (IOM) publication series, likes to ask, "When did the first guideline appear in writing?" And the answer to that question is actually 200 years B.C. with the use of the Hammurabi code. The Jews were asked to prepare foods in a Kashrut manner. The Torah prohibits consumption of blood.* This is the only dietary law that has a reason specified in the Torah: we do not eat blood because the life of the animal (literally, the soul of the animal) is contained in the blood. This applies only to the blood of birds and

---

* Lev. 7:26-27; Lev. 17:10-14.

mammals, not to fish blood. Thus, it is necessary to remove all blood from the flesh of kosher animals.

The first step in this process occurs at the time of slaughter. The remaining blood must be removed, either by broiling or soaking and salting. Liver may only be koshered by the broiling method, because it has so much blood in it and such complex blood vessels. This final process must be completed within 72 hours after slaughter and before the meat is frozen or ground. Most butchers, and all frozen food vendors, take care of the soaking and salting for their customers, but it is left to the person to verify this to make sure they are in compliance with the guidelines.

Guidelines have sprung up throughout the ages and they were advanced for hospital readmissions in the 1800s. They are again being scrutinized by the Centers for Medicare & Medicaid Services (CMS) in the health reform bill being assembled as we speak. Florence Nightingale and Ernest Codman were pioneers in this field.

In 1863, Florence Nightingale (1820–1910) published the third edition of *Notes on Hospitals* that detailed her experience in managing wounded soldiers during the Crimean War. She attempted to apply these same guidelines to the commercial population. In 1855, six months after arriving in Scutari, Turkey, at Barrack Hospitals, she cut hospital death rates from 42.7 to 2.2%.*

"Accurate hospital statistics are much more rare than is generally imagined," wrote Ms. Nightingale, "and at best they only give the mortality which has taken place in hospitals with no cognizance of those cases which are discharged in hopes of learning of the condition progress or, to die immediately afterwards, a practice which is followed to a much greater extent by some hospitals than others." Early American physician and researcher Ernest Amory Codman (1869–1940) began tracking outcomes and readmissions while still a clerk going to medical school at Harvard. Dr. Harvey Cushing (the soon to be recognized neurosurgeon) became concerned about anesthesia rates, graphing patients every 5 minutes. Over time they developed the first intraoperative anesthesia charts. Codman then began studying postdischarge patients, reviewing whether or not they did return to health. He labeled this "end results idea," which was "merely the commonsense notion that every hospital should follow every patient it treats, long enough to determine whether or not the treatment has been successful, then inquire into the 'if not, why not' with a view of preventing similar failures in the future" (Codman 1934).†

---

* I. B. Cohen, "Florence Nightingale," *Scientific American* 250, no. 3 (1984): 128–137.
† Ernest Amory Codman, *A Study in Hospital Efficiency: As demonstrated by the Case Report of the first five years of a private hospital*, Oak Brook Terrace, IL, Joint Commission on Accreditation of Healthcare, 1995.

Both Codman and Nightingale were tracking not just the incidence of illness, as many of our claims systems and utilization management systems do today, but rather looking at *why* some patients were healed and others were not. They then found a root cause and determined what could be done to reduce the likelihood of a poor outcome.

One of the principal reasons AcademyHealth was formed in 1960 was a joining of two research foundations. The mission was to carry forward a national discussion on qualified studies in care improvement between nongovernment researchers and government funding sources to see that foundations and grant-making organizations had a means to connect with some of the nation's best and brightest thinkers. Engineering and reengineering to identify and remove waste has continued to be a principal focus. The Academy will continue to lead much of the work in cost-effective analysis and comparative economics.

Though much of this work, as well as the work by Health Affairs and the Commonwealth Fund, advocates for solid scientific methods in population management and redesign, there are still concerns about projected savings and dollars earned by hospital pools, medical groups, or health plans to see whether they should undertake a health promotion of comparative performance analysis of providers associated with their organization.

The amazing thing is that after years of original study by Nightingale, Codman, and others, we still have a problem with discharge planning.

In addition to the discharge and transitional care gap in the delivery system, there is an ongoing gap in daily services that can be attributed to lack of efficient coordination or just plain unnecessary care. A 2005 report from the National Academy of Engineering and the Institute of Medicine, *Building a Better Delivery System: A New Engineering/Health Care Partnership*, found that "an estimated thirty to forty cents of every dollar spent on health care ... a half trillion dollars a year ... is spent on costs associated with: overuse, underuse, misuse, duplication, system failures ... and inefficiency."* It also found that just over half of patients receive evidence-based care, and each year 98,000 patients die and 1 million are injured as the result of medical errors. The complexity of medicine has increased to the point where no one person can ensure that it is delivered reliably and safely; instead, standardized approaches are needed to guide patients from provider to provider throughout the system.

This theme continues to be carried out in 2009 and 2010 with health reform discussions about how money can be saved through health care reengineering of both process and eventuality outcome.

---

* Proctor Reid, et al., "Building a Better Delivery System: A New Engineering Healthcare Partnership," (Washington, D.C.: The National Academies Press, 2005), 8.

Savings Estimates

United Health Group, the largest private contractor for Medicare Advantage in the United States, compiled a lengthy report and series of recommendations on how the government could reengineer its delivery system requirements for Medicare fee-for-service (FFS) to do what managed care companies are doing to reduce costs but at the same time maintain or improve quality.

Option 1: Member Incentives to Use Highest Quality Providers

Academic research from Dartmouth, Rand, and many other centers has consistently demonstrated that the use of evidence-based care is variable, as are the resulting clinical outcomes and efficiencies. These variations are evident across geographies, between hospitals, and within all specialist and primary care providers, and persist despite the availability of evidence-based standards covering many conditions and treatments.

Option Description

Analysis of physician outcome data, treatment data, and cost data can inform the assessment of quality and efficiency for certain kinds of health episodes, which reflect all of the procedures, testing, and drugs used to treat a health "episode" (e.g., cardiac bypass surgery). By developing a rating system that accounts for quality and efficiency, it is possible to bring better information into the process for patients and providers. These premium provider networks, as United calls them, apply evidence-based science and specialty society guidance across 20 medical specialties in 39 states, covering nearly 20 million United members. For example, United can identify nearly 100,000 physicians who consistently produce superior clinical outcomes at up to 20% lower costs, because of the quality and appropriateness of their work. However, the performance curve is continuous, so networks can be tiered in many different ways.

To encourage members/beneficiaries to use the highest quality and most efficient physicians, network tiers can be developed and patient financial incentives can be applied. Patients pay lower copays for top-tier physicians than for bottom-tier physicians. In this way, patient choice helps drive higher savings. These incentives could be added to the FFS Medicare program.

Health plans could use their performance data and care management programs to create virtual network overlays on fee-for-service Medicare. Participation in these programs would be entirely voluntary for seniors, who might, however, benefit from lower Part B premiums and lower cost sharing when they choose to use a premium designated provider who scored better on quality and efficiency. The bulk of the remaining savings would accrue directly to Medicare. Medicare should also begin to contribute its data to a sector-wide effort combining public and private payer data to produce valid and relevant physician and hospital performance measures.

Basis of Savings Estimate

We estimated the savings from providing information to seniors on quality and efficiency variations to influence their choices, as well as from an optional program by which seniors who chose to use higher performing providers would benefit from a 10% cost advantage in their Medicare premiums. Savings are based on the results of current United Health Group programs using a quality and efficiency measurement system coupled with a member incentive program that promotes the highest quality and most cost-effective physicians. However, United and CMS have made conservative assumptions about the uptake of these programs inside original Medicare. Because the program is voluntary, United has modeled the potential effects of only a small proportion of the Medicare FFS population shifting to higher performing providers. This would still yield over $37 billion in savings over a 10-year period, with a phase-in over 5 years. Stronger incentivization with more gain sharing with seniors would produce much more substantial savings, as well as likely stimulate stronger improvements in physician performance right across the delivery system.

Option 2: Transitional Case Management Program

One of the biggest gaps in care takes place when patients leave the hospital. Patients can have difficulty remembering or following instructions from physicians. They may also have trouble arranging necessary follow-up visits and may not be aware of social and community support services available to them. In some cases, patients may be inappropriately discharged to a setting that does not provide a sufficient level of follow-up care. These care gaps often lead to expensive and avoidable hospital readmissions.

Option Description

Transitional case management programs serve as a bridge between the hospital inpatient admission and discharge to home for individuals and their caregivers. They help to facilitate a safe transition for those individuals who have a high risk of being readmitted. Special attention is given to those with chronic health conditions and complex discharge plans with a focus on ensuring that the patient and caregiver have a discharge plan, understand their discharge plan, and have the necessary resources to execute the discharge plan. At the time of discharge, case managers assist in determining the most appropriate discharge setting (e.g., skilled nursing facility or home care). Case managers also ensure continuity of all discharge orders including medications, therapies, and wound treatments. Case managers help patients schedule appropriate follow-up visits with a personal physician. They also connect patients with social and community service evaluations and referrals. The level of case manager interventions increases with the level of complexity of follow-up care for the patient.

Option 3: Gaps in Care Reduction Programs

Patient care in the United States is often managed by multiple physicians across a range of specialties. Frequently, there is little coordination among clinicians, which creates opportunities for patients to miss important preventive interventions or inadvertently stray from prescribed courses of treatment. These unnoticed and unidentified gaps in care can lead to sicker patient populations requiring significantly more intensive treatment, including hospitalization. Poor patient management from gaps in care also increases the cost of care for these patients.

Option Description

Gaps in care programs use predictive modeling tools and comprehensive patient encounter data to identify missed preventive care, gaps in prescribed courses of treatment, and gaps in evidence-based recommended interventions. When care gaps are identified, proactive communications are sent to both the patient and the relevant physician. These notifications result in savings by identifying and addressing gaps in care early, before serious problems develop. This tool keeps patients healthier and avoids higher acuity treatments and hospital admissions.

Basis of Savings Estimate

Based on results from United Health Group's Gaps in Care program, the Medicare program could also see savings. This patient notification process could be incorporated into the Medicare program in several ways, but we see it effectively done through a system that emphasizes the role of the primary care physician. The 10-year savings score assumes a 2-year phase-in of this program, which would then be deployed across original Medicare.

Option 4: Integrated Medical Management

The senior population has a significantly higher disease burden than the general population. This increased risk magnifies the impact of missed preventative care and inappropriate or delayed care. Financial and logistical barriers to care can result in missed opportunities to detect and treat ailments before they become more serious. In addition, insufficient applications of evidence-based standards can result in unnecessary, inappropriate, and expensive interventions.

Option Description

Integrated medical management programs combine a number of elements that ultimately result in lower avoidable hospital usage. These programs include annual preventative care assessments and interventions, as well as benefit designs that lower member costs for appropriate care and reduce access barriers. They also include programs to apply evidence-based guidelines to hospital utilization to reimburse providers differently and to help patients make decisions appropriate for them. Combined, these programs result in significantly lower inpatient admissions and lengths of stay.

Basis of Savings Estimate

Based on hospital inpatient admits in United Health Group Medicare Advantage plans versus inpatient admits in the Medicare FFS program, standardized for geography and Hierarchical Condition Categories (HCC) (as a proxy for patients' health care needs), United estimates the potential savings to original Medicare of $100 billion over 10 years, assuming a 4-year phase-in.

Option 5: Medical Home Care Delivery Model and Physician Incentives for Coordination

The prevalent care delivery model in the United States is both fragmented and complex. Patients are now largely responsible for gathering, organizing, and communicating critical health care information to a variety of physicians across multiple clinical encounters. No single clinical professional is responsible for ensuring that care is coordinated, comprehensive, and appropriate. This fragmented delivery model can lead to higher costs of care, driven by unnecessary hospitalization, duplicative tests and services, and noncompliance with treatments. In some cases, patients may even be harmed by disjointed and uncoordinated care.

Option Description

The medical home care delivery model effectively designates a single clinician or medical practice as the responsible entity for organizing patient information and coordinating care. This approach reestablishes the important patient–physician relationship by having patients receive long-term comprehensive care from a primary care physician, or "medical home," instead of episodic care from multiple disconnected physician encounters. Patients select a personal primary care physician who will treat ailments, manage chronic conditions, incorporate preventive and wellness initiatives, and coordinate care, as appropriate, with other professionals. By providing appropriate comprehensive care that reduces duplicative treatments and testing, decreases inpatient admissions and readmissions, and reduces inappropriate utilization of the emergency room and specialty care, this delivery model can help reduce system costs.

Physicians are incentivized to act as a patient's medical home through the payment of a monthly fee on a per member, per month basis. Physicians are also eligible for additional retrospective bonus payments on a quarterly basis for achieving certain quality and cost targets. These incentives are critical to make this model most effective.

Basis of Savings Calculation

Established physician incentive programs in Medicare Advantage, as well as projections for current United Health Group medical home pilot programs for privately insured members, contribute to United's estimate of savings for the Medicare FFS population. Were a voluntary system for physicians and Medicare beneficiaries able to bring in two thirds of FFS beneficiaries, and depending on the design of the bonus incentives, savings could fall into a wide range. Savings would be higher if requirements were introduced for physicians to participate and Medicare beneficiaries to join.

Option 6: Care Coordination

Significant waste in the current health care delivery system is driven by a lack of care coordination and partial adherence to evidence-based care. The current fee-for-service model for provider reimbursement can exacerbate this problem, by providing incentives for more volume, as opposed to providing more appropriate and efficient care. Incentive systems do not currently exist within the Medicare program to lead primary care physicians to support comprehensive, cost-effective care to their patients.

Option Description

The physician additional compensation program rewards medical groups for providing comprehensive, high-quality, and cost-effective care for their patients. The program focuses on primary care physicians but allows for the inclusion of specialists within multispecialty groups. The financial structure of the program is simple: A portion of CMS revenue is placed into a pool every month. Medical costs incurred by the practice are withdrawn from the pool, and at the end of the year, any savings are shared between the physicians and the health plan, which is able over time to incorporate those savings into the prices incurred by employers and individuals. The physicians have no downside risk if costs are higher than projected, but if there is no surplus, the group gets no bonus. Unlike the medical home pilot, no monthly participation fees are paid. Cost savings are generated as physicians focus on providing appropriate levels of care, resulting in improved outcomes and a reduction in the number of unnecessary treatments and unplanned admissions to the emergency room.

Basis of Savings Calculation

Based on actual results observed over a 10-year period in ongoing United Health Group physician gain-sharing programs, United estimates that a similar program serving the Medicare FFS population would lead to both higher quality care and lowered system costs. If a voluntary system for physicians and Medicare beneficiaries could eventually cover half of FFS beneficiaries, savings estimates could be as set out above. Depending on the design of the bonus incentives, and the health of the enrolled seniors, savings would fall into a range. Savings would be higher if requirements were introduced for physicians to participate and Medicare beneficiaries to join. The 10-year savings score assumes a 3-year phase-in of this program, which would then be deployed across original Medicare.

Option 7: Specialist Data Sharing

In many markets, significant outcome and efficiency variability exist across specialist practitioners. Typically, poorly performing physicians are not aware of their performance relative to their peers. Physicians generally receive very little regularly reported comparative performance data. In the absence of comparative data, physicians have little external guidance on opportunities for improvement, which allows performance disparities to persist. Ultimately, this results in poor outcomes and inefficient use of health care resources.

Option Description

Utilizing rigorous clinical and statistical evaluation techniques, quality and efficiency measures are calculated for specialist physicians. These scores are based on episodes of care, which reflect all of the procedures, testing, and drugs used to treat a health episode (e.g., cardiac bypass surgery). Personalized scorecards are created and shared with individual physicians to demonstrate their performance relative to local, regional, and national averages. By leveraging the desire of physicians to perform at high levels, this data sharing reduces costs and improves the quality of care by encouraging clinically proven practices for treatment of a variety of conditions. Under this particular program, no incentive payments are made to drive improvement.

Basis of Savings Calculation

Based on actual reductions in medical costs resulting from ongoing United Health Group data-sharing programs, we expect that required data sharing with physicians in the Medicare program could have similar results. In future iterations, CMS RAC (Recovery Audits Contracts) audits could be used as further incentive to drive increased adoption of best practices. Physicians could be required to view such a scorecard as part of initiatives to reform the physician payment system. The 10-year savings score is based on results in cardiology and assumes a 5-year phase-in of this program, which would then be deployed across original Medicare. Savings from deploying the program across a wider range of specialties would be correspondingly greater over time.

Summary of Selected Savings Options

These are but a few areas where payers like United have developed a savings program based upon changing beneficiary behavior or reducing unnecessary services. The examples above total $137 billion of a total of reengineering and waste reduction plan that could easily reach $540 billion.

United's examples and our own work all revolve around the use of guidelines, process standards, and protocols, much of which are already used by the majority of physicians. However, the few who are not in line with the norms could create large savings using a combination of guidelines and technology.

Incentivizing Member/Beneficiary Use of High-Quality Providers 2010–2019 Savings

Option 1: Member Incentives to Use Highest Quality Providers—Assessment of quality and efficiency of providers using episodes of care analytics measured against evidence-based standards and efficiency benchmarks. Provides members with incentives to use highest quality physicians. ~$37 billion

Option 2: Cancer Support Programs—Voluntary guidance on cancer treatment best practices and patient options, including hospice care and case management to prevent hospital readmissions between therapy sessions. ~$5 billion

Option 3: Transplant Solutions Program—Voluntary guidance for patients on selecting the best transplant centers in the nation for their condition. ~$0.7 billion

Reducing Avoidable and Inappropriate Care

Option 4: Institutional Preadmission Program—Provision of on-site nurse practitioners at skilled nursing facilities to manage illnesses and prevent avoidable hospitalizations. ~$166 billion

Option 5: Transitional Case Management Program—Follow-up with patients after leaving the hospital to reduce readmissions by checking on recovery progress and supporting adherence to discharge plans and recommended medical care. ~$55 billion

Option 6: Advanced Illness Program—Provides information and guidance to patients and their families about both their condition and the benefits of further treatment options including palliative care at the end of life. ~$18 billion

Option 7: Disease Management for Congestive Heart Failure—Voluntary coaching for members with higher-acuity chronic illness to ensure treatment compliance. ~$25 billion

Option 8: Gaps In Care Program—Voluntary intervention for members with chronic illness but relatively good health to ensure ongoing treatment compliance. ~$1.4 billion

Option 9: Integrated Medical Management—Application of clinical evidence-based care management tools with targeted preventative care and patient education tools to reduce admission rates. ~$102 billion

Incentivizing Physicians to Encourage High Quality Care

Option 10: Patient-Centered Medical Home—Establish a primary care physician as the central ongoing coordinator of patient care. Reduces inappropriate or duplicative treatments while ensuring that needed anticipatory care is provided. ~$20 billion

Option 11: Physician Additional Compensation Program—Rewarding physicians for providing comprehensive medical care and utilizing resources appropriately. ~$24 billion

Option 12: Specialist Data Sharing—Sharing comparative quality and effectiveness data with physicians to induce behavioral change toward evidence-based clinical practice. ~$15 billion

Applying Evidence-Based Standards to Reimbursement Policies

Option 13: Radiology Benefit Management—Application of clinical evidence to determine clinically appropriate diagnostic radiology studies. ~$13 billion

Option 14: Radiology Therapy Management—Application of clinical evidence to determine clinically appropriate usage of radiology therapies. ~$5 billion

Option 15: Prospective Claims Review—Analysis of claims before they are paid to detect upcoding, duplicate billing, and billing for nonexistent patients. ~$57 billion

Potential savings to the federal government by applying these selected programs are provisionally estimated at $540 billion during 2010–2019.

These estimates are created from the United Health database and our discussions with actuaries and CMS staffers. Again, a small sample of members were used to model this, because Medicare is a voluntary program, but by inferring estimates on a cost per thousand basis across the spectrum of services and costs, we judge these estimates to be conservative.

Guidelines and Episodes of Care

We have seen how guidelines for select procedures and groups of services/procedures have been used; now, let's look at the more detailed analysis of these tools and their application.

Many of these techniques and methodologies may be familiar to the reader. You will notice that much of the reporting still centers around hospital inpatients. This was driven by the formation of diagnosis-related groups (DRGs) in 1984. The advantage of DRGs is the ability to link diagnoses to a specific set of services. The disadvantage is that DRGs cannot be backed into a capitation calculation nor can they be adjusted easily to predict care use as Principle Inpatient Diagnostic Cost Group (PIP DCGS) because DRGs rely on short-term costs and procedural data, especially if surgery is indicated. This calls for a more adjusted approach to reflect differences in populations and contrasting outcomes and to examine performance of individual patients, populations, or subgroups of these populations.

As discussed on page 14, Dr. Wennberg finds geography to play a more important part in who does and does not receive what kind of care.

Much of the data contained in risk adjusters is used for report cards, payment tiering, and outcomes analysis to use as a baseline for future improvement. Risk adjusters by themselves may only truly report variance of up to 10% of the population, but this is far superior to just demographics. In other words, like statistics, the use of the correct adjusters must be selected based upon what it is the researcher, health plan, or provider group wants to examine. The risk adjuster approach is able to level the playing field by making a predictable budget from a population with select diagnosis and demographic factors. This means that as a sicker population is managed, there are more dollars and resources available. This is attractive to payers and providers and offers some flexibility to alter these adjusters as modern medicine makes more technology available. (In our definition of technology we include not only medical devices but also drug therapies.)

Grouping Bundles of Services

In the MedPac report of 2008* a discussion of wrapping provider payments for acute and ambulatory care together was discussed. The goal of this was to develop a better package of services based upon acuity and to also begin the process of having physicians and hospitals be at risk for patient care versus competing with one another for procedural billing. A grouper used to bring these two providers together was called Episode Treatment Groups™ (ETG™), an invention of Symmetry Technologies in New Mexico. The attractiveness here was not just the clearly established outcome and diagnosis but also the meta analysis for medical review material presented with each ETG.

---

* MedPac Annual Repot to Congress, June 2008.

A. The ETG methodology is a patented case-mix adjustment and episode-building system that uses routinely collected inpatient and ambulatory claims data. The resulting clinically homogenous groups, of which there are approximately 600, adjust for severity by the presence of complicating conditions, comorbidities, and other characteristics of a patient's condition that affect resource utilization. The ETG methodology is similar to that of the DRGs but with several important differences.

B. Treatment as an inpatient, outpatient, or both. Specifically, the characteristics of the ETG methodology are as follows:

1. Manageable Number of Groups—The ETG episode of illness patient classification system is composed of nearly 600 statistically stable clinical groups. The ETGs were constructed using a nationally representative 60 million record claims database representing all illness types.

2. Case-Mix Adjustment—ETGs adjust for patient severity, intensity, and complexity by accounting for differences in patient age, complicating conditions, comorbidities, and major surgeries.

3. Clinical Homogeneity—ETGs are clinically homogeneous so that each patient's illness and severity level are medically consistent with others belonging to the same ETG. Consequently, direct comparisons of treatment patterns can be made among providers within the same ETG.

4. Episode building—ETGs combine inpatient, ambulatory, and pharmaceutical claims to build a complete treatment episode from onset of symptoms until treatment is complete. Rather than relying on a fixed time frame, each episode's treatment duration is flexibly determined based on its ETG-specific *clean period*, or time period in which there is an absence of treatment. This ensures that all appropriate treatment and cost information has been collected and correctly assigned to one complete illness episode.

5. Concurrent and Recurrent Episodes—Using the service unit of an individual claim or encounter form as input, ETGs identify and track the treatment of different illnesses that may exist during a single patient encounter. As a result, ETGs separate and identify concurrently occurring illnesses and assign each health care service to the clinically appropriate episode. In addition, should a patient be successfully treated but suffer a recurrence of the same illness, the ETG software identifies the recurrent episodes.

6. Shifting Episode Assignment—ETGs account for changes in a patient's condition during the course of treatment. Once a change in condition has been identified, the patient's entire episode may shift from the initially defined ETG to the ETG that includes the change in condition. In this way, the progression of an illness is identified.

7. Pharmaceutical Claims—Unique to the ETG methodology is its ability to assign pharmaceutical claims data to the appropriate illness episode using the 11-digit National Drug Code (NDC) that contains highly specific information regarding each drug type, its manufacturer, dosage, and route of administration. Using a sophisticated hierarchical approach, the ETG methodology evaluates each prescription drug claim against each of the concurrently occurring episodes for which the particular drug could be prescribed and then assigns the drug claim to the most clinically appropriate episode.

Value-Based Purchasing and Performance-Based Contracting

The transition from the current payment by DRG to a more performance-based plan requires some strategy work by hospital management to work with physician leadership to be able to obtain the necessary data and begin the evaluation process to determine what gaps remain in reporting clinical information.

At the present time most hospitals are already reporting data under the CMS Reporting Hospital Quality Data for Annual Payment Update (RHQDAPU) Program. This pay for information is different than what the future holds. At the present time, information, as well as Medicare Advantage actual payment and clinical utilization data, has been reported into a profiling system that is now identifying key measures of performance and using benchmarking data to do comparative analysis of quality and costs. What most hospitals and physicians do not understand is that this dimension of value-based purchasing (VBP) is just the beginning. Once baselines are set for care, appropriateness based upon severity and payment level will also be created, placing a not-to-exceed number on payments. This payment level linked to severity of illness is the real threshold to a bidding system where Medicare can start bidding out the best value hospitals, leaving other higher cost providers with lower values with few patients. Volume will increase for the best contractors. The structure for this is already in place with demonstration projects of accountable care organizations, Beacon communities, and similar projects.

This RHQDAPU information gathering program is a transition to the government's performance payment system called *value based purchasing*.

There is a version of value-based purchasing being followed by employers at this time and we will discuss this later in the book, but the issues right now are the performance measures and payment alterations being planned for 2010 based upon this year's data collection. This version of performance-based contracting

(PBC) has been made part of the legislative package passed by Congress several years ago. A short introduction is in order.

In 2006, Congress passed Public Law 109-171, the Deficit Reduction Act of 2005 (DRA), which under Section 5001(b) authorized CMS to develop an approach to value-based purchasing for Medicare hospital services commencing FY2009. Value-based purchasing in the DRA applies only to subsection (d) hospitals and does not apply to critical access hospitals or to other hospital types that are not paid under the Inpatient Prospective Payment System (IPPS). However, the DRA 2010 is changing to include all forms of payment to facilities.

The Medicare Hospital VBP program builds on the important groundwork established by Medicare's RHQDAPU program and, in 2010, has expanded the measures and complexity.

Since FY2004, RHQDAPU has provided differential payments to hospitals that publicly report their performance on a defined set of inpatient care performance measures, as originally mandated under the 2003 Medicare Modernization Act and expanded under DRA Section 5001(a), The Tax Relief and Health Care Act of 2006 expanded the RHQDAPU and in 2010 VBP is further expanded.

CMS Goals for the VBP Program

- Improve clinical quality
- Address problems of underuse, overuse, and misuse of services
- Encourage patient-centered care
- Reduce adverse events and improve patient safety
- Avoid unnecessary costs in the delivery of care
- Stimulate investments in structural components and the reengineering of care processes system-wide
- Make performance results transparent to and useable by consumers
- Avoid creating additional disparities in health care and work to reduce existing disparities

This program includes measures for hospital outpatient services (by FY2009) and ambulatory surgery centers (by FY2010); see Table 6.1. CMS proposes to replace the current hospital quality reporting program—RHQDAPU—with the VBP program. Building on the foundation of the RHQDAPU program, the new VBP program would encompass both public reporting and financial incentives for better performance as tools to drive improvements in clinical quality, patient-centeredness, and efficiency.

Table 6.1   FY2009 Candidate Measures for VBP Financial Incentive

Clinical Quality—Process-of-Care Measures		*Entered RHQDAPU*
Acute Myocardial Infarction (AMI)		
AMI-1	Aspirin at arrival[a]	11/2004
AMI-2	Aspirin prescribed at discharge[a]	11/2004
AMI-3	ACE inhibitor (ACE-I) or angiotensin receptor blocker (ARBs) for left ventricular systolic dysfunction[a]	11/2004
AMI-4	Adult smoking cessation advice/counseling[a]	4/2005
AMI-5	Beta blocker prescribed at discharge[a]	11/2004
AMI-7a	Thrombolytic agent received within 30 minutes of hospital arrival	4/2005
AMI-8a	Primary percutaneous coronary intervention (PCI) received within 90 minutes of arrival	4/2005
Heart Failure (HF)		
HF-1	Discharge instructions	4/2005
HF-3	ACE inhibitor (ACE-I) or angiotensin receptor blocker (ARBs) for left ventricular systolic dysfunction	11/2004
HF-4	Adult smoking cessation advice/counseling[a]	4/2005
Pneumonia (PN)		
PN-2	Pneumococcal vaccination status	11/2004
PN-3b	Blood culture performed in emergency department before first antibiotic received in hospital	4/2005
PN-4	Adult smoking cessation advice/counseling	4/2005
PN-6	Appropriate antibiotic selection	9/2005
PN-7	Influenza vaccination status	1/2006
		(continued)

Table 6.1 FY2009 Candidate Measures for VBP Financial Incentive (continued)

Clinical Quality — Process-of-Care Measures		*Entered RHQDAPU*
Surgical Care Improvement/Surgical Infection Prevention (SCIP/SIP)		
SCIP-Inf-1	Prophylactic antibiotic received within 1 hour prior to surgical incision	9/2005
SCIP-Inf-3	Prophylactic antibiotics discontinued within 24 hours after surgery end time	9/2005
Clinical Quality—Outcome Measure		
	30-Day AMI mortality	6/2007
	30-Day HF mortality	6/2007
Patient-Centered Care Measures		
	HCAHPS	12/2007

[a] Denotes topped-out measure. All of the process-of-care measures with the exception of influenza vaccine and the prophylactic antibiotic selection measure were used in analysis that supported development of the proposed performance assessment model.

Beyond these candidate measures, the measure set for FY2010 would also include hospital outpatient measure currently under development, as required by Section 109 of the Tax Relief and Health Care Act of 2006.

The design of the proposed VBP program is predicated on the following assumptions:

- The VBP program would start in FY2009 (October 1, 2008).
- A specified percentage of hospital payment would be conditional on hospital performance assessed using VBP incentive payment measures.
- The VBP program could include measures for different purposes: incentive payment, public reporting, and measure development. All measures used for incentive payment would also be publicly reported.
- Hospitals would be required to submit data on all measures applicable to their patient population and service mix to qualify for incentive payment.
- The VBP program would reward hospitals that improve their quality performance as well as those that achieve high levels of performance.

■ The VBP program would use both financial incentives and public reporting to drive quality improvement.

■ The VBP program would build on the existing measures and on the data submission, validation, and public reporting infrastructure of the RHQDAPU program.

■ The VBP program would transition from and replace the current RHQDAPU program.

■ The VBP program would not include additional funding beyond the annual payment updates (APU).

■ The VBP program would move rapidly to achieve a comprehensive measure set by expanding the measures available for assessing clinical quality, including HCAHPS to begin to assess patient-centered care, and efficiency measures. It is anticipated that the VBP program would also incorporate hospital outpatient measures as required for the RHQDAPU program by the Tax Relief and Health Care Act of 2006.

Overview of Performance Assessment Model

■ A hospital must submit data for all VBP measures that apply to its patient population and service mix, regardless of whether the measure is for incentive payment, public reporting, or measure development.

■ The hospital receives a performance score on each measure for incentive payment.

■ The hospital receives 0 to 10 points for each measure based on either the attainment or improvement scoring criteria.

■ The hospital's overall VBP performance score is determined by aggregating the scores across all VBP measures for which it has a minimum number of cases.

■ The overall performance score, reflected as a percentage of points earned out of the total possible points for which the hospital is eligible, is then translated into the incentive payment using an exchange function.

Each measure has a benchmark and an attainment threshold that are determined from the distribution of national hospital performance on that measure during the previous reporting period. Because these scoring cut points are determined from actual hospital performance, they provide realistic markers of performance expectations. These parameters and the attainment range and improvement range they define are used to determine a hospital's score on each measure. The methodology used to determine these parameters is described below.

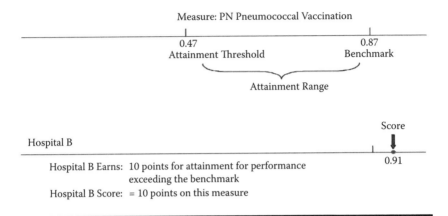

Figure 6.1 Benchmark calculation.

Setting Benchmarks and Attainment Thresholds

To provide an empirical basis for designing and testing of the performance assessment model, a database was created containing the 20 RHQDAPU process-of-care measures reported on Hospital Compare by more than 3,000 IPPS hospitals for 2004 and 2005.

Scoring Performance Based on Attainment

For each VBP measure that counts toward incentive payment, a hospital could earn from 0 to 10 points for attainment based on where its score for the measure fell relative to the attainment threshold and the benchmark. All attainment points would be rounded to the nearest whole number (*e.g.*, attainment points of 9.6 would be rounded to 10 points).

■ If the hospital's score is equal to or greater than the benchmark, then the hospital receives 10 points for attainment.
■ If the hospital's score is within the attainment range (greater than the attainment threshold but below the benchmark), then the hospital receives a score between 1 and 9 based on a discrete linear scale established for the attainment range.
■ If the hospital's score is equal to or less than the attainment threshold (i.e., the lower bound of the attainment range), then the hospital receives 0 points for attainment.

In Figure 6.1, Hospital "B" is scored on the pneumonia measure "patients assessed and given pneumococcal vaccine." The benchmark calculated for this measure was 0.87, mean value of the top decile in 2004, and the attainment threshold was 0.47, performance of the median hospital in 2004. Hospital B's measure rate in 2005 was 0.91, which exceeds the benchmark; thus, Hospital B would earn the maximum of 10 points for attainment. Hospital B's improvement from its previous year's score on this measure is not relevant and would not be calculated, because it has earned the maximum 10 points for the measure.

Basis of Incentive Payments

The VBP incentive is calculated as a percentage of the DRG payment with the percentage allocated to the VBP incentive payment established annually. The incentive is a percentage of the base DRG payment only, with geographic and DRG relative weight adjustments. This is intended to link the incentive payment directly to the clinical services provided during a patient stay.

This method will be refined and may be influenced by other payment components such as capital costs, Disproportionate Share Hospital (DSH) payments, and Indirect Medical Education (IME) payments as needed.

This approach represents a change from the RHQDAPU program, which ties payment to the annual payment update. Similar to the mechanism used in the RHQDAPU program, the VBP payment incentive would be tied to the reimbursement each hospital receives for the hospitalization of a Medicare patient. This means that the performance metric of quality will now be tied to a patient's annual budget that can be measured in costs per thousands and budgeted on a per member per month basis.

CMS is evaluating candidate VBP measures based on the following selection criteria, many of which already serve as a basis for evaluating the suitability of measures for public reporting and accountability purposes:

■ Importance
■ Scientific acceptability
■ Feasibility
■ Improvability
■ Usability
■ Controllability
■ Potential for unintended consequences
■ Contribution to comprehensiveness

Small Numbers on Individual Performance Measures

Under the current RHQDAPU program, many hospitals report a small number of cases in the measure denominator for one or more of the measures proposed for use in VBP. Small numbers on individual measures occur for a variety of reasons, including low patient volumes, the use of sampling, and the use of discretionary exclusions for patients who are otherwise eligible for a measure.

For hospitals with small numbers of cases that can be scored for a given performance measure, the performance estimate that is calculated could be highly variable. Very low numbers of cases provide only limited approximations of the true underlying performance of the hospital. CMS is aware that some hospitals may have too few cases for certain measures to produce a stable estimate of performance (Table 6.2).

Though this transition continues to race forward to a fully implemented payment modification for hospitals, there are many aspects to this process, including public reporting on the Healthcare Compare website, that make both quality and some pricing transparent. This is intended to assist consumers as well as health maintenance organizations (HMOs) and insurance companies in identifying top-performing hospitals based upon a comparison of regional and national performance benchmarks (Figure 6.2). It is also a means for private payers including unions, voluntary employee benefits agreements (VEBAs), and similar trust funds for public employers to begin reporting data to their customers, thereby justifying the rationale for creating a high-performance network within a broader network. By paying the benefits at 100% for a top-performing hospital's services and 80% or less for a lower performing hospital, consumers can be shifted away from both hospital and doctor to assure themselves of maximum coverage with no out-of-pocket costs by seeing the top-performing doctors and hospitals.

What the Regulations Are Saying about Pay for Performance

At the present time the regulations for Medicare Advantage health plans have expanded to include the following descriptions. Much of this planning is intended to connect with the value-based purchasing initiative already in place from CMS. Hospitals and physicians who understand these requirements will have a better chance to participate in Medicare Advantage knowing the expectations of the Medicare plan and the federal government.

Table 6.2 Effect of Small Numbers by Hospital Bed Size

Number of Measures Able to Be Scored	All Hospitals		1–99 Beds		100–199 Beds		200+ Beds	
	Number of Hospitals	%	Number of Hospitals	%	Number of Hospitals	%	Number of Hospitals	%
0 Measures	49	1.4	42	3.5	7	0.7	0	0.0
1–2 Measures	165	4.9	154	13.0	10	0.9	1	0.1
3–4 Measures	82	2.4	70	5.9	10	0.9	2	0.2
5–6 Measures	303	9.0	170	14.3	83	7.7	50	4.5
7–8 Measures	289	8.5	235	19.8	46	4.3	8	0.7
9–10 Measures	491	14.5	276	23.2	171	15.9	44	3.9
11–12 Measures	551	16.3	182	15.3	276	25.7	93	8.3
13–14 Measures	899	26.6	49	4.1	315	29.4	535	47.6
15–16 Measures	556	16.4	11	0.9	155	14.4	390	34.7
	3,385	100.0	1,189	100.0	1,073	100.0	1,123	100.0

Note: Data represent a count of hospitals having a minimum of 10 cases to score a measure.

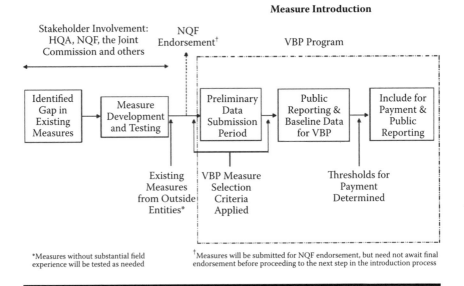

Figure 6.2 CMS measure development and testing.

The federal definition of pay for performance in the House Resolution Bill 3590 as of this writing is as follows:

(a) In General—Section 1853 of the Social Security Act (42 U.S.C. 1395w-23), as amended by section 1161, is amended—

   (1) in subsection (j), by inserting "subject to subsection (o)" after "For purposes of this part"; and

   (2) by adding at the end the following new subsection:

(o) Quality Based Payment Adjustment—

   (1) HIGH QUALITY PLAN ADJUSTMENT—For years beginning with 2011, in the case of a Medicare Advantage plan that is identified (under paragraph (3)(E)(ii)) as a high quality MA plan with respect to the year, the blended benchmark amount under subsection (n)(1) shall be increased—

      (A) for 2011, by 1.0 percent;

      (B) for 2012, by 2.0 percent; and

      (C) for a subsequent year, by 3.0 percent.

   (2) IMPROVED QUALITY PLAN ADJUSTMENT—For years beginning with 2011, in the case of a Medicare Advantage plan that is identified (under paragraph (3)(E)(iii)) as an improved quality MA plan

with respect to the year, blended benchmark amount under subsection (n)(1) shall be increased—

    (A)   for 2011, by 0.33 percent;

    (B)   for 2012, by 0.66 percent; and

    (C)   for a subsequent year, by 1.0 percent.

  (3) DETERMINATIONS OF QUALITY—

    (A)   QUALITY PERFORMANCE—The Secretary shall provide for the computation of a quality performance score for each Medicare Advantage plan to be applied for each year beginning with 2010.

    (B)   COMPUTATION OF SCORE—

(i) FOR YEARS BEFORE 2014—For years before 2014, the quality performance score for a Medicare Advantage plan shall be computed based on a blend (as designated by the Secretary) of the plan's performance on—

(I) HEDIS effectiveness of care quality measures;

   (II)   CAHPS quality measures; and

   (III)   such other measures of clinical quality as the Secretary may specify.

Such measures shall be risk-adjusted as the Secretary deems appropriate.

    (ii)   ESTABLISHMENT OF OUTCOME-BASED MEASURES—By not later than for 2013 the Secretary shall implement reporting requirements for quality under this section on measures selected under clause (iii) that reflect the outcomes of care experienced by individuals enrolled in Medicare Advantage plans (in addition to measures described in clause (i)). Such measures may include—

(I) measures of rates of admission and readmission to a hospital;

   (II)   measures of prevention quality, such as those established by the Agency for Healthcare Research and Quality (that include hospital admission rates for specified conditions);

   (III)   measures of patient mortality and morbidity following surgery;

   (IV)   measures of health functioning (such as limitations on activities of daily living) and survival for patients with chronic diseases;

   (V)   measures of patient safety; and

   (VI)   other measure of outcomes and patient quality of life as determined by the Secretary.

Such measures shall be risk-adjusted as the Secretary deems appropriate. In determining the quality measures to be used under this clause, the Secretary shall take into consideration the recommendations of the Medicare Payment Advisory Commission in its report to Congress under section 168 of the Medicare Improvements for Patients and Providers Act of 2008 (Public Law 110-275) and shall provide preference to measures collected on and comparable to measures used in measuring quality under parts A and B.

(iii) RULES FOR SELECTION OF MEASURES—The Secretary shall select measures for purposes of clause (ii) consistent with the following:

(I) The Secretary shall provide preference to clinical quality measures that have been endorsed by the entity with a contract with the Secretary under section 1890(a).

(II) Prior to any measure being selected under this clause, the Secretary shall publish in the Federal Register such measure and provide for a period of public comment on such measure.

(iv) TRANSITIONAL USE OF BLEND—For payments for 2014 and 2015, the Secretary may compute the quality performance score for a Medicare Advantage plan based on a blend of the measures specified in clause (i) and the measures described in clause (ii) and selected under clause (iii).

(v) USE OF QUALITY OUTCOMES MEASURES—For payments beginning with 2016, the preponderance of measures used under this paragraph shall be quality outcomes measures described in clause (ii) and selected under clause (iii).

(C) DATA USED IN COMPUTING SCORE—Such score for application for—

(i) payments in 2011 shall be based on quality performance data for plans for 2009; and

(ii) payments in 2012 and a subsequent year shall be based on quality performance data for plans for the second preceding year.

(D) REPORTING OF DATA—Each Medicare Advantage organization shall provide for the reporting to the Secretary of quality performance data described in subparagraph (B) (in order to determine a quality performance score under this paragraph) in such time and manner as the Secretary shall specify.

(E) RANKING OF PLANS—

(i) INITIAL RANKING—Based on the quality performance score described in subparagraph (B) achieved with respect to a year, the Secretary shall rank plan performance—

(I) from highest to lowest based on absolute scores; and

    (II) from highest to lowest based on percentage improvement in the score for the plan from the previous year.

A plan which does not report quality performance data under subparagraph (D) shall be counted, for purposes of such ranking, as having the lowest plan performance and lowest percentage improvement.

    (ii)   IDENTIFICATION OF HIGH QUALITY PLANS IN TOP QUINTILE BASED ON PROJECTED ENROLLMENT—The Secretary shall, based on the scores for each plan under clause (i)(I) and the Secretary's projected enrollment for each plan and subject to clause (iv), identify those Medicare Advantage plans with the highest score that, based upon projected enrollment, are projected to include in the aggregate 20 percent of the total projected enrollment for the year. For purposes of this subsection, a plan so identified shall be referred to in this subsection as a "high quality MA plan."

    (iii)   IDENTIFICATION OF IMPROVED QUALITY PLANS IN TOP QUINTILE BASED ON PROJECTED ENROLLMENT—The Secretary shall, based on the percentage improvement score for each plan under clause (i)(II) and the Secretary's projected enrollment for each plan and subject to clause (iv), identify those Medicare Advantage plans with the greatest percentage improvement score that, based upon projected enrollment, are projected to include in the aggregate 20 percent of the total projected enrollment for the year. For purposes of this subsection, a plan so identified that is not a high quality plan for the year shall be referred to in this subsection as an "improved quality MA plan."

    (iv)   AUTHORITY TO DISQUALIFY CERTAIN PLANS—In applying clauses (ii) and (iii), the Secretary may determine not to identify a Medicare Advantage plan if the Secretary has identified deficiencies in the plan's compliance with rules for such plans under this part.

  (F) NOTIFICATION—The Secretary, in the annual announcement required under subsection (b)(1)(B) in 2011 and each succeeding year, shall notify the Medicare Advantage organization that is offering a high quality plan or an improved quality plan of such identification for the year and the quality performance payment adjustment for such plan for the year. The Secretary shall provide for publication on the website for the Medicare program of the information described in the previous sentence.

In the overall health reform process these points are raised over and over again and are subject to Kathleen Sibelius the HHS Secretary and former commissioner of insurance for the state of Kansas. It is with her purview to select which measures will be law and what changes would be made over time. In addition, 2008 funding of the Episodes of Care task force with $10 billion tells us that the government is serious about bundled care and incorporating Agency for Health Research and Quality (AHRQ) and similar measures within these bundles. This will define care packages but also define reimbursement.

Chapter 7

Challenges

The Pay-for-Performance Rumors and Issues

Many seminars and books will tell you that setting in motion the performance-based contracting enterprise is a complex process. On top of that, who sets the standards is a challenge to assure that all parties, providers, and patient populations are scored properly and that money is connected to performance and not just activity. A discussion on whether to implement pay-for-performance (P4P) programs for the Medicare population continues to be debated despite all the demo projects and Medicare Advantage experiments to the contrary. Thus, several points made by Michael Cannon of the CATO Institute as well as from our own experience bear repeating.*

Defining Quality

As we said earlier, defining this idea of quality in words and process is probably the most difficult thing for health plans and providers to do. Many clinical guidelines have been advocated by our work as well as that of many other knowledgeable people, but the definition is still elusive.

Most work has relied on four types of quality measures. Clinical outcomes are what most of us think of when we are looking at performance. Patient outcomes, in terms of infection rate and readmissions, are also measures used since Codman. Some of the problems with these measures are the intervening

---

* Michael Cannon, "Pay for Performance: Is Medicare a Good Candidate?" *Yale Journal of Health Policy, Law & Ethics* (2006).

variables. We discuss this more with risk adjusters and groupers, but severity of illness and the work in which they are engaged or the stress factors in a family cannot necessarily be measured by clinical norms. Finally, another limitation is time. The lag time on mortality statistics or the need to have a more immediate influence on the quality aspects of care has many researchers looking deeper inside these definitions to find out what the root causes and driving forces in clinical outcomes are.

Can we look to this as a reproducible finding? Does this mean that all patients with this diagnosis at the same age and gender and predisposition should get this treatment? This march toward a more mechanical definition is what has practitioners (and patients) afraid that comparative economics and "cookbook medicine" may lessen the effectiveness of outcomes, making the standard of care mediocre instead of robust.

Process Points

Adherence to guidelines allows comparisons of data and process points (i.e., checking blood pressure or beta blockers for heart attack, eye exams for diabetes patients), which are all part of this mix of pay-for-performance discussions. Adherence to these measures results in pay increases or decreases very similar to the early pay-for-performance models.

Structural Factors

Structural factors take into account the delivery system resources and setting. This may include equipment available in a university setting that may not be available in a rural town or expertise of the medical staff.

For example, a neurotrauma in a geographic area where neurosurgeons do not present a problem. There are some, like Leapfrog and Bridges, who have come to the conclusion that having e-prescribing of hospitals with state-of-the-art information technology (IT) may be desirable, but these factors have limits.* Because the hospital has an advanced cardiac care unit does not mean that all of the best benchmarks are used. Availability of technology may assume that all resources are used optimally, which, we have found, is not always the case. Gaps in care delivery and process are not just a function of size of hospital or number of physicians with new technology.

---

* http://www.leapfroggroup.org/about_us/other_initiatives/incentives_and_rewards/ bridges_to_excellence.

Patient Satisfaction

"Patient satisfaction is influenced by patients' expectations and their understanding of the available alternatives."* This weakens this promise of this measure because much of these expectations can be influenced by the provider about to be judged. I have had doctors argue with me that patient satisfaction should not be a quality or performance measure because "patients have no idea what's good for them." This, again, settles the argument that physicians, not patients, have the influence in arranging or delivering a certain level of care.

Any one of these factors could be described as a measure. Collectively, they do represent a new look at the dimensions of care which, though more complex, are nonetheless more accurate.

Evidence-Based Quality Data

"A fundamental assumption of EBM is that practitioners who practice based on an understanding of evidence from applied health research will provide superior care compared with practitioners who rely on understanding of basic mechanisms and their own clinical experience. So far, no convincing direct evidence exists that shows this assumption is correct."†

The quest for good evidence-based data has been a barrier to the science of performance measurement and because third parties have limited access to these data points, arranging for payment based on a common definition of success is very difficult. As we stated in the earlier chapters, this is a science of limited followers because we lack reliable data and the willingness of those involved to invest in care guidelines and benchmark evaluation.

"Inaccurate findings are apparently not difficult to come by in medical literature. Recent analysis indicates that one third of frequently cited clinical studies are either incorrect or overstate the results of clinical interventions."‡

In our discussion of the future of P4P, we will present the potential use of P4P data and findings as a move away from mere insurance and clinical improvements and into the area of life sciences. More pharmaceutical companies are seeking solid outcomes data to gain Food and Drug Administration (FDA) approval and to justify the efficacy of their drugs. Health plans will benefit from this as

---

* Michael Cannon, "Pay for Performance: Is Medicare a Good Candidate?" *Yale Journal of Health Policy, Law, & Ethics* (2006).
† R. Brian Haynes, "What Kind of Evidence Is It That Evidence Based Medicine Advocates Want Health Care Providers to Pay Attention To?" *BMC Health Services Research 2*, no. 3 (2006).
‡ John P. A. Ioannidis, "Why Most Published Research Findings Are False," *PLoS Medicine 2*, no. 8 (2005): e124.

well because most plans have their own formulary or contract with a formulary, many of which are owned, at least in part, by pharmaceutical companies.

This loop of providers to plans to pharmaceutical companies back to plans may be the means by which insurance companies and health plans will be able to update their guidelines on an ongoing basis, a chore that many plans have not done for fear of controversy. Seeing this as a responsibility to their own members to assure that the best benchmarks and guidelines are used and that substandard care is not rewarded may be the impetus needed.

Outliers

A one-size-fits-all guideline may have adverse effects on those who fall outside the mean in terms of care. Immediately one thinks of the comorbidities of the elderly and the potential for multiple chronic conditions. Though there is a correlation between age and number of medications, many of today's medications are engineered to be taken for a very specific malady and, as such, may not have been tested for long-term effects of interaction with various other drugs.

Drug-induced diabetes is a good example. When seniors begin to lose weight and take better care of themselves the diabetes goes away. Was it the drug? The health habits? Or was diabetes misdiagnosed?

Plans that encourage physicians to treat outliers like normal patient populations run the risk of not only doing harm to the patient's health but creating a large financial cost to the plan to fix something that should not have occurred in the first place.

While giving a lecture to second-year students at the University of Illinois School of Medicine, the first question I was asked was, "What if the patient is not fitting the norm?" This was followed by "What if money is taken away from my practice because this outlier really needed individualized treatment and not the normal protocol?"

Identifying Optimal Target Incentives

Payers who are looking to use aggregated paid claims data as a means to develop protocols may have a difficult time really building targets and incenting the desired behavior of physicians. If incentives force the patient to not seek needed care or build inequities into the system between private or public payer groups, the goals of improvement will not be achieved.

In an integrated care setting like Health Partners or Kaiser, the group is rewarded for performance, thereby eliminating the need for apportioning out the steps of clinical intervention in the treatment process. But in a nonintegrated setting, patients will see more than one doctor, receive prescriptions from more than one doctor, and may obtain second opinions for their needs. Which provider should receive some or all of the incentive for good care and which provider should be having their incentive removed if care is not adequate? This apportioning of bonuses and sharing in a successful savings needs to be developed *before* the process is put in place.

What Types of Performance Targets?

Some targets can be referred to as *absolute targets*. Determining performance is simple. Either you did or did not give beta blockers to 80% of patients who fit the definition of a patient with acute myocardial infarction (AMI).

But what if a provider is already achieving 80% of AMI patients? Is it worth it to try for 85% or even 100% for the same payment? We worked with a large health plan that was achieving an average readmission rate of 17%. I asked what it would take to get that to 15%, and she asked me why? Why get below the average when the average is acceptable and there really is no great reward for being best?

We find that this mediocre goal is the wrong information to communicate and that a higher standard may be better, even if the group takes a bit longer to achieve it. In this case, it may not be about money; it may be more about the physician's own resourcefulness to innovate and answer his or her own question, "Why are we not at 95% of patients with AMI receiving beta blockers?"

This speaks to the relative performance measure where providers are assembled and set their collective goals based upon local practice patterns. This may result in a migration of the bottom performers to try to achieve the top deciles, or it could result in the bottom getting further and further away from the top performers, only because the top performers will try to improve while the bottom providers do not. This can get very sticky for P4P that rewards improvement only. In the above case, the top performers make *less* than the bottom performers who eventually may improve.

Size of Financial Incentives

In several Premier examples and demo projects, the use of 1 and 2% income increases or income reduction seemed to be enough to start changing some behavior, but the question that remained was if the incentives could be higher for primary care practitioners (PCPs) and specialty care doctors, would the results also have been more rapid and dramatic? Would cooperation from independent doctors be any easier to establish? Would the end result of savings turned back to providers in a larger sum have made a difference in performance?

Many argue that 2% of the bottom line for a multi-million-dollar hospital is usually equivalent to annual profit, and 2% of PCP gross revenue amounts to $1,000. This is why the Physician Quality Reporting Initiative (PQRI) was forced to establish a pay-for-information incentive at 5%, because most PCPs see no reason to change their reporting and coding unless they can get $3,000 or more.

In coming legislation, a discussion combining the use of gain sharing and pay for performance will reestablish a gain of several thousand dollars per physician if they can establish guidelines for care that are followed by all surgeons in a department. There is a way to return some of these savings to the hospital, which under prescribed circumstances is able to share these same savings with the physicians.

The Health Reform Bill HR3590 Patient Protection Act stated that those participating in pay-for-performance programs, including clinical integration, would be able to qualify for gain sharing to be incorporated into the pay-for-performance revenue payment system. This was voted down by Stark proponents, but it is logical to fit this situation of performance-based contracting to offer yet another opportunity for participation as part of the performance-based contracting environment.

In the interim, the current laws *do* offer a prescribed manner to share these savings from hospitals with doctors. This could be made part of a performance and reward system.

Cost Effectiveness

This is one of those terms that gets lost in translation because everyone thinks they know what it means. But in health care it is clear that we do not all agree on what this means.

As we discuss in other chapters, efficient care is often calculated wrong and effective care today may be an old guideline tomorrow as various panels and groups of experts continue to pour of comparative data to determine where an optimum level of care is achieved. As fewer and fewer dollars exist in this finite system of care, other services like preventive screenings and diagnostic treatments are becoming limited, with the idea that if only a few lives are saved by a test given to all, maybe the test given to only those with probable diagnosis or predisposition to the disease should be included in the testing. This sacrifices a few lives for the many, but the few who do die use resources at an alarming rate when in fact the entire episode could have been avoided by the test being shared with everyone. We all pay for this one way or the other, because the final days of life continue to be the most expensive use of inpatient and outpatient resources.

Commitment

A question that usually occurs in the first 10 minutes of discussion about performance-based medicine is "Will providers buy in?"

We get this question for hospital administrators talking about doctors but also managed care companies and employers who advocate an immediate implementation of P4P, recognizing just how interdependent we all are on each stakeholder in the system to understand their roles and responsibilities in contributing to the new delivery system.

Unfortunately, many providers are forced into rapid implementation by competitors or purchasers and in the absence of planning and building a high-performance vision find themselves in the awkward position of not fully grasping "why" we are doing this and only focusing on the "what" of how it affects their own facility or practice. This brings us to a discussion of some issues and situations to avoid in development and implementation of the performance contracting strategy.

The Vision

Before the words *pay for performance* are uttered in a complete sentence, physicians and hospitals will want to know where the standards come from and against what benchmarks they are to be measured. Are these standards derived from actuarial analyses that are strictly looking for cost reductions, or are there some evidence-based medical standards being used here? Committing an error here can make for a short meeting, because providers are, and have been, suspicious of payers' goals and if the performance-based initative is imminent, all questions will be based on fear and resistance grows quickly.

A solution depends on the group and their current circumstances. Are they truly integrated clinically? Have they had a bad experience as a Physician Hospital Organization (PHO) or other type of arrangement between physicians and hospitals? Do they have data that is representative of their strengths and weakness, or have they spent all the IT money on billing and expensive equipment to do more production of procedures? This resistance can shut down a very successful performance plan before it gets started. The vision of having to do something because a managed care company or employer says it wants to save money is not a valid or durable foundation to build this type of venture. Successful performance-based contracting requires a firm understanding of the total environment of payers' and consumers' needs. A fundamental grasp of value-based purchasing as seen by payers gives us a glimpse into the environment of the future.

This view of the outside environment and future of hospitals' and physicians' positions in a competitive and constantly shifting environment of federal and state rules, technology assessment seems endless. There are, however, serious consequences of payers moving business elsewhere or developing their own primary care entity to drive referrals outside of the service area if a common vision of collaboration cannot be reached.

Just Another Program

This is just another quality strategy using today's buzz words. Though physicians in study after study have a decided interest in quality and a desire to make themselves quality leaders in their region, many well-planned quality improvement plans (QIPs) are still not in use, and resistance is high if someone should doubt the doctor's skill and potential to claim this title of quality provider. Performance-based contracting is the actual outgrowth of many early quality works done by experts and actually allows physicians and hospitals to participate in the revenue from savings, assuming that they can come to grips with the role of the purchaser.

Let's assign this process to the quality department? Or managed care department, or operations?

Where does this fit?

Putting the cart before the horse does not work out well when suddenly a department is assigned the accountability to "do this" performance measurement and, without tools, resources, or even a vision, is held accountable for results. The issue here is that this is not just managed care as it was commonly practiced. This is integrating clinical and quality measurement, biostatistics admissions data, emergency department data, and medical records help as well as billing departments, billing and collections data to start forming a new platform of data that is used in making decisions, not just presenting reports. The "who" follows the "what," which follows the "why" we are doing this. In other words, the venture has no clear goals, vision or statement of what it intends to do.

We will discuss more of this in our chapter on getting started.

Lean Engineering

As hard as it is to believe, there are still some hospitals, medical groups, and health plans that still have this only half right. They are taking bits and pieces and implementing them, but only part way, saying that it is a process, so it is never done. As we discussed in the efficiency definition, we are starting from some false assumptions, and unless we really do the root cause analysis, we are never going to be done because we never started down the right path to begin with. Lean engineering, as discussed earlier, represents the opportunity to reengineer and reorganize process points to follow guidelines. Right now most performance is just that—process against guidelines—but as the guidelines become more sophisticated in detail and what works versus what does not work become actual goals of performance. Patient outcome can be measured. This leads to changing the patients' health status using successful process guidelines linked to outcomes measures of a clinical nature.

International Classification of Diseases

A change that will help this is the change from the *International Classification of Diseases*, 9th revision (ICD-9) to the 10th revision (ICD-10).* Though ICD-9 and similar codes represent a way to document and bill for patient care, the ICD-10 represents a way to see how clinical management is working to elevate the patient's severity level.

This level of "granular" data actually is used internationally by National Institute for Health and Clinical Excellence (NICE) and other countries who have been using ICD-10 for years. Though people hesitate to get ahead of reform, it is a necessary survival step to move to ICD-10 to bill Medicare by 2013.

Ramping up to these multiple codes and this intense service requires some sophisticated electronic data management tools, most of which the hospital and health plans have not yet invested in because the majority of investment in IT has been around revenue cycle management and billing. This will need to change.

Web-Based Processing

As reported by William Boyles in *Health Market Survey*, "Doctors, Hospitals May Waste Tens Of Billions In Fed Funding."† A spot survey of health IT vendors at the biggest IT trade show in April 2009 found common agreement that about 60% of companies hoping to bid for federal funding under the new economic stimulus bill are already obsolete and may not survive.

---

* CDC. International Classification of Diseases. 9th Revision (ICD-9) 10th Revision (ICD-10). Atlanta, GA: September 1, 2009.
† William Boyles. "Doctors, Hospitals May Waste Ten of Billions in Federal Funding." *Health Market Survey*. Washington, D.C.: Interpro Publications Inc. April 18, 2009, p. 4.

Several respondents agreed that the entire health IT industry was built on the assumption that health data systems can be kept private, generating maximum profit and product differentiation. This idea is ending quickly as the new federal law mandates a higher standard.

The biggest risk is to Medicare, which will pour almost $20 billion of federal IT funds into doctors' offices, hospitals, and medical clinics that are still being sold "new" products that will be obsolete within 12 months. A second category is venture capital firms and banks, which still have not realized that they are backing IT startups that are already obsolete and cannot possibly compete under new federal benchmarks without rewriting the entire application at great cost.

Hundreds of health IT vendors in the United States will be out of business in 2 years due to their inability to meet new federal standards enacted by the economic stimulus law. Most of the biggest vendors will survive but will have to make major changes in their current products to make them accessible across the entire health system.

Right now the majority of IT products are designed to operate with proprietary software and hardware, and most do not even exchange data on the Internet or wireless devices. Basically, hospitals buy a product and then use it only for their own patients running on their own computers, causing massive duplication and waste system-wide. This problem is much bigger than how to pay for the new system.

One sector that is much further along in buying and using the latest standards is insurers and health plans and some large hospitals and large employers. For example, Kaiser and other large carriers use a product from Epic that is catching on fast as one that can adapt to the national data exchange requirement. Other competing products are also moving fast to avoid becoming obsolete.

Kaiser chief George Halvorson gave a sobering keynote speech to 1,000-plus delegates at the HIMSS Annual Conference on April 6, 2009, in Chicago, Illinois. "It would be breathtakingly stupid to put health care data on the computer and end up with the same sets of isolated, inaccessible, non-interactive information silos we have now with paper medical records. We need all of the information about each patient. We need that information all of the time—whenever and wherever care is being delivered."

Many health care providers, third-party processing entities, and insurance companies have agreed to follow industry standards of internal processing with very little left to chance in losing or repeating data. The wireless environment and web-based processing was a new area. However, everyone, from the government to patient level have heeded accurate, understandable clinical and billing information will require that the delivery system move to a much more integrated web-based environment.

Grants from the Centers for Medicare & Medicaid Services (CMS) are available for physicians who want to purchase electronic medical records (EMRs) but they must meet the standards of "meaningful use," which means that the EMR must be web based and be able to connect with providers, billing companies, health maintenance organizations (HMOs), insurance companies, pharmacies, and hospitals to report patient status and bill and reevaluate health status improvement to begin to capture episodes of care, not just components for a visit or procedure. We discuss episodes of care elsewhere in the book, but using bundled care packages or globals connected with a budget of fees for executing this package represents a way for providers to get paid for not just production but also performance and outcome.

Unfortunately most "big iron" companies have continued to sell large-scale institutional processing machines that centralize everything and attempt to link all of the work done by providers. Getting data in and out quickly has been the issue, and security, once thought of as the privacy issue barrier to web-based care, is no longer the barrier, with encryption and Health Insurance Portability and Accountability Act (HIPAA) documentation permitting each stakeholder to be accountable to only use this data for a specific purpose.

Change Management

A July 2009 survey at McKinsey discussed the fact that the majority of hospital leaders were either not prepared or not interested in preparing their organizations for the future.

> Only 30 percent of executives representing the health care industry in the United States say their companies are ready for reform and changing economic conditions, according to a McKinsey survey on how prepared industry players—payers, providers, and pharmaceutical companies—are for change. However, 76 percent say the impact of reform on the industry will be significant, and 54 percent say the same about the effects of the current economic crisis.*

Many of the reasons varied from economic conditions beyond their control including fee cuts for Medicare and managed care to competition for physicians that left them unable to recruit enough primary care to establish a specialty base

---

* http://www.mckinseyquarterly.com/overhauling_the_US_health_care_payment_system_2012.

that would keep occupancy at optimum levels. Some had established a satisfactory ability in their minds to respond to change after it happened but few were willing or able to actually anticipate change and prepare contingency plans for changes as we are discussing today. Dr. Isham of Health Partners states that he has run into a "mindset" of people's preconceived notions for or against the performance-based payment idea.* Our own experience in working with hospitals, physicians, and employers reveals a misunderstanding of what could be a firm foundation of cooperation between providers and purchasers.

In 1966 employers in Minneapolis gathered to discuss health care and saw the value of

1. Pitting providers at each other to keep costs down and quality up
2. Having each provider-sponsored entity own their own insurance entity in order to have an incentive for savings
3. Telling providers that this was the desired form of care and that they would offer this plan to their employees if the providers built this kind of delivery and financing system[†]

Group Health Plan was a model the employers liked as a not-for-profit HMO with multispecialty clinics as their base and operating as a cooperative since 1958. Group Health Plan had an advantage. Soon others emerged and, by 1973, Nicollet Eittel Health Plans sponsored by the Nicollet Clinic had formed, MedCenters Health Plan sponsored by St. Louis Park Medical Center had formed and, SHARE Health Plan sponsored by the Samaritan Hospital and Clinic. Soon the nongroup physicians became concerned as patients selected the medical groups with insurance plans endorsed by General Mills and other larger employers. Physicians Health Plan sponsored by the Hennepin County Medical Society became the response to these plans. Even Blue Cross attempted to retain business by building a product line called HMO Minnesota.

HMOs flourished as the laboratory of innovation and in St. Paul, Minneapolis, the Twin Cities grew as a national?

As patient choice grew, hospitals were forced to become more attentive to the changes in the market and soon consolidation began to occur as hospital networks and cartels tried to leverage their size to get better reimbursement.

In 1980 there were 42 hospitals in the greater Twin Cities market and by 1988 there were four large systems and some HMOs began buying clinics and hiring doctors. Based on these many choices, employers once again spoke up and said we

---

* Interview by William De Marco with Dr. George J. Isham, June 6, 2009.
† *Twin City Health Care Development Project*, State of Minnesota Office of the Governor Wendell Anderson http://www.mnhs.org/library/tips/history_topics/87hmos.html

want to pit the HMOs against one another and pick one and only one vendor to cover their patients. This forced the consolidation of four HMOs under the banner of Health Partners. One of their first moves was to buy Regions Hospital, the largest county facility in the area. When asked why, the response was, "Because they can manufacture primary care." Indeed, this was true: as a teaching hospital and nursing school this hospital had many advantages and left their competing hospital without a contract for the largest HMO in the state.

We present this story so that people understand that what employers force HMOs to do has an effect on hospitals and physicians and as insurance companies and health plans get larger. The end result is larger plans get larger and eventually can shift patient base in favor of providers who offer value and quality because the health plans and the insurance companies need to have this proven outcome to sell to employers and unions. As the market shifts to a more individual market of policyholders who purchase insurance from a health exchange this topic of price quality and value becomes more critical to planning the delivery system of the future.

Comparative Effectiveness and Ethical Limitations

We will discuss the comparative economics of health care's future in a upcoming chapter but it is important to point out here that as decisions are made to offer access to care these guidelines may change over time. Over time the guidelines do change, physicians pressured by new technology that makes it easier to do noninvasive tests before surgery, do preventive measures before heavy-duty pharmacy is introduced, and assist patients with simple recovery therapy to return home as soon as possible without infection and relapse.

These are choices made by patients and doctors. Many may disagree that guidelines are only formed by physicians, but patients have the option to listen and comply with the doctor's recommendations or deviate from them. An example would be a physician's recommendation to follow a regime of antibiotics. Patients make a decision to stop taking drugs because "I feel better" so why continue to take this drug? The research behind comparative effectiveness goes back to 2003 in the United States according to Research Fellow Kalipso Chalkidou et al. in their paper "Comparative Effectiveness Research and Evidence-Based Health Policy: Experience from Four Countries":*

> In 2003, senior officials from the Agency for Healthcare Research and Quality (AHRQ) and the Center for Medicare and Medicaid Services (CMS) described serious gaps in the generation of

---

* K. Chalkidou, S. Tunis, et al. *Milbank Quarterly.* Volume 87. 2. 2009. 340 Wiley Periodicals, Inc.

information needed by decision makers in health care in the United States: "Neither of the major sources of funding for clinical research in the United States—the National Institutes for Health and the medical products industry—has as a primary mission the goal of ensuring that studies are performed to address clinical questions important to decision makers."

Four years later, the head of the Congressional Budget Office testified before the House Ways and Means Subcommittee on Health on the potential impact of comparative effectiveness research (CER) on health outcomes and expenditure:

> Better information about the costs and benefits of different treatment options, combined with new incentive structures reflecting the information, could eventually yield lower health care spending without having adverse effects on health . . . even if it did not bring about significant reductions in spending, more information about comparative effectiveness could yield better health outcomes from the resources devoted to health care.*

Comparative effectiveness research is a relatively new and distinctly American term. Other countries still use terms such as *health technology assessment* or *evidence-informed policymaking* to describe essentially the same activity.

Different U.S. organizations have suggested different definitions of CER. Throughout this article, we use the definition from a recent Institute of Medicine (IOM) report:

> [Comparative evidence research is] the comparison of one diagnostic or treatment option to one or more others. In this respect, primary comparative effectiveness research involves the direct generation of clinical information on the relative merits or outcomes of one intervention in comparison to one or more others, and secondary comparative effectiveness research involves the synthesis of primary studies to allow conclusions to be drawn.†

---

* Congressional Budget Office Testimony 2007, p. 2.
† Institute of Medicine (IOM), CER and Evidence-Based Health Policy 341 (2007), pp. 7–8.

In order to include comparative costs, we also qualify the IOM definition with that of the American College of Physicians: "the evaluation of the relative (clinical) effectiveness, safety, and cost of 2 or more medical services, drugs, devices, therapies, or procedures used to treat the same condition."*

CER is an analytic activity that is explicitly guided by the information needs of decision makers. A final qualification: by "CER entities" we are referring to formal structures that use CER to make or inform decisions about health services and technologies covered by payers.

The relationship between decision making and CER is of central importance: CER entities set (mostly secondary) CER priorities and use (primary and secondary) CER findings to inform their (mandatory or advisory) decisions about specific aspects of health policy and practice. There is currently no such CER entity (or group of entities) in the United States. Instead, most of the current discussion pertains to research organizations established to generate primary or secondary CER rather than to a CER decision-making or decision-informing entity.

Since publishing this paper, the U.S. federal government has moved forward in creating and funding the Office of Comparative Effectiveness Research. Part of the funding for this is already in place from previous legislation and another several million dollars are earmarked for additional funding from the health reform legislation.

Just what role the government has in identify or endorsing evidence-based care guidelines is of concern to physicians and others. The advantage of care guidelines or practice guidelines is that if these are observed consistently throughout medicine, malpractice judgments would be reduced because negligence cannot be proven if doctors follow protocol.

However, if the guideline cannot be followed due to lack of local resources, availability of specialty care, or adequate capacity of the delivery system to manage admission or discharge properly, then would this constitute substandard care?

Moreover, because guidelines affect specific candidates or groups of populations with a specific disease, would the guideline change over time as research discovers that screenings for such things as breast cancer between ages 40 and 50 only saved a few lives per thousand patients screened whereas more intense screening in the 50 and over population yielded more saved lives? How does the government and its committees change guidelines that are almost sure to be used by lawyers in prosecuting cases of malpractice but is also going to be followed by insurance companies requiring doctors to appeal on individual cases?

Great doctors have a hard time keeping up.

---

* American College of Physicians 2008, p. 1.

Insurance companies pay for treatments but not all treatments. They also have underwriting rules to determine one's past illnesses and standards to rate a patient based upon occupation, age, gender, and lifestyle. This is similar to assigning FICA scores to customers at a bank.

As for profit, insurance companies (a relatively new phenomenon) oblige their stockholders and create a profit margin by managing coverage of benefits and treatments of what is necessary and what is not. Some of this is necessary because overtreatment can be just as dangerous as undertreatment, and there are frills and frivolous services that are overused.

For example, the first step in back pain is alternating heat and cold possibly followed by a $200.00 X-ray. But if the hospital owns a magnetic resonance imaging (MRI) machine, the first test will be a $4,500 MRI. So capacity and expert knowledge fit here, but in the absence of a community pattern of practice or a guaranteed if–then–therefore logic, the outcomes are different, as are the treatments and therefore the costs.

Everything from physical exams to days in the hospital may be cut in an attempt by insurance companies to save money. Insurance companies evaluate their benefits with their employers every year to see where they can cut benefits that are not heavily used.

The mental health area is a good example. No claims submitted to the insurance company means no use. So the benefit is excluded. Doing this, however, is missing the real issue that people pay for it out of their own pockets to avoid having the employer see claims revealing that the person is depressed or worse. Cutting the benefit only makes things worse in that these emotional illnesses usually manifest themselves in physiological ways.

And then there is the government, which is setting minimum standards for care and education to get a license to practice. Offering coverage to make sure at least some mental health is covered for all and then trying to supervise pricing so consumers are fairly treated. Most of these city and county governments and large private employers are looking to the insurance industry to come up with a long-term plan to conserve dollars and slow the cost of premium growth.

They have three choices:

1. Slow the approval of medical devices and drugs that are used in the market because this is the chief driver of rising costs. (Someone must draw the line between what is a necessary drug or medical device and what is not necessary and then fund research and medical education to use this properly.)
2. Cut back the amount of coverage, which forces patients to bear up under rising out-of-pocket costs for services that were heretofore covered (increased deductibles like a health savings account).

3. Establish a method to prospectively determine costs of services (fee caps) and allocate public and private money for necessary services based on individual patient need (like a Medicare/Medicaid program without the fraud).

To do any of this requires new rules. Some of these rules have been in place for decades, and new ones are being drawn up as we speak.

Here is a crash course on the assumptions used to score whether or not you and I will get care in the future.

- New technologies, both private and public, drive new needs for benefits and coverage.
- Consequences of choosing correct benefits can be negative or positive.
- What benefits are appropriate at what costs (new rules)?
- If it is true that older people are sicker, should we not charge them more? But how much?
- Create Disability-Adjusted Life Years (DALYs) that will show the entire disease burden and then multiply this unit of disease burden times the age-weighted equation $W = (C) (x) e - Bx$, where x = the age of the person benefiting from a change in DALYS and e = 2.71, the natural constant.

One can see in Figure 7.1 that, over time, as people become older and less productive, one loses points. The scoring gives greater weight to those with fewer illnesses who are younger and more productive. This follows our current thought process, which is why employed people can get insurance and the rest of the population cannot: we favor productivity.

Under cost utility analysis (CUA) an analysis of a health outcome using various health assessment tools has also created QALYs, or quality adjusted life year, (Figure 7.2). Elements such as pain and mobility are compared to the population of people with similar issues, a calculation of QALYs is made, and costs per DALY are used to arrive at a score that enables:

1. The insurance company to arrive at alternative tests and services and a budget for you based upon your needs, which could be very intense if you are young and productive because getting you back to work will assure you of many years of productive health QALYs.
2. Develop a treatment protocol that relieves discomfort with minimal costs. A man with prostate issues may forgo the surgery and earn QALY points in favor of watchful waiting. It has been proven here, as well as in other instances, that with or without surgery the results are the same. I can make this argument for breast cancer detection with a low human epidermal growth factor receptor (HERR) count. Drugs, chemo, and other treatments

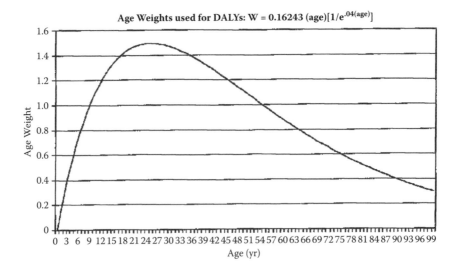

Figure 7.1 Age versus Dalys.

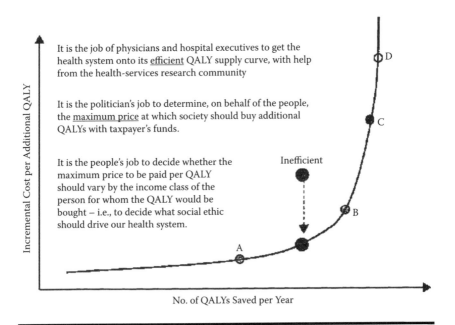

Figure 7.2 Cost versus QALYs saved per year.

drive the cancer out or make it encapsulated, so it cannot spread. Why operate and reduce a woman's self-esteem when in 10 years, surgery or no surgery, the result is the same?—That is, *no cancer*.

3. Determine a budget that says you are 98 years old and need a hip transplant but we are not going to do this because there is no way your quality of life will be improved in a significant way for your remaining life expectancy. Your QALYs are too high, and we need the money elsewhere.

This has become the new science of comparative utility where economics are driving medicine and though many of us are in favor of heath science research into comparative economics, in other words best practices in health care, this goes beyond best practices when patient's needs are scored like a FICA score.

An argument can be made that if we had a great fire and people had to negotiate with the fire department to put it out or rescue you from a 10-story window, this could not work and it shows the flaws in the ethical arguments.

In insurance parlance this can be described as lifestyle benefits, but the reality is that the insurance company or the government can track a patient's health status, running annual checks on your budget for care and if the patient should exceed it, there could be a penalty or a charge.

A QALY example is illustrated below.

Lung Volume Reduction Surgery as a QALY Example

Lung volume reduction surgery (LVRS) is a palliative therapy for patients with severe emphysema. It was developed in the 1950s, though it was not widely accepted; a 1957 study showed that despite 75% of patients reporting clinical improvement, there was a lack of objective documentation of benefit and an operative mortality of 18%. In 1995, Dr. Joel Cooper of Washington University (St. Louis)* reported a modification to the procedure after favorable results from a small, uncontrolled study in 1994. LVRS began to rise in popularity and the mainstream press wrote about the procedure.

In 1994–1995, CMS asked the Agency for Healthcare Research and Quality (AHRQ) to review LVRS. AHRQ found no compelling evidence of benefit, and CMS learned from an internal claims review that mortality at 6 months for LVRS was 17%. In December 1995, CMS announced that it would not pay for the procedure—it would, however, collaborate with the National Institutes

---

* Joel Cooper, M.D., et al., "Report of the Xenotransplantation Advisory Committee of the International Society for Heart and Lung Transplantation," *The Journal of Heart and Lung Transplantation*, Vol. 19. 12, (December 2000). pp. 1125–1165.

of Health (NIH) and sponsor a multicenter randomized control trial (RCT), and CMS would pay for the procedure (CMS usually only pays for routine care in trials). In 1996 Congress passed a law requiring CMS to provide a report that included an analysis of all available data for LVRS as well as recommendations regarding Medicare coverage. In 1997, a congressional hearing was held where Dr. Cooper and Rep. Jim Ramstad (R-MN) criticized the policy for not covering LVRS outside of the trial. Just before the trial, Dr. Cooper pulled out of the trial, saying it was unethical to hold a controlled study, given the "obvious" benefits.

The findings, published in the New England Journal of Medicine May 2003, showed no improvement in survival for surgical patients but differential improvements in exercise capacity and respiratory-specific quality of life for a percentage of the surgical patients. One subgroup showed statistically significant improvements in survival for the surgical cohort; surgical patients in three of the four subgroups had improvements in exercise capacity and quality of life compared with medical therapy patients. Findings from subgroup analyses of a single clinical trial are considered relatively weak evidence, particularly in situations where the trial fails to show a hypothesized benefit for the experimental group. The FDA does not accept subgroup analyses, instead requiring a second trial focusing on the subgroup. The cost-effectiveness during the 3 years following the initiation of treatment was judged to be unfavorable, at $189,000 per QALY.

CMS, at the same time the trial was published, announced a national coverage memorandum for three of four subgroups listed above; the final coverage policy was implemented in January 2004.

In *Health Affairs*,* authors Ramsey and Sullivan point to pressures (political, advocacy, professional) as well as the fact that those in the surgical arm of the trial did demonstrate statistically significant improvements in pulmonary functioning, exercise capacity, and respiratory-specific quality of life compared with those in the medical arm.

Over time as public records and private records are collected and analyzed, the baseline equated to diagnosis will be entered into a formula. But controversies are already occurring over cost and quality. Why? Because patients and doctors will want to know whether there are maximum prices or different prices for the poor and the rich. Will there be different guidelines for patients based on socioeconomic issues of how useful a person's occupations, skills, and training are to the future of the general population?

---

* S. D. Ramsey and Sean Sullivan, "Evidence Economics, and Emphysema: Medicine's Long Journey with Lung Volume Reduction Survery," *Health Affairs*, Vol. 24.1 (2005) pp. 55–66.

These points play directly into the performance-driven environment when researching what is behind the care guidelines and standards used. Is there a utilitarian ethical scoring process that isolates the patient in one symptom or diagnosis while not considering other related and sometimes unrelated illnesses? Many of these will need to be discussed at the federal level but also at the local level among physicians, hospitals, and health plans to come up with a solution that has equity and virtue, not just a scientific single score.

This chapter has covered a series of challenges that will need further study and will need further funding to truly represent the dynamics of what comparative economics holds for all of us. Many pay-for-performance systems are just now starting to understand the true long-term implications of their decisions on not just quality but availability of resources needed to sustain quality long term. For example, latest equipment, new operating methods requiring technology that today may not even exist will all have an impact on what level the performance measure is set. This rapid change will either complicate the fundamental flaws in performance-based management or will accelerate to an end the actual usable knowledge and conceptual understanding of how all the linkages between research and practice are accepted by medical practitioners in the future.

> A physician takes an oath to put his patient's interests ahead of his own. A corporation is legally bound to put its shareholders' interests first. And this is part of the inherent conflict between health care as a business, part of our economy, and health care as a public growth industry. That means higher health care bills. That means more and more middle-class people cannot afford health care in this country. (Maggie Mahar)*

---

* www.healthbeatblog.org (January 2009).

Chapter 8

International Reform

We continue to see that governments around the world share a similar perspective when it comes to pay for performance (P4P). They feel that they have no extra money budgeted to pay for reform but see that by creating savings through pay for performance they can create a pool of money to fund additional government programs. This allows health care expenditures to become budget neutral.

To begin on this course requires the government to institute guidelines as a means of managing payments. The better the outcome or performance, the better the pay. This also works in reverse, with the lower performing providers seeing a reduction in pay, which translates into savings. The balance sought by most politicians is to identify those procedures that can create the most meaningful savings without ruffling too many feathers of their provider community.

This delicate balance must be observed by health maintenance organizations (HMOs) and insurance companies here in the United States as well, because providers who are normally independent thinkers and see themselves as scientists (and not businessmen) can suddenly begin thinking as one and put a stop to the progress health reform offers.

To score savings and then redeploy these dollars in the delivery system does not require the government to come up with extra money but rather to be effective in gleaning large amounts of savings from the current system. Recent Office of Management and Budget (OMB) estimates in the United States came up with three key expense areas that must be contained in reform proposals to actually reduce costs and thereby fund implementation over time. They are as follows:

1. Technology reporting and comparisons that build best practice benchmarks enforced by medical societies and payers. ($100 billion)
2. Guideline development and refinement of coordination of services enforced through payment and recognition programs. ($250 billion)
3. Elimination of waste and fraud from the system by using private contractors and delegating the management of this "rationing" and rewarding to companies who can also create savings. ($400 billion)

Competition through Improved Performance

The short-term investment needed to set in motion options for patients and providers to reengineer and innovate to compete for savings dollars is easily recovered through this process as well as by reshaping chronic care management for the 20% of patients who will use 80% of the services/dollars in the system.

The long-term impact of being able to reassess the disease detection and management system for simple viruses as well as to anticipate disease in individuals will alter the course of events that define quality of life. This will also place into the system checks and balances to look for palliative care solutions for some and rehabilitation for others. Inasmuch as the "scoring" of these illnesses will be interpreted with the ability to use nanotechnology to later rid the body of breast cancer, prostate cancer, and other illnesses of predetermination, it would seem likely that we can leave the traditional institutional model behind and recast the delivery system to connect with the home and family, offering home health and respite care for those able to be at home and save the inpatient care setting for the very ill.

This does not sit well with some hospitals because they see P4P possibly leaving inpatient care behind. The problem is that most U.S. hospitals have no effective means to increase the volume of patients while decreasing the frequency and use of unnecessary services. Pay for performance could be used here to drop hospital inpatient stays while increasing the number of patients who really need hospitalization for an acute care episode or chronic illness setback. This improves the quality of the admission, reduces denials, and usually raises income per patient. In other words, savings for performance can be earned without sacrificing a large part of existing revenues simply by reengineering the patient pathway and hospital resources.

Because the savings from performance can incent these behavioral changes and, in part, promote a bit more predictability into the care and cost, many physicians, hospitals, and regulators are truly of the belief that "extra dollars" will leave the system unless savings and a means to harvest these savings are in place. This means that for payers, including national governments, this approach to performance-based contracting will cost very little and bring about large dividends early in the transition as the "low-hanging fruit" is harvested.

The Netherlands

The Netherlands began to overhaul its health system in 1987 after a government committee concluded that the best approach was managed competition, an idea first proposed by Professor Enthoven of Stanford. The country had four different coverage schemes. The wealthiest third of the population was required to get health insurance without government assistance. Some in this group received help from employers in the form of paid premiums, and others paid the whole bill themselves. The bulk of the Dutch population was covered under a compulsory state-run health insurance scheme financed by deductions from wages. Civil servants and older people were insured under two separate plans within this state-run scheme. In late 2004, the Dutch House of Representatives passed a law to usher in mandatory health insurance and switch people on state-run insurance to private carriers.

The government closely regulated hospital budgets and doctors' fees but provided few incentives to cut costs. When hospitals lost money on a particular kind of care, they rationed it. Many patients ended up on waiting lists.

According to Gautam Naik, reporter for the local press,

> The Dutch system features two key rules, all adults must buy insurance, and all insurers must offer a policy to anyone who applies, no matter how old or how sick. Those who can't afford to pay the premiums get help from the state, financed by taxes on the well-off. The system hinges on competition among insurers. They are expected to cut premiums, persuade consumers to live healthier lives, and push hospitals to provide better and lower-cost care.*

In order to prevent insurers from seeking only young, healthy customers, the government compensates insurers for taking on higher-risk patients. This subsidy varies, but insurers get a risk equalization, or what we have discussed as a risk-adjusted payment in previous chapters. This payment is for covering the elderly and those with certain conditions, such as diabetes. This is the beginning of building a P4P program. By documenting risk levels and patient populations, the government has created its own division of health data. Understanding

---

* Gautam Naik, "Dutch Treatment: In Holland. Some see Models for U.S. Health Care System," *Wall Street Journal*, September 6, 2007.

risk has altered the underwriting principles, which has lowered costs to both subscribers and government.

Consumers also benefited from a premium war as insurers made a grab for market share. The Dutch health ministry had predicted that insurers in 2006 would price the annual mandatory premium at an average of €1,106, or about $1,500. Instead, market forces set it at €1,028, 7.6% lower. This year, it has risen to €1,103, partly because of an ease in the price war. That is still less than the €1,134 the government predicted for 2007.

The real test of the Dutch approach is yet to come: Can insurers push hospitals to lower their costs and improve their quality or will the hospitals do as they have done in the United States and consolidate or form cartels to negotiate against insurers? Insurers have clout because they can direct large numbers of patients toward particular hospitals. But, in a holdover from the old system, insurers can currently negotiate prices for only 10% of the services hospitals offer. This number has increased each year but there will be a cap on this at 50% of services in the near future, which is a barrier to true competition. Like those in the United States, Dutch hospitals used to receive fixed prices for their services and received more money for more service regardless of quality, so they had little incentive to improve their care.

This one-size-fits-all scenario reminds us of the diagnosis-related groups (DRGs) that are standard regardless of whether the outcome is good or bad. Innovation to improve care is now in place with more dollars for more resources but also a level dollar amount for cases that can be managed.*

Germany

About 90% of the people in Germany are covered by the Statutory Health Insurance (SHI) fund and the rest are members of private insurance funds, according to research conducted at NICE.† This is consistent with the guiding principles of the health insurance fund in Germany. These core principles include: obligatory membership in the sickness insurance fund; non-state governance of the system; and joint contribution to the insurance fund of an

---

* R. Busse and A. Riesberg, *Health Care Systems in Transition* (Germany, 2004: WHO Regional Office for Europe on behalf of the European Observatory on Health Systems and Policies). Available at http://www.euro.who.int/Document/E85472.pdf.

† C. Altenstetter and R. Busse, "Health Care Reform in Germany: Patchwork Change within Established Governance Structures," *Journal of Health Politics, Policy and Law* 30, nos. 1-2 (2005): 121–142.

individual by both the employer and employee.* The increase of new pharmaceuticals and medical technologies in the market and the decrease in the income of the health insurance fund raised debates on the exclusion or inclusion of some of the pharmaceuticals (lifestyle drugs; e.g., Viagra) and other medical services (e.g., some dental treatments). The need for more cost control and transparency in the process of reimbursing drugs by the SHI fund was recognized and led to the German health care reform legislation in 1992 along with the addition of a cost containment policy to the health care agenda and obligatory quality assurance measures for health providers. Several changes and reforms followed the legislation, which also introduced the optional family doctor model and the concept of DRGs in hospitals. There were initiatives in 2000 that required using health technology assessments to evaluate the medical services in outpatient care. However, it was not until the health care reform in 2003† that a structured evidence-based policy-making process for the whole health care system was developed in an attempt to improve the quality of health services, the transparency of decisions on exclusion or inclusion of pharmaceutical or medical technologies from the Statutory Health Insurance fund, and patient participation in the health care system.‡

The main evidence-based policy making entity in Germany is the Federal Joint Committee (G-BA, Gemeinsamer Bundesausschuss), which includes the Federal Association of Contracted Physicians (KBV and KZBV, Kassenärztliche und Kassenzahnärztliche Bundesvereinigungen), the German Hospital Federation (DKG, Deutsche Krankenhausgesellschaft), the Top Organization of Health Insurance Funds (Spitzenverband Bund der Krankenkassesn), and patient representatives. This committee is currently composed of three impartial chairs, five members representing the health insurance funds (physicians,

---

* C. Altenstetter and R. Busse, "Health Care Reform in Germany: Patchwork Change within Established Governance Structures," *Journal of Health Politics, Policy and Law* 30, nos. 1-2 (2005): 121–142; C. Altenstetter, "Insights from Health Care in Germany," *American Journal of Public Health* 93, no. 1 (2003): 38–44; C. Diederichs, K. Klotmann, and F. W. Schwartz, "The Historical Development of the German Health Care System and Respective Reform Approaches," *Bundesgesundheitsblatt Gesundheitsforschung Gesundheitsschutz* 51, no. 5 (2008): 547–551.

† C. Altenstetter and R. Busse, "Health Care Reform in Germany: Patchwork Change within Established Governance Structures," *Journal of Health Politics, Policy and Law* 30, nos. 1-2 (2005): 121–142.

‡ R. Busse and A. Riesberg, *Health Care Systems in Transition* (Germany, Copenhagen: WHO Regional Office for Europe on behalf of the European Observatory on Health Systems and Policies. Available at http://www.euro.who.int/Document/E85472.pdf; C. Altenstetter and R. Busse, "Health Care Reform in Germany: Patchwork Change within Established Governance Structures," *Journal of Health Politics, Policy and Law* 30, nos. 1-2 (2005): 121–142.

dentists, and hospitals), five members representing the providers of health care, and up to five patient representatives. The Federal Joint Committee has a detailed process for making decisions about the health services of the Statutory Health Insurance fund based on the best available evidence. Its responsibilities include making evidence-based decisions about exclusion of pharmaceuticals and lifestyle drugs from the Statutory Health Insurance fund, inclusion and exclusion of other medical care services in outpatient care, and exclusion of medical services in hospital care. Moreover, it makes decisions on disease management programs for chronic diseases, reference price setting, over-the-counter exemption lists, inclusion (for specific indications) or exclusion of off-label medications from the Statutory Health Insurance fund, cost-effectiveness analyses, and quality assurance of in- and outpatient care. The directives developed by the Federal Joint Committee are legally mandatory for payers and providers of health care and insurers.*

For an independent evaluation of benefits and additional benefits of health care services (pharmaceuticals, surgery, diagnosis, etc.), the health care reform legislation commissioned the Federal Joint Committee to establish a nonprofit, nongovernmental, independent, private law foundation body that has the legal capacity and is responsible for creating and maintaining the Institute for Quality and Efficiency in Health Care (Institut für Qualität und Wirtschaftlichkeit im Gesundheitswesen, IQWiG; http://www.iqwig.de).

IQWiG was established on June 1, 2004, and is responsible for undertaking the evaluation of benefits and cost benefits of medical services based on international standards of evidence-based medicine in a transparent, scientific, inclusive, independent, and consistent way. The cost effectiveness evaluation was further defined on June 1, 2007, with the implementation of the health care reform of 2007, to develop methods for cost–benefit evaluation of drugs in order to define a ceiling price for drugs† and support competition between Statutory

---

* Federal Joint Committee (Der Gemeinsame Bundesausschuss). Available at: http:// www.g-ba.de; GB-A Verfahrensordnung des Gemeinsamen Bundesausschusses [The rules of the procedure in GB-A]. Available at: http://www.g-ba.de/downloads/62-492-83/ VerfO_2006-04-18.pdf (accessed July 14, 2008); V. Paris and E. Docteur, "Pharmaceutical Pricing and Reimbursement Policies in Germany," OECD Health working paper No. 39. Available at: http://www.oecd.org/dataoecd/6/57/41586814.pdf (accessed November 15, 2008).
† IQWIG, "Methods for Assessment of the Relation of Benefits to Costs in the German Statutory Health Care System," Version 1.1. Available at: http://www.iqwig.de/ download/08-10-14_Methods_of_the_Relation_of_Benefits_to_Costs_v_1_1.pdf; IQWIG, "Allgemeine Methoden" [General methods], Ver. 3.0. Available at: http://www. iqwig.de/download/IQWiG_Methoden_Version_3_0.pdf.

Health Insurance funds (Gesundheitsreform 2007 "Gesetz zur Stärkung des Wettbewerbs in der gesetzlichen Krankenversicherung").*

Since 2003, the Federal Associations of Health Insurance Funds have the opportunity to make specific agreements with pharmaceutical companies for a discounted price as long as the provided service/drug follows the Federal Joint Committee directives.† The pharmaceuticals used in the hospitals are mainly reimbursed through the DRGs, and not separately, and the hospitals could negotiate a volume and price agreement directly with the industry.‡

The current process of evidence-based policy making in Germany is focused on the decision of the reimbursement of pharmaceuticals or medical services from the Statutory Health Insurance fund and developing and improving disease management programs. IQWiG is not commissioned to develop guidelines for medical practice. Physicians and dentists can still prescribe treatments that are not included in the Statutory Health Insurance fund; however, the patient may need to pay the cost for the treatment if it is not included.

The current structure of the institute includes eight departments along with an Institute Management Department. The departments are as follows:

- Pharmaceutical
- Medical Biometry
- Health Economics
- Health Information
- Quality of Healthcare
- Nondrug Interventions
- Communication
- Administration

Funding of IQWiG

Fifty percent of the funding of the institute ("system levy") comes from a levy on every hospital case invoiced (every hospital visit to be reimbursed) and 50% from an additional percentage increase in remuneration for medical and dental outpatient services reimbursed by SHI. The levy in the outpatient sector is

---

* Health Reform 2007 "Law on strengthening of competition in the national health insurance."
† V. Paris and E. Docteur, "Pharmaceutical Pricing and Reimbursement Policies in Germany," OECD Health working paper No. 39. Available at: http://www.oecd.org/dataoecd/6/57/41586814.pdf (accessed November 15, 2008).
‡ V. Paris and E. Docteur, "Pharmaceutical Pricing and Reimbursement Policies in Germany," OECD Health working paper No. 39. Available at: http://www.oecd.org/dataoecd/6/57/41586814.pdf (accessed November 15, 2008).

itemized separately in the invoice issued by the hospital and is not included in the overall sums or in the corresponding revenue balances.

For the levy on each hospital case, the proportions contributed by the associations of Statutory Health Insurance funds, physicians, and dentists, as well as details on the forwarding of these funds to a body to be named, are determined by the IQWiG. Germany uses DXCG (or Diagnostic Costs Groups) to analyze the inpatient and outpatient services. This grouper integrates a case mix adjuster and helps to adjust population data by diagnosis and provider.

Principles and Values, Aims and Objectives

IQWiG evaluates evidence on topics that are important for the quality and efficiency of the medical services undertaken in the Statutory Health Insurance fund. Its advice serves as the basis for national decision making on policy and reimbursement of medical services; IQWiG also develops health information for the general public.*

The tasks of IQWiG are stated in paragraph §139a of the Social codebook and include

1. Search for, assessment and presentation of current scientific evidence on diagnostic and therapeutic procedures for specific diseases
2. Preparation of scientific reports and expert opinions on quality and efficiency issues of Statutory Health Insurance fund, taking age, gender, and personal circumstances into account
3. Appraisal of evidence-based clinical practice guidelines on the epidemiologically most important diseases
4. Issue of recommendations on disease management programs[†]
5. Provision of understandable evidence based information for patients and public

Current Status

Despite best efforts to reduce costs and improve quality Germany faces a 7.5 billion euro (US$10.96 billion) deficit in the public fund in 2010. The fund covers 10 million Germans at a cost of 170 billion euro.

---

* P. T. Sawicki and H. Bastian, "German Health Care: A Bit of Bismarck Plus More Science," British Medical Journal 7 (2008); 337. doi: 10.1136/bmj.a1997.

† http://www.iqwig.de/download/139a_The_Institute_for_Quality_and_Efficiency_in_Health_Care.pdf; IQWIG, "Allgemeine Methoden" [General methods], Ver. 3.0. Available at: http://www.iqwig.de/download/IQWiG_Methoden_Version_3_0.pdf.

In October of 2009 Germany's center right parties agreed to fund public health reform by 2011 by using taxpayers' money and contributions on income-dependent components. The parties agreed to keep the country's health fund, which pools the fixed rate insurance contributions for employers and workers at 14.9% of a worker's gross income. Although workers who exceed their annual budget for health care may be charged extra for these services, the total out-of-pocket cannot exceed 1% of total gross income.

German Chancellor Merkel's* center right government is at odds with itself according to *Wall Street Journal* reports following the election in September, and though many favor no change to the fund, a group within the coalition government has made radical new proposals to dismantle the fund in favor of new approaches. Although this may happen over time, we do favor the outcome because the data on cost and utilization is firmly in the hands of the government, so decisions will be made using actual experience data.

Turkey

In April 2008, we were invited by Professor Dr. Sabahattin Aydin, Health Ministry of Turkey, to participate in the first global pay-for-performance summit in Ankara, Turkey.

We discovered that the Turkish government has had a pay-for-performance system in place since 2003. Though it is still refining aspects to this very sophisticated scoring and payment methodology, we were very impressed with the fact that this pay-for-performance system did not just cover clinical care process but also management process. They have actually used the performance definitions to not only remove waste from the system but, of equal importance, balance the number of physicians needed with the population's overall needs. Now think of this for a moment. If we could somehow use guidelines to stabilize utilization here in the United States—that is, bend the cost curve—the government could start to predict with certainty the number of physicians needed by specialty and, by using demographic forecasting, begin to predict the number of primary care needed in a given area. This formula, when turned over to medical schools and state and federal budget authorities, could set a stable budget for medical education for physician training as well as physician extenders, technicians and navigators.

In developing equations and methods to reward providers, the government can attest to an actual cost of labor for each procedure. This means that demand has increased for services, allowing the government to seek and hire more salaried

---

* "Mrs. Merkel Wins, Germany Loses," *Wall Street Journal*, October 25, 2009, Opinion Europe column.

physicians, which has also stimulated research in the private, independent physicians to become more efficient and expand their availability through additional workers.

These dimensions of the pay-for-performance realm are very far ahead of other countries that are using pay for performance as a means to offer bonus dollars to doctors in exchange for better outcomes.

In studying this performance-based medicine project, we saw a system-wide change supervised and promoted by the government but with the intention to shift all care decisions, both clinical and administrative, to move in the same direction. In other words, we are not talking about rationing as the key goal but rather developing a patient-oriented performance system. One of the most prioritized steps taken to this end is the performance-based contribution payment, which aims to establish a payment and pricing system that will encourage service providers to deliver productive and qualified health care services. This performance-based contribution payment system was first a pilot implementation. Ten hospitals from July 2003 have been implemented; across Turkey since 2004, it has also covered the primary care.

Implementation

Implementation of the program actually went relatively smoothly. The Ministry picked a handful of very clear quality measures to be carried across the system. This formed a basis to add more measures and more procedures over time, similar to the value-based purchasing system now in process in the United States (see Figure 8.1).

> There are mainly two phases of the implementation which have been conducted up to now. One-year practice made in 2004 facilitated the adaptation of health care professionals and facilities to the new condition and paved the way for inspections and audits to sustain the measurement of performance. Considering the changes and experience, a limited number of quality criteria easily measurable in domestic conditions were tested and the most eligible ones were put into practice in the year 2005. By these smooth changes, it is aimed to elevate the consciousness about providing qualified health care and to motivate the infrastructural settings (Figure 8.1).

Measurement

Measurement was developed based on three categories of care: labor intensive, individual, and group performance. Scoring is done at these three levels and rewards are also calculated at three levels. This separates the very unusual cases out but leaves a chance for individual and group rewards to be examined.

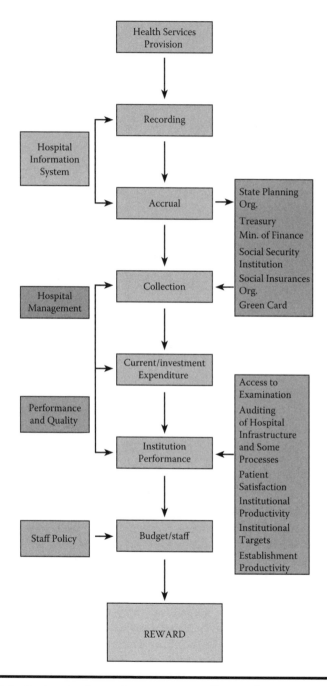

Figure 8.1 Factors having an impact on rewarding performance.

Because feedback is done monthly (as opposed to quarterly or semi-annually), there is a sense of urgency to change process and behavior rapidly.

"As the first step, an innovative model was developed by means of directives that envisage identifying individual performance at primary care facilities and hospitals and to make contribution payments based on this performance and in this implementation many different parts are involved" (*Performance Management in Health*, pp. 29–30).* "Labor-intensive medical services, according to their significance and frequency, were scored and the services given by practitioners were made measurable on a monthly basis" (*Performance Management in Health*, p. 30).†

Individual services given by practitioners were made measurable as much as possible and the system was promoted by strengthening patient–practitioner relations and the patient's right to choose his or her practitioner. Considering the fact that delivery of health care services is a team product, nonclinic practitioners, other health employees, and managers were scored in accordance with the average score of their institutions. So total performance of the institution is reflected upon all employees.

As for the monthly revenues at institutions, which are distributed to employees as legal contribution payment, every other employee could have a share based on his/her individual performance and score. So, employees make contribution to and have a share in positive values produced by their institutions. As for calculating the scores of practitioners, a difference is emphasized between two groups, working in the public sector, on a part-time and full-time basis. So, full-time working in the public sector is subsidized. Providing that the incentives, which aim to prevent hospital infections within the main framework identified, are achieved on a regular basis, then practitioners of relevant branches will be awarded, as well. The necessity of a registry and information system which could provide a proper follow-up of service quality and quantity is a common known fact. For regular collection of monthly data, keeping the services of employees under record, transmitting these records to reimbursement agencies and calculating the score distribution of institutions in a transparent and realistic way, hospital information systems have rapidly begun to become widespread. Hospital information systems, though not being a provision in this directive, turned out to be a natural outcome of the directive. This is the first time that health care services

---

* Ministry of Health of the Republic of Turkey: Performance Management in Health. 2008.
† (Ibid.)

have been kept under numerical records to such an extent and in such detail so far.

This implementation does not measure financial performance directly. However, the monetary value of calculated scores remains quite similar to the monetary surplus value that is created by the institution each month. For this reason, this implementation indirectly influences financial performance, like decline in per unit costs, savings in current expenditures, check of the patient's hospital admission date, and increase in the investment in curative devices and infrastructure.

At training and research hospitals, additional scores are given to clinic chiefs, deputy chiefs, chief interns, and specialists provided that they make publications of a definite number. Clinic chiefs and deputy chiefs at training and research hospitals are also given additional scores provided that they give certified theoretical and practical trainings of a certain level. Thus, uncompetitive performance criteria are used in the field of scientific publications and specialty training.

Commissions, which are set up in provincial health directorates for primary care facilities and at hospitals, with the participation of representatives from different professions, determine the amount of contribution payments to personnel by considering income–expense balance, debts, credits, fiscal status, and needs of the institution.

Thus, participation of different groups and levels in hospital management is encouraged and the capacity of on-site administration is promoted (Figure 8.2).

In order to ensure that health care services given in health facilities are being documented accurately on a regular basis, it is understood that by coordinating the care and the administration of this care, both team executives and practitioners are rewarded and a group think approach to care delivery and care improvement is achieved. When we asked whether there were negative penalties for those practitioners who did not accept new technology or benchmarks we were told that negative attitudes detected in measuring performance might be punished.

Turkey is different than many other countries. It has many problems that originally triggered this move to build such a far-reaching plan. The key opportunity I see is to improve the ratio of patients to doctors by improving demand for skilled care. Staffing ratios in other countries point out the plight of the Turkish system, had change not occurred.

> Here, while expecting a high quality in health services, sufficient health manpower, one of the most important inputs, appears as an important subject. The number of the doctors and nurses per individual is very important from this aspect. 0.5 nurses are left per

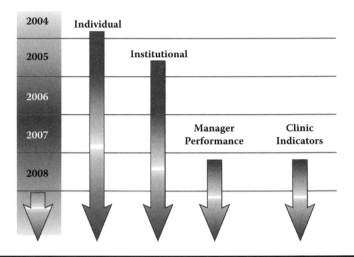

Figure 8.2 Development of performance-based supplementary payment system.

bed in Turkey. This number is attained merely by the late contractual personnel policies of the Health Ministry. This rate is, as an example, 0.62 in Taiwan (9), 7.9 in Japan (17), 2.3 doctors left per 1,000 individuals in the USA (18). While an average of 2.9 doctors are employed per 1,000 individuals in the OECD countries, this number is higher in Europe (13). Among the 52 countries of the World Health Organization Europe Zone, Turkey is the last with 1.3 doctors employed per 1,000 patients.*

Results

The scope covered by performance based supplementary payment includes the following:

■ 975 hospitals affiliated to the Ministry of Health
■ 6,400 local health centers
■ Approximately 310,000 staff, 58,162 of whom are practitioners

---

* *OECD Annual Report 2008*, Ministry of Turkey, 2008, http://www.oecd.org/data oecd/39/19/40556222.pdf.

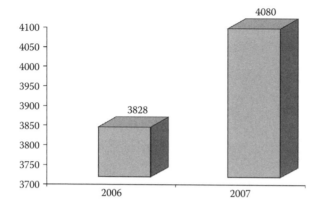

Figure 8.3 Average supplementary payments of specialist doctors in year 2006 and first 8 months of 2007.

Looking at the fee structure and compensation above salary, dollars have slowly increased, indicating that large-scale results are still ahead of the government. This has required some modification of ceilings but has also sent the message to practitioners that the government wants to see this dollar amount rise (Figure 8.3).

Performance Models of Care

According to the Ministry of Health's publication,* the performance system has been implemented within the context of three different models. These models have been explained in detail in the regulation, which were issued in the Hürriyet Daily News on May 12, 2006, titled "Regulation Regarding Making Supplementary Payment from Revolving Fund Proceedings to Health Staff Who Works Within the Ministry of Health Institutions and Establishments." Following is an excerpt.

> In the first model, there are application principles and procedures towards primary health care services. This regulation has been prepared taking into account the treatment and protective health care services depending on the nature and structuring of primary health care services, as well as the issue of service provision in rural areas.

---

* Prof. Dr. Sabahattin Aydin and Dr. Mehmet Demir, *Performance Management in Health; Performance Based Supplementory Payment System*, Ministry of Health of Republic of Turkey, 2008.

For primary level establishments, protective health services scores and regional administrative scores increasing towards the total area have been defined in the regulation in addition to the criteria related to treatment health services.

In the second model, two models pertinent to state hospitals and training and research hospitals have been defined. While both models have similar aspects, there are certain different application principles. One of the main difficulties is to score 5120 medical processes being performed in health institutions. To do this, a relative value scale was designed. Among these processes, those episodes that are totally completed from beginning to end by a specific provider are given a score (For example: examination, surgery, intervention processes, etc.). Processes performed by devices and auxiliary health staff were not scored, even though they were under the responsibility of the practitioner. It was observed that the scoring often times was inconsistent within the episode of care (Figure 8.4).

To build the global care reimbursement of a patient, a series of components was added in and the coefficient reflects the severity and intensity of the case. As is the situation with government-run systems, the government takes a share of the hospital income before the bonus is calculated (Figure 8.5).

The accrued fund for bonuses continues to prove that there are changes happening in the delivery system to make care more efficient. With savings there are also patient volume increases. Despite these increases, the length of stay continues to be steady or goes down and the number of physicians working part-time and then becoming full-time has also increased (Figure 8.6).

The Ministry is now meeting with the surrounding countries of Macedonia, Greece, Bulgaria, Moldova, Cyprus, and others in proximity to Turkey who are members or candidates for membership in the European Union. Our research on the economics of Turkey indicates that a Western and Eastern expansion of this country's influence is occurring. Although independent, they are making great strides to connect with other governments and leveraging economics and history to create the connection between Europe and Asia. To this end, we believe that the Ministry of Health is ahead of most countries, in both its understanding and use of reimbursement attached to performance.

We thank Eroğan Yilmaz, Director of the Performance Management and Development Department of the Health Ministry, and Professor Dr. Julide Yildirim, Gazi University, Ankara. Their guidance in helping me understand this pioneering and creative system of care in Turkey was instrumental to this part of this book.

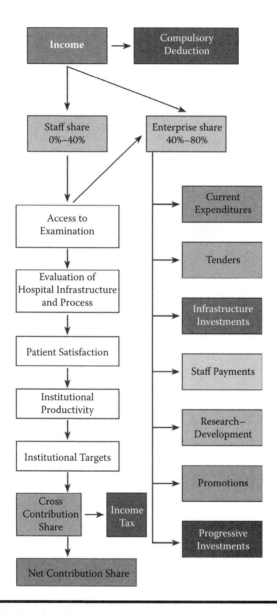

Figure 8.4 Institutional performance.

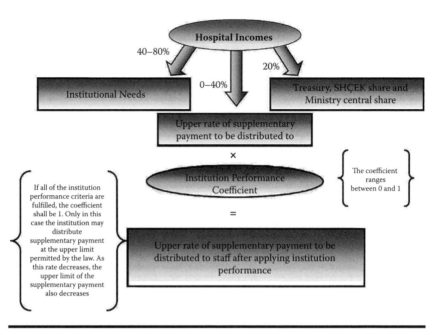

Figure 8.5 Payment distribution.

Year	Total Accrument (YTL)	Supplementary Payment (YTL)	Rate (%)
2000	608.000.000	114.000.000	19
2001	1.024.000.000	226.000.000	22
2002	1.961.000.000	431.000.000	22
2003	2.919.000.000	523.000.000	18
2004	4.827.000.000	1.275.000.000	26
2005	7.542.000.000	2.157.000.000	29
2006	9.480.762.776	2.923.134.053	31

Figure 8.6 Total accrual payment.

Costa Rica

Most Costa Rican citizens subscribe to the government-sponsored national health care system maintained by the Caja Costarricense de Seguro Social (CCSS, Department of Social Insurance). The CCSS has the responsibility of providing quality, low-cost health care to all of Costa Rican working citizens and their dependents. Not only does the CCSS provide universal health care coverage to its citizens, but noncitizens are also permitted to partake in the system.

There is a network of 29 hospitals throughout Costa Rica that provides modern, reliable medical service. Doctors at these hospitals usually receive their initial training in Costa Rica and obtain more advanced training in their specialty in other countries. There are also more than 250 small clinics scattered throughout Costa Rica that provide quality health care to even the remotest parts of the country.

There are several choices for health insurance coverage in Costa Rica. One can buy into the CCSS services for a small monthly fee and have access to all of its hospitals, clinics, and services. The fee is based on income. It covers preexisting conditions, prescriptions, doctor visits, hospitalization, dental, and eye care, and there is no dollar limit to annual coverage. The drawback to this coverage is the long lines and waits associated with public hospitals and clinics. Non-Costa Rican citizens can also buy health insurance from the Instituto de Seguro Nacional (INS, National Insurance Institute). This private health insurance permits the insured access to private hospitals. Rates vary depending on age and gender, and the policy only covers up to $18,000 annually. It also does not cover preexisting conditions. Private hospitals are often less crowded and provide more personalized service, usually without the long wait associated with public hospitals. Many doctors work for both the CCSS and have private offices as well. Quality health care is available with both options.

Costa Rica's Public Plan is funded in part by its citizens and in part by the government to pay for social services, formerly allocated to their national army in the 1950s to pay for social services. The government funds the basic services directly and the additional services are funded by a pool, not unlike a health savings account.

Each citizen is offered a basic health plan by the national insurance company INS. INS is a quasi-government insurance company in that its board is comprised of the state's banking officials appointed by the government. Rate setting and annual evaluation of utilization are part of the governance body's responsibility and therefore under government control.

Originally, citizens were given an annual amount to pay for their noncovered services. This amount was usually managed by individuals or banks in an attempt to maximize the money as an investment and stretch these dollars further. Brokers, as they are called, are paid a percentage of the amount they earn for their clients, and citizens use their services wisely to help conserve this fund which can be rolled over annually.

Recently, the single-payer system has been challenged by the Caribbean Area Free Trade Agreement (CAFTA). The CAFTA trade agreement states that the government may not have a monopoly on any business and must invite in competitors. INS has had such a monopoly, so in the last year the country has admitted four new insurers, as well as authorized Health Savings Account (HSA) collectors to move into the country.

Add to this the fact that many immigrants from neighboring Nicaragua have been using the system without paying into it, and this leads to providers oftentimes not being reimbursed or, if they are, the state has no way to recover these utilization costs but to raise rates.

As the citizens purchase supplements and additional migrants travel into Costa Rica, the thought is that costs will increase to a point where the INS may no longer be sustainable. It may have to cut back benefits or increase out-of-pocket costs to the citizens, many of whom would not be able to participate and would be forced from the rolls and from the insurance pools.

Steps are being taken to remedy this situation, but the concept of a single payer for basic services and supplements from private payers is ripe for a performance-based setting. Many of the new insurance rules and many large employers on the island are calling for some standardization of care and cost to incent quality while not adding to the cost of care for the patient or the government.

As the Population Grows Older

Overall many countries including Switzerland and Italy are working toward a more performance-based model of reimbursement and care management. They have learned as we are just learning that there are ways to change the behavior of both physicians and patients using reimbursement and quality indicators to accomplish what rigid policies and price controls cannot. The very supply of physicians and allied professionals is shrinking globally at a time when the populations everywhere are aging and in need of more sophisticated care.

Can we afford to grow old? This is the question being asked everywhere. The government's willingness and ability to offer benefits and alternative financing for care is now a priority.

Chapter 9

Getting Started

Developing a planned approach to performance-based contracting is desirable versus a reactive approach of suddenly dealing with a contract renewal from a large payer that forces a rapid response. As we have explained, the performance-based approach really combines several disciplines including clinical analytics, claims analysis, integrated team reporting, medical chart review, and cost versus charge analysis. All of this will help the provider organization understand its own opportunities for improvement as well as explain in terms of effectiveness and efficiency just what the options are to reveal the root cause of how care is now provided and what needs to change if participating in a value-based purchasing (VBP) demonstration. While this analysis is going on at the internal level it is important to note what employers and health plans are looking for on the outside of your organization.

First, the employer needs. What are the issues of performance and how do your large employers define value-based health care? Some employers are new to the concept even though they are reading all the Institute of Medicine (IOM) reports and related value-based purchasing (VBP) publications. Both of these bodies of knowledge are vital to read before talking to employers about your interest as a hospital or physician group in building a performance-based contracting strategy.

Employers who do understand this possibility will place specifications in their contracts with managed care companies. And they will cover the four pillars of VBP created by the Bush administration. These pillars include the following:

Four Cornerstones

The Executive Order is intended to ensure that health care programs administered or sponsored by the federal government build on collaborative efforts to promote four cornerstones for health care improvement:

1. Interoperable Health Information Technology

Interoperable health information technology has the potential to create greater efficiency in health care delivery. Significant progress has been made to develop standards that enable health information systems to communicate and exchange data quickly and securely to protect patient privacy. Additional standards must be developed and all health care systems and products should meet these standards as they are acquired or upgraded.

2. Measure and Publish Quality Information

To make confident decisions about their health care providers and treatment options, consumers need quality of care information. Similarly, this information is important to providers who are interested in improving the quality of care they deliver. Quality measurement should be based on measures that are developed through consensus-based processes involving all stakeholders, such as the processes used by the AQA (multi-stakeholder group focused on physician quality measurement) and the Hospital Quality Alliance.

3. Measure and Publish Price Information

To make confident decisions about their health care providers and treatment options, consumers also need price information. Efforts are underway to develop uniform approaches to measuring and reporting price information for the benefit of consumers. In addition, strategies are being developed to measure the overall cost of services for common episodes of care and the treatment of common chronic diseases.

4. Promote Quality and Efficiency of Care

All parties—providers, patients, insurance plans, and payers— should participate in arrangements that reward both those who offer and those who purchase high-quality, competitively-priced health care. Such arrangements may include implementation of pay-for-performance methods of reimbursement for providers or the offering of consumer-directed health plan products, such as account-based plans for enrollees in employer-sponsored health benefit plans.*

This managed care-driven approach is in direct line with the value-based purchasing that employers will demand. More sophisticated employers and employer coalitions will require a detailed outcome, whereas smaller networks may be less sophisticated but are easily influenced by the Bridges of Excellence or other database approaches to measuring both safety and clinical outcomes.

Managed care and health plans have an incentive to protect their business relationships with employers. Employer premiums are directly related to number of lives covered and this, of course, relates to the income of the insurer. We are just now seeing a firm grasp by insurance companies as to how the difference in physician and hospital performance can be fed into an underwriting and pricing strategy to lower costs by restricting access to select providers. By building these restrictions into the benefit plan, patients are told that they should see the specific provider who is the "best practices" provider determined by the administrative and medical record samplings review of a given service area.

Now that the origin of how a market shifts to pay for performance is understood, one can conclude three points:

1. Once employers decide that their costs and value of benefits are unsatisfactory, they will take action by asking their managed care contractor or third-party administrator to take action.
2. Once a Third Party Administrator (TPA) or insurer feels that their revenue is at risk of loss from a large, unhappy employer, no cost is too much to create a data-driven solution that eventually links benefits to provider performance, which shifts patient flow to a smaller group of high-performance physicians and hospital services.
3. Once one or two employers determine that they are saving money by using the VBP approach, the number of enrollees exposed to select providers increases dramatically and patients begin to change use patterns to avoid large out-of-pocket copays or deductibles for not picking the right doctor.

Our experience shows that patient loyalty is worth $17 to $25 per month in premium differences. That is, if a patient sees an extra cost for seeing their own doctor they will switch rather than pay the out-of-pocket difference.

---

* George W. Bush Executive Order, August 11, 2008.

Clinical Integration as Defined by FTC

An active and ongoing program to evaluate and modify the clinical practice patterns of the physician participants so as to create a high degree of interdependence and collaboration among the physicians to control costs and ensure quality.*

Introduction to Planning

Planning steps to get the performance-based medicine approach to managed care contracting requires physicians and hospitals to first look at what is now being done. Is the hospital now engaged in the quality measurement process? Many hospitals already are reporting data to the Centers for Medicare and Medicaid Services (CMS) and also have some quality management programs (Figure 9.1).

Are physicians involved in Physical Quality Reporting System (PQRS) or pharmacy trials? Perhaps the newly contemplated Electronic Medical Record

Figure 9.1 Demonstration project funded before reform.

---

* Federal Trade Commission Definition used to approve Greater Rochester IPA as a clinical integration model.

⌈ Inventory of Health Plans ⌉

Health Plans
Fully insured 39%
Self administered 44%
Other 17%

Figure 9.2   Percentage of revenue by payor.

⌈ Inventory of Health Plans ⌉

- ■ **Self Funded Plans**
- ■ Administrated Services Only (ASO) 88%
- ■ Self administrated by company 12%

Figure 9.3   Percentage by type of coverage.

(EMR) is able to develop excellent clinical and utilization reports if set up correctly by a certified vendor Certified Commission for Health Information Technology (CCHIT). How is data being collected? What are the goals of such plans? Better control on process? Better options in reimbursement? Attempt to control patient throughput? Remember, internally, a medical group should be able to learn who their customers are.

An inventory of these plans (Figures 9.2 and 9.3) in process or recently completed may surprise you as each department is trying to connect the dots of what process could be introduced to make their department more efficient.

Take the four buckets of dollars discussed earlier.

1. Blue Cross Blue Shield (BCBS)
2. Self-pay
3. Public pay, Medicare, and Medicaid
4. Commercial and managed care

An analysis should now be done to determine how many BCBS (Figure 9.4) are covered with a fully insured plan and how many are covered by an Administrative Services Only (ASO) (Figure 9.5) contract (BCBS does claims processing only). Now, which commercial and managed care private pay companies by name are represented and how many encounters and referrals does this constitute? If you are able to group services appropriately, this will tell you approximately how many patient lives each company within the payer group represents. If you can

■ **ASO by Blue Cross**
■ School District 1000 contract holders
■ County Government 900 contract holders
■ City workers 500 contract holders
■ Acme manufacturing 500 contract holders

Figure 9.4   List of ASO client administration employers insurance plans.

■ **ASO by local TPA**
■ Ace building supplies 150 contract holders
■ Local fastener manufacturer 200
  contract holders
■ Local University 500 Contract holders

Figure 9.5   Local third party claims payer administrating employers.

merge this with primary and specialty care visit data, you will get a precise measurement of total value of each actual employer to your health care system. These are your vulnerabilities. If one or more of these top referral sources for doctors and hospital services should switch to a pay-for-performance (P4P) format, the shift away from your health system could be devastating.

Many large, family-owned local corporations (Figure 9.6) are selling to larger industrial enterprises as owners retire or see little chance to be a leader in the economic decline. This means that the purchaser may have a totally different insurance and criteria for contracting with providers. We have witnessed this in

■ **Fully Insured Plans**
■ Hardware store 25 contract holders
■ Grocery store 100 contract holders
■ Local alliance of merchants 150 contract holders

Figure 9.6   Companies who buy insurance and are not self-funding.

> **Summary**
>
> - Total labor market #
> - Total insured #
> - Total insured seeing your clinic or hospital #
> - Source of total insured by company name
> - Who are the biggest employers your organization relies upon
> - Which network brings you the largest proportion of patients?

Figure 9.7 Estimate % of market share by payer.

urban and rural markets where a sudden sale or closure of a large employer shifts patient volume but also recasts reimbursement floor and ceiling using regional or national usual and customary paid claims data.

Claims data alone are not useful. Only claims that have actually been paid will give payers data they will use, which is why charge masters are not as relevant as paid claims data in determining pricing strategies for negotiation.

Once you have discovered employers who have a great value to your organization they become your top target purchasers.

Now, consider that there are employers who will fall into the surprise list. These are large, self-funded employers who do not use the volume of services you perhaps thought they did. Dig deeper and find out from your emergency staff, medical records, billing, and admissions departments whether there is any unresolved conflict/fallout with this employer/carrier at some point. What was the shift and why? Was the conflict resolved or not? This may explain why you may or may not get a call back from that employer when you call to make an appointment (Figure 9.7).

In my 30-plus years of consulting I have only had one medical group administrator who, when we explained what we were doing, actually was able to make one-on-one calls with 30 CEOs in 10 days and arrange 20 appointments over a 30-day period of time. In all other cases few knew who to call or what data they had to work with. Again, we would encourage the C-level staff who sponsor this process to read all of the Institute of Medicine materials and value-based purchasing material available from CMS.

Environmental Scan

The next step is to reach outside the hospital or physician group to determine what is happening with employers. Are employers getting good information on utilization? Are they getting answers from your group about unpaid claims and workers' comp challenges? Do we have a "go to" person for employers and managed care to contact if a problem or question should arise? If large employers see that your provider organization will talk about both the strengths and weaknesses of your organization you have extremely valuable information to bring back to your team. Hearing the same complaint and/or the same compliment may also help you reevaluate your value proposition and determine what can be done to fill gaps.

Managed Care's Involvement

Not unlike employer issues, managed care has its role in helping your organization to enter or expand your performance-based strategy. Most plans have hospital and physician utilization measured against some metrics. Several plans have this broken down by physician and hospital, so obtaining a profile of a provider organization can be fairly accurate, assuming that the plan has a considerable volume of members going to your facility.

Sharing the data can and should be done following Health Insurance Portability and Accountability Act (HIPAA) and HITECH rules for deidentified data because what you are looking for is the grouping of populations by disease, age, and gender to begin mortality and morbidity calculations. These data fields can be compared by procedure or by diagnosis-related group (DRG) but may miss three points.

1. The health maintenance organization (HMO) does not have all the data. They have a sliver of the population they enroll that your doctors and hospitals may service but unless you are the only hospital with which they have contracted, the population of members is split between several medical staffs and several facilities.
2. Severity adjusting data may be difficult, because the number of providers seeing a specific patient could be 10 doctors. Many of these doctors may not show up in the data because if the patient has a large deductible he may have gone outside the network to a doctor he chose to see due to reputation or price. Without this early diagnosis information, the episode is not complete. In a bundled payment environment primary care practitioner (PCP) referrals are going to be vital.
3. If one can obtain the HMO data, that data can not only be compared to benchmarks but also to competitors, some of whom may produce the same services at a more efficient price or effective outcome.

If you can get payers and TPAs who represent payers to share their data along with MedPar and other databases that may be available for state government data or pharmacy data, you can now begin to see patterns emerge. They emerge with little variation for some procedures but with great variation for others.* Looking at these variations is the key to assigning a benchmark and reengineering the procedures that will be attractive to the HMO.

Feasibility and First Steps

Before getting to the task of launching your performance-based contracting strategy, we recommend that a feasibility study be constructed to determine the gaps and resources needed to carry this out. This allows the testing of internal capabilities and competencies before the payers or employers do, beginning to build some assumptions as to net new growth, and sharing performance bonuses with various payers and HMOs. To know what you want is important in moving into a negotiation. Without this foundation of a feasibility analysis, the business planning step will be flawed and probably not materialize. Feasibility must unite the internal resources and the external reality of the market to make sure you are ahead of the needs of the market but able to manage the resources.

Issues will include

- Organizational and governance
- Technical, such as clinical protocols and benchmarks
- Management—how will this strategy be administrated and managed by current or proposed staff?
- Financial—how will reduction in unnecessary admissions be made up by additional market share for patients with less severe yet billable services?

Right now you have a 17% managed care adjustment. However, when you add in the cost of money lost due to slow payment of 60 or 120 days, the denied payments due to inappropriate care or undocumented care, plus the loss of income to these billings that are just uncollectible and written off, your managed care payer segment is closer to 38–44%.

Each practice or institution is unique in its payer mix. Organizational structure within the structure management occurs at different paces and urgency. Sometimes, the pace is predictable and unintended delays or lack of understanding slows decision making so that quality decisions cannot be

---

* Medicare Participating Database.

made. Competitors move forward and opportunities are forfeited to an otherwise good strategy. Successful organizations, as discussed in the Adizes Management approach, follow a proven set of milestones.* The corporation evolves into a series of related enterprises or institutes. In some organizations an entirely new corporation holds the agreements and does the data analysis to avoid being held hostage by hospital/physician politics and to be seen as impartial in reporting data and payment. As this core data group assimilates a larger volume of data, it has more information, and reporting it can generate more sophisticated drill-down capabilities to expose areas where the reengineering of a DRG or episode of care can be accomplished. Quality measurement within the health system will take a larger portion of interest as more dollars can be made and shared between payers and providers if efficiency and effectiveness of care merit such a savings budget. Organizations formed and forming for this purpose include the following:

- ICSI
- Intermountain
- Cleveland Clinics Institutes of Care
- Pittsburg Health System
- Baylor Health System Dallas

These entities, in some circumstances, have formed with physicians, hospitals, employers, and health plans to review data and develop a better understanding of the trends and remedies on which the providers intend to work. Indianapolis, Indiana, is a good example, with at least three large groupings of payers and providers all gearing toward performance. The employer coalition in St. Louis forced the five HMOs in the area to share data, and this combined database is being monitored to look for best practices. In Colorado, a similar goal has been to have the employers lead the market in bringing doctors and hospitals together.

What Are We Trying to Prove?

Put another way, what are we attempting to disprove? Charles Jacobs, head of Interqual, says to clients that it is what makes you different that makes you sell.† Certainly performance differences exist now and in the future as all pay-

---

* Ichak Adizes, *Corporate Lifecycles: How and Why Corportions Grow and Die and What to Do About It.* Paramus, N.J.: Prentiss Hall, 1989.
† Discussions with William De Marco on various projects, November 15, 1982.

ers and the government pit providers against one another to reduce cost and reengineer quality.

Geisinger's "proven care" guarantees there will be no readmission due to infection of medical problems. This means that they will absorb all or most of any follow-up care that occurs because a patient did not take medication as prescribed, got an infection, or just had a relapse. The Geisinger plan has a focused desire to keep its patients healthy because it avoids expense. So, in this model, from the moment a heart surgery begins an episode of care by a patient with a PCP or cardiologist, all of the paperwork, drugs, presurgical instruction, surgical equipment, staffing in the operating room, follow-up bed care, and discharge planning has to be perfect. In addition, follow-up care by a nurse and/or social worker, further rehab follow-up, and assurance that the patient is compliant with his doctor's orders are all part of the warranty. If the patient does not fulfill his part of the bargain the warranty is violated. Here, there is no variation of treatment protocols and all waste has been removed. The coordinator cannot miss a thing.

Is this revolutionary? Probably not. Many provider-sponsored health plans have had to reengineer many aspects of their care systems in this way. Health Partners, Dean Care, and others are all managing the risk of delivery and financing, and this is also the intention of the Health Reform bill with accountable care organizations (ACOs).

The upside risk is only related to how good the care can be delivered with a promise of sharing additional margins with the doctors and hospitals if the providers can offer a quality outcome at a lower price than what Medicare has been paying in claims for the same procedure. The downside risk does not exist as it does with pay for performance because the CMS rules do assure payment for services rendered.

Legal Issues That Might Affect What You Are Trying to Do

We do not intend to offer legal advice but business advisory services associated with the legal aspects. Most providers can read up on aspects of antitrust issues on websites, including the Health Care Lawyers Association website,* and begin to understand the questions for which they will need answers in determining the feasibility of a strategy. In short, the federal government views every provider with a separate tax ID number as a competitor in some way. Therefore, to allow

---

* www.Healthlawyer.com

competitors to collectively negotiate with payers or set some sort of pricing on their services, the government has said that if an organization is clinically and/ or financially integrated, it may be able to conduct business as a single entity and negotiate with payers as a single entity.

Most Physician Hospital Organizations (PHOs) and Independent Practice Associations (IPAs) are able to set pricing using the messenger model of circulating sample pricing, and if the participating doctor does not reject this offer in a set number of days he is in the pool that will contract. To all plans this is very cumbersome because they want a definitive answer to their proposed arrangements. If, however, the provider is sharing some risk through capitation or fixed pricing, then the challenge is waived because the provider is taking risk. This means that prices should be competitive to consumers. This community benefit is key in understanding the regulations.

By the same token, if a physician group or PHO says that they do not want to share financial risk through capitation, the other option is to be clinically integrated.

It is a very sophisticated process to integrate the clinical information of doctors and hospitals and prove through the very processes we discuss here that the quality of care is being reengineered and improved, which will have a community benefit as the care becomes proven instead of unproven.

These antitrust guidelines are not safe harbors or guarantees that you will not be investigated or reviewed in some fashion but offers a pathway to get to an example for what the department despite in building a good network.

Tasks to Move toward an Integrated Care System

We have been asked many times to list the tasks to move toward an integrated care system that can benefit from sharing savings with payers. Much of this depends upon the situation and how you are organized at present. What we do know is that those organizations that set up the integrated entity outside of hospital and physician organizations have a better chance of survival. The reason for this is that hospital politics will sabotage any effort to reduce unnecessary care. The locus of management within the physician IPA or Management Sources Organization (MSO) may also create issues in terms of care guidelines and economics of care management.

In general, the route to performance payment that is sustainable goes through the clinical integration pathway. Here is a set of tasks and subtasks that come to mind. Again, this list is not exhaustive, and in fact it is just a starting point.

Feasibility Study for Nonaligned Hospitals and Physicians

Tasks and Resources

I. Legal development

   Phase 1: Assess laws governing physician hospital organizations in your state

   Task 1: Assess state laws governing the organization of health corporations

   Subtask 1.1 Identify and assess state and federal legislation regarding antitrust

   Subtask 1.2 Review medical and hospital service corporation laws

   Subtask 1.3 Identify and assess other legal mechanisms that may need to be changed to operate an independent joint venture with physicians

   Subtask 1.4 Determine applicability of health reform legislation

   Task 2: If shared savings is a goal review state insurance and managed care statutes

   Task 3: Review prohibitions against advertising with ACO

   Task 4: Investigate restrictions against the corporate practice of medicine and explain to ACO steering committee

   Subtask 4.1 Form physician organization (PO) as provider organization

   Subtask 4.2 Review governance process

   Subtask 4.3 Create shareholder agreements

   Subtask 4.4 Create participating physician agreements

   Task 5: Assess health planning requirements

   Subtask 5.1 Analyze state certificate of need (CON) requirements

   Task 6: Identify restrictions on the use of allied health professionals

   Task 7: Explore other state statutes and legal developments in local area

   Task 8: Assess requirements of the federal law and regulations if Medicare contract is desired

   Task 9: Determine the ACO relationship to the PO

   Subtask 9.1 Determine the ACO's organizational roles and responsibilities

   Subtask 9.2 Document proposed organization structure's conformance with state legal requirements for PO

   Task 10: Determine management agreements between PO and management entity that will collect and administrate data

   Task 11: Prepare and negotiate provider agreements

Task 12: Develop payor agreement and marketing materials

Subtask 12.1 Develop payor agreement with employers

Subtask 12.2 Develop marketing materials

Task 13: Develop contractual agreements comprising the ACO's risk control program

Subtask 13.1 Analyze standard business insurance needs for PO

Subtask 13.2 Analyze malpractice and corporate liability insurance needs for PO

Subtask 13.3 Analyze options to reduce the risk of insolvency through reinsurance and stop loss with payor and PO

II. Organizational and management development

Task 1: Assess alternative organizational models and administrative structures

Subtask 1.1 Determine the relative use of regional versus corporate resources

Subtask 1.2 Develop a plan for identifying, assessing, recruiting, and retaining key staff in your area

Subtask 1.3 Develop a plan for management delegation, development, evaluation, and succession at local and corporate level

Subtask 1.4 Develop a preliminary plan to fulfill information technology and management information system requirements

Subtask 1.5 Medical organization and ACO plan management development process

Task 2: Build a base of community support and develop a plan for managing external relations

Task 3: Lay foundation for a well-rounded, strong board of directors

Subtask 3.1 Identify and recruit board members in your local area

Subtask 3.2 Determine the board's role in relationship to local management

Task 4: Recognize the need to accommodate growth

III. Health service delivery development

Phase 1: Analyze the existing provider network

Task 1: Inventory service area physicians

Task 2: Inventory service area hospitals

Task 3: Catalog other existing health care delivery resources

Phase 2: Assess the climate of support for bundled payment and direct contracting

Task 4: Sample physicians' attitudes toward ACOs

Task 5: Establish rapport with local and state health organizations and agencies

Task 6: Establish communications with institutional and other providers

Task 7: Assemble evidence of provider network support

Phase 3: Design preliminary provider configuration for the ACO

Task 8: Make a preliminary selection of organizational model type
- Not for profit
- For profit
- LLC

Task 9: Analyze alternative physician reimbursement mechanisms
- Fee-for-service
- Clinical benchmarking
- Incentive arrangements
- Global payment
- Bonus
- Impact on malpractice liability insurance
- Guaranteed access to ACO members
- Quality improvement and utilization management programs
- Terms and conditions of payment

Task 10: Analyze alternative hospital and other inpatient facility reimbursement mechanisms
- PO relationships with institutions
- PO relationships with other medical groups/IPAs
- PO contracts with reinsurer
- PO contracts with carve out services

Task 11: Analyze plans for ancillary and other outpatient services
- Laboratory and X-ray
- Home health care
- Pharmacy
- Physical, occupational, and speech therapy
- Dental
- Optometry
- Other

Task 12: Begin planning for the quality improvement and utilization management plans

Phase 4: Develop provider network

Task 13: Determine physician staffing needs

Subtask 13.1 Select the primary care delivery system configuration

Subtask 13.2 Determine the number and specialty of physicians and other health professionals

Task 14: Develop and implement physician recruitment programs

Subtask 14.1 Recruit the medical director

Subtask 14.2 Implement physician recruitment program

A. Physician recruitment in PO

Task 15: Develop physician contracts

Task 16: Develop inpatient hospital agreements

- Location
- Scope of services
- Religious affiliation
- Teaching affiliation
- Reputation
- Quality of care
- Charges to health plans
- Affiliations of medical group

Task 17: Develop contracts for ancillary services

Phase 5: Develop facility arrangements

Phase 6: Develop quality assurance/utilization management methods

Task 18: Establish organizational responsibility for QI and Utilization Management (UM) programs

Task 19: Establish QI program

Task 20: Establish UM program

- Episode of care instruction by specialty
- Build strong support for PCP management and reimbursement of this management
- Construct reporting path for EMR and non-EMR physicians
- Construct data base reporting elements in compliance with CMS rules
- Build a multispecialty team to oversee quality benchmarks and enforce peer review

Task 21: Identify data collection and analysis methods in procedures

- ACO member enrollment
- Encounter or service claim
- Referral authorization
- Hospital/inpatient authorization
- Ancillary service claim

IV. Marketing development

Phase 1: Develop the framework for the marketing plan

- Environmental analysis
- Competitive analysis of other delivery systems in the area
- Market segments of Medicare, large commercial, small commercial, Medicaid, unions
- Marketing mix forecast of the payor segments most desired
- Marketing strategy as to how to communicate to these segments

- Enrollment forecasts of population matched to delivery system capacity
- Community support to understand the high performance nature of your organization

Task 1: Analyze the service and marketing environment

- Service area including other regional partners
- Market area focus on the retention of current market

  Subtask 1.1 Define and analyze the geographic characteristics of the service area

  Subtask 1.2 Examine and analyze demographic characteristics of the service area population

  Subtask 1.3 Define and analyze the economic base of the service area

Task 2: Collect market survey data

  Subtask 2.1 Survey employer groups and unions

  - Union/employer group segmentation
  - Sampling of representative groups
  - Personal interview
  - Telephone survey
  - Mail survey

  Subtask 2.2 Survey competing ACOs and HMOs

  - Model type
  - Stage of development
  - Current enrollment
  - Years in operation
  - Growth over past 5 years and projected 5 years
  - Expansion plans of marketing effort or facilities
  - Marketing segments served in major employer groups
  - Penetration by other HMOs within these groups
  - Benefits
  - Premiums
  - Locations
  - Number of physicians, names, and specialties
  - Percent of surveyed employers presently offering HMOs
  - Reputation in the community among employers and consumers
  - Marketing management strategy of non- Medicare Advantage (MA) program participants

  Subtask 2.3 Survey the public sector

  - Medicaid
  - Medicare

- Other

Task 3: Analyze the competition

Subtask 3.1 Analyze market shares

Subtask 3.2 Analyze the health benefit consumption patterns of the marketplace

Subtask 3.3 Analyze the public sector

Subtask 3.4 Analyze competition from other HMOs

- Number of HMOs of each model
- Federal qualification status if applicable
- Current enrollment and past growth
- Benefit package of each HMO
- Premiums and payments charged by HMO
- Inpatient and outpatient locations of ACO and HMO
- Service area of each
- Marketing strategy of each

Task 4 Determine priority market segments

Task 5: Develop marketing mix

Subtask 5.1 Design the preliminary plan

Subtask 5.2 Set the price and reimbursement strategy

Subtask 5.3 Select the highest priority target market

- Select target audiences and appropriate objectives
- Conduct market research
- Choose promotional tools
- Devise promotional plan

Task 6 Formulate the marketing strategy

Subtask 6.1 Set the objectives of the marketing strategy

Subtask 6.2 Identify the most attractive primary and secondary market targets

- Number of employees residing in the service area
- Receptivity of management
- Complexity of the accounts' decision-making and administrative procedures

Subtask 6.3 Institute a system of market planning and control

- Long-range plan
- Annual plan
- Develop control procedure for predictability

Task 7: Commercial forecast enrollment

Subtask 7.1 Develop an account penetration model and apply it to all targeted accounts

- Employ out-of-pocket cost differential by contract type
- Benefit differential

- Account size
- Industrial category
- Account receptivity
- Existing HMOs

Subtask 7.2 Determine the 5-year potential of secondary market segments

Subtask 7.3 Determine the additional members who will enroll in later years

Task 8: Draw conclusions regarding market viability before proceeding to phase 2

Phase 2: Develop the marketing program

Task 9: Create a marketing department

Subtask 9.1 Define departmental functions

- Sales
- Account services
- Member services
- Advertising/promotion
- Marketing planning and control

Subtask 9.2 Determine staff requirements

Subtask 9.3 Design the organizational structure

Subtask 9.4 Staff and administer the marketing department

Task 10: Develop the marketing budget

Subtask 10.1 Determine the marketing budget

Subtask 10.2 Evaluate the marketing budget

Task 11: Implement the marketing program

Subtask 11.1 Scheduling the accounts

Subtask 11.2 Selling the employer/union

Subtask 11.3 Enrolling the employee

Subtask 11.4 Servicing the account

Subtask 11.5 Re-enrolling the account

V. Financial development

Phase 1: Conduct budget and actuarial analysis

- Fixed costs
- Semi-variable costs
- Variable costs
- Capitation development

Task 1: Estimate hospitalization costs

- Bed day utilization per 1,000
- Hospital per diem rates

Subtask 1.1 Formulate actuarial assumptions

Subtask 1.2 Calculate average per diem rate

Subtask 1.3 Calculate average per diem rates for all hospitals, by admission type

Subtask 1.4 Calculate overall average per diem rate

Subtask 1.5 Compute hospitalization capitation rates

Subtask 1.6 Estimate monthly and quarterly hospitalization rates

Task 2: Estimate the cost of physician services

Part A—Estimating physician costs in medical groups

Subtask 2.1 Establish costs in charges for physician services

Subtask 2.2 Determine in-house and referral physician mix

Task 3: Estimate bundled medical costs

Task 4: Estimate administrative costs

Subtask 4.1 Estimate administrative staff and fringe benefits

Subtask 4.2 Estimate professional service costs

Subtask 4.3 Estimate facility occupancy costs

Subtask 4.4 Estimate information technology costs

Subtask 4.5 Estimate cost of risk reduction through reinsurance

- Emergency out-of-area fund
- Continuation of coverage should health plan operation cease

Subtask 4.6 Estimate bad debt experience

Subtask 4.7 Estimate recruitment cost

Subtask 4.8 Estimate liability insurance and reserve requirements

Subtask 4.9 Formulate promotional strategy

Phase 2: Project financial requirements

- Establish competitive pricing structure
- Project revenue by source
- Develop pro forma statements
- Estimate the size of the loan and/or capitalization plan required

Task 6: Develop pricing analysis

- Variable costs
- Fixed costs
- Using multiple coverage and benefit packages
- Using multiple provider tiers
- Cost loading
- Copayments
- Rate change policy

Subtask 6.1 Compute contract mix and average family size

Subtask 6.2 Develop PMPM for each contract type

Subtask 6.3 Create forward scenario using Medicare actuarial assumptions

Subtask 6.4 Identify sources of subsidy that meet Medicare requirements

Task 7: Project revenue from savings, Medicare, and commercial
Task 8: Prepare pro forma operating statements and compute breakeven
Task 9: Size up the capital requirements
    Subtask 9.1 Calculate commercial loan/investor requirements
    Subtask 9.2 Develop annual schedule of loans to new entity
    Subtask 9.3 Calculate interest expense and interest income
Phase 3: Develop cash management plan
Task 10: Conduct cash flow analysis
    Subtask 10.1 Calculate cash impact
    Subtask 10.2 Complete the cash flow
    Subtask 10.3 Complete the account balance sheet
Task 11: Prepare the pro forma balance sheets
Task 12: Conduct sensitivity analysis and test the financial viability of the plan
Task 13: Refine and update financial planning assumptions
Task 14: Recognize potential financial problems
VI. Summary recommendations
Task 1: Assemble final recommendations
Task 2: Develop additional sources for capitalization for ACO as needed
Task 3: Assemble business plan for ACO*

Financial Steps

Early on, the joint venture of physicians and hospitals may need to come to grips with just who will pay for the startup of the enterprise and how they will be paid back before any dividends or bonus payments are made. Some organizations have characterized this as a loan and others have characterized it as an investment, converting a convertible debiture to a stock ownership once feasibility and an implementation plan are underway.

Regardless of how startup costs are paid, the ownership of the enterprise that leads the critical pathway to integration must have solid physician leadership. There is no good way for hospitals to tell doctors how to practice medicine, but there is a good way for hospitals to offer support and tools for doctors to lead this transition.

---

* © De Marco & Associates, 2010.

Planning Steps

Always start with a feasibility study. Every project we have been involved with in which a feasibility study was agreed to stood the test of time, whereas everyone who raced into clinical integration without really understanding the complexities of both reimbursement and behavioral change failed. The feasibility study should bring together all essential assumptions and facts about what the organization intends to do and present a business case for why a specific vision should move forward.

General Issues to Avoid

Avoid the squabbling about startup costs and arguments about what the government may or may not do. Rather, look at the move to clinical integration and performance-based contracting as a necessary evolution and an opportunity to take the high moral ground as a quality leader in the community.

Issues to Decide upon Early On

Having said that it is not all about money, it is important that everyone understands how the money may change under integration. Everyone needs to agree that some waste will be cut in exchange for a share of the savings to replace this income, and it may be important to discuss why we are doing this again.

No Guarantee That Any of These Steps Will Produce a Result

The risk factor in all integrated delivery system formations is that there is no absolute guarantee that everything will work the way it is promised. People will get frustrated along the way and some may even try to scuttle the ship from time to time, because this change is permanent and represents a threat to all who are human and have any insecurity about their position in the organization. The government, HMOs, and insurers are going to do what they are going to do. Just remember, learning to live in a lean environment is a requirement for survival.

Chapter 10

The Future of Performance-Based Medicine

Once We Have Baseline

The emphasis throughout our book has been to make sure that there are ambitious but realistic goals in setting benchmarks. These benchmarks serve as a baseline for the patient population and measuring above or below average care for this population will be the scoring process used to generate and share savings. Measuring and reporting of utilization data against commonly accepted norms, therefore, is a foundation for behavioral change for the consumer, physician, hospital executives, and the health plan.

This is where the focus on performance actually creates its own environment for change. Acceptance of medical leadership and management creates a means to build a platform of data and billing information to test and simulate clinical and financial results over time. Using clinical guidelines that are shared with physicians, health plans, and patients reduces the current conflicts of denials and delays in payment, eliminates the mystery of consequences if a patient is not compliant, and builds a framework to offer an early warning system for providers, patients, and health plan. This signals a disease grouping that may result in a catastrophe if case management does not intervene. This allows us to return to the agenda of preventive care and health promotion with an actual stake in the quality and financial outcome.

Operating Your Performance-Based Strategy

The strategy we will discuss requires you to have already run an analysis of your paid claims information and grouped these data elements into a bundled grouper such as an episode treatment grouper (ETG), Medstat episode grouper (MEG), or similar tool to begin to select top-performing physicians and services on a risk-adjusted basis. These top performers will leave behind a pattern of process steps that are similar in that they can be matched to a series of steps that get them to a diagnosis and then, using the diagnosis link, select services for select episodes where a series of tests, visits, follow-ups, and interventional strategies are performed regularly for a similar population of people with similar diseases/complaints.

Taking top performers in two or three specialties and primary care management can create some reporting information that actually sets some realistic goals for measurement using local norms of your top providers as the benchmarks and national specialty society norms or Agency for Healthcare Quality and Research (AHQR) norms to develop the rationale as to why this is good medicine.

It is now time to share this information with physicians either through your benchmarking consortium administrator or through the medical director of the group to be discussed.

Like a tool for discovery, the data can be laid out with the guidelines and then the performance to show how far some providers may be from that norm. In some groups there may be minor changes, whereas in others the changes may be substantial. What we have learned in doing this is that the larger the chunk one attempts to digest, the more problems. These problems can be up to and including pushback from the table by physicians who cannot fathom that they have learned or done something wrong. This is why the grouper concept offers a true definition of the patient, her health status, and a factoring of complexity that mere procedure codes and diagnosis-related groups (DRGs) do not.

Episode Treatment Group

The Episode Treatment Group™ (ETG™) methodology is a patented case-mix adjustment and episode-building system that uses routinely collected inpatient and ambulatory claims data. The resulting clinically homogenous groups, of which there are approximately 600, adjust for severity by the presence of complicating conditions, comorbidities, and other characteristics of a patient's condition that affect resource utilization.*

---

* Dang, DK, Pont, JM, Portmoy, MA; *Episode Treatment Groups: An Illness Classification and Episode Building System – Part II*; Med Interface, 1996 Apr:9(4):122-8

The ETG methodology is similar to that of the DRGs but with several important differences. Perhaps the most obvious is that ETGs identify and classify an entire episode of care regardless of whether the patient has received medical treatment as an inpatient, outpatient, or both. Specifically, the characteristics of the ETG methodology are as follows:

1. Manageable number of groups—The ETG episode of illness patient classification system is composed of nearly 600 statistically stable clinical groups. The ETGs were constructed using a nationally representative database including 60 million record claims representing all illness types (Table 10.1).
2. Case-mix adjustment—ETGs adjust for patient severity, intensity, and complexity by accounting for differences in patient age, complicating conditions, comorbidities, and major surgeries.
3. Clinical homogeneity—ETGs are clinically homogeneous so that each patient's illness and severity level are medically consistent with others belonging to the same ETG.

Consequently, direct comparisons of treatment patterns can be made among providers within the same ETG (Figure 10.1).

Episode building—ETGs combine inpatient, ambulatory, and pharmaceutical claims to build a complete treatment episode from onset of symptoms until treatment is complete. Rather than relying on a fixed time frame, each episode's treatment duration is flexibly determined based on its ETG-specific "clean period," or time period in which there is an absence of treatment. This ensures that all appropriate treatment and cost information has been collected and correctly assigned to one complete illness episode.

Concurrent and recurrent episodes—Using the service unit of an individual claim or encounter form as input, ETGs identify and track the treatment of different illnesses that may exist during a single patient encounter. As a result, ETGs separate and identify concurrently occurring illnesses and assign each health care service to the clinically appropriate episode. In addition, should a patient be successfully treated but suffer a recurrence of the same illness, the ETG software identifies the recurrent episodes.

Shifting episode assignment—ETGs account for changes in a patient's condition during the course of treatment. Once a change in condition has been identified, the patient's entire episode may shift from the initially defined ETG to the ETG that includes the change in condition. In this way, the progression of an illness is identified.

Table 10.1 Characteristics of Patient Classification Systems

Patient Classification Method	Developer	No. of Terminal Groups	Clinical Homogeneity	Statistically Stable	Severity (Casemix) Adjustment	Episodic Structure	Episodic Shifting on Acuity
ETGs	Symmetry Health Data system	600	Yes	Yes	Yes	Yes	Yes
MEGs	The MedStat Group	630	Yes	Yes	Yes	Yes	Yes
Diagnosis Clusters (DECs & PTEs)	Value Health Sciences & PPSI	1.800 & 125	Yes	No	Yes	No	No
CCI	HealthChex/HCIA	20	No	No	Yes	No	No
ACGs	Johns Hopkins/ CSC	52	No	Yes	No	No	No
DxCGs, DCGs & HCCs	DxCG, Inc.	80	Yes	Yes	No	No	No

Source: Data from Casemix Consulting, LLC.

MPC: Pulmonology

(1) Employer/Plan	(2) # of episodes	(4) Clinical demand index (S)	(5) Actual charge per episode	(6) Clinically adjusted (CA) charge per episode*	(7) % of peer group charge (CA)
A	1921	1.872	$232	$124	100.6%
B	1356	0.845	$119	$140	113.8%
C	789	1.232	$107	$87	70.6%
D	661	0.852	$88	$103	83.7%
E	473	0.916	$113	$123	100.1
Peer Group National Benchmark	5,445	1.000	$123	$123	100.0%
				$136	
				$70	

*The calculation for column 6 is a result of dividing column 5 by column 4.

Figure 10.1 ETG office change comparison by employer/healthplan. (Data from the Delta Group, Inc. 1999. 1999 HCFA 1500 Claims Data, Greenville, N.C.).

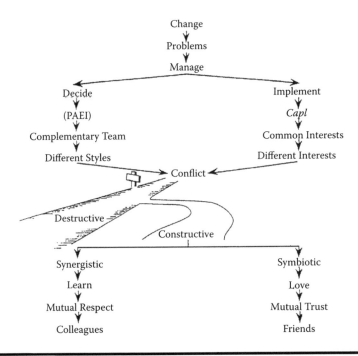

Figure 10.2   The human paths to successful change management. (Data from Odizes Institute. © 1997. Carpineteria, CA.)

Pharmaceutical claims—Unique to the ETG methodology is its ability to assign pharmaceutical claims data to the appropriate illness episode using the 11-digit National Drug Code (NDC) that contains highly specific information regarding each drug type, its manufacturer, dosage, and route of administration. Using a sophisticated hierarchical approach, the ETG methodology evaluates each prescription drug claim against each of the concurrently occurring episodes for which the particular drug could be prescribed and then assigns the drug claim to the most clinically appropriate episode.

As it relates to payment data, Figure 10.2 shows that employer/plan A has the highest clinical demand index, 1.872, indicating that employer/plan A has the highest demand for resource consumption based on the severity, intensity, and complexity of its patients. Consequently, after adjusting for this higher clinical demand, employer/plan A's average charge per episode decreases from $232 to $124, allowing for an accurate comparison of financial outcomes to be made across employers/plans.

The balance is to find some generally acceptable norms and point out where the patterns of good care coming from the group are. The top performers of some procedures can be named. The naming of bottom performers is not a good idea and should be discussed using code numbers for various players. The purpose here is not to put people on the defensive by saying what is happening is wrong but rather to say that this behavior is inconsistent with a high-performance group. By creating better processes we get better outcomes, which means less waste and more dollars set aside for successful pay for performance or sharing of serious savings under the accountable care organization payment method.

In many cases the sharing of serious dollars between primary and specialty care and the hospital may signal the change of behavior that is desired because the change is linked to a pay plan versus merely trying to reduce expenses for an insurance company.

Sharing Benchmarks and Eliminating Unhealthy Conflict

We are taught in school that all conflict is bad, yet as we grow in maturity and understanding of the group think process, we are eventually brought to the conclusion that conflict can be positive, especially if one's expectations are not being met because of one's own behavior.

Using Discussions of Quality to Create Productive Conflict

In our process of earning trust between providers and payers the transition will not occur without some conflict. Conflict comes in all varieties, including the following:

- Conflicts of interest
- Lack of balance
- Lack of respect
- Normal versus abnormal
- Constructive conflict

In general, the point at which something as complex as health care becomes manageable only happens as organized decision making is allowed and balanced by different styles of personalities for different projects. There are usually producers who are always working toward results, administrative types of management who work toward the coordination and monitoring of the operation, entrepreneurs who are the visionaries and motivators of reason and urgency to choose one option over another, and integrators who bring together different styles of personalities or management styles to flow in a single direction.

The decision to carry out an implementation plan has other forces to deal with that are collectively and sometimes singly able to stop the ball rolling or condemn the decision even before it is made. These include people who coalesce the group's interests, those who by rank or acknowledged role have authority to approve or carry out a decision, and those who have the power from inside and sometimes outside to support or stop a good decision from being implemented. There are also those who influence all these players and therefore can be directly linked to success or failure of an otherwise well-thought-out decision.

Let's touch on each of the above conflicts to understand what they are.

In the conflicts of interest we see different managerial types in conflict with others. You may have an operations director who sees that the visionary is not following the rules, an administrator who thinks that producers of results are wasting more money than they should to get results. In our current situation providers and executives who are compensated more by producing more tests and encounters will run into the visionary executive or the plans by outside groups to see costs of care reduced by utilization cutbacks and inspection of true quality outcomes. The compensation and goals must change to reduce unnecessary treatments or the tendency to always offer the most expensive treatments to resolve a patient's complaint.

In a lack of balance situation you may have the deck stacked by management to have all the administrative types block a decision without input from producers or entrepreneurs and, as such, have a decision that is unbalanced measuring input is lacking from all sources and will certainly fall prey to those with power who see their needs are not met or those who influence outcomes knowing that the end result will not serve the organization as a whole. This is the core failure of capitation when brought into the care environment. Physicians thought that under capitation they would have some influence over the decision-making as to what the quality definitions were and found that their needs as producers and visionaries were not met so they had the power to block this and coalesce many other physicians against the hospital and the managed care company who were (they thought) controlling this terrible decision making to cap costs and limit good medicine from being practiced.

When there is lack of respect, all efforts are derailed until trust is rebuilt and done so in a manner that all managerial types see or earn an advantage and all forces that can sabotage the outcome of implementation are then appeased in some way with information and a balance of promises. Though all of us in health care seem to abhor risk in favor of the guaranteed outcome, it is also apparent that the market forces including the regulators are demanding change of a permanent nature. Purchasers, including employers and Medicare, are doing this by linking reimbursement to patient outcome. This means that the hospital and the physician must work cooperatively to create this high-performance delivery system but the lack of respect from past deals that went bad or missteps by previous CEOs or medical staff are all on the minds of those who are listening to this transition to a focus of care quality and harvesting of savings now being offered by the government and some health plans. Trust is built slowly and communication between all parties is expected, with decision making shared by physicians and hospitals in making and setting benchmarks and the means to achieve these benchmarks.

Normal vs. Abnormal Conflict

There are normal conflicts in the hospital–physician relationship. Trying to assess how to resolve normal conflicts requires the respect for the other partner's situation and a mutual goal of trying to grow the business with more patients or more incomes and reducing expenses by elimination of denied or stalled payments. Guidelines do help avoid payment delays and denials because the benchmarks are clearly prescribed in advance of services. This prospective pathway is a means to offer top quality and get paid for it and the more that doctors and hospitals work closely at precision documentation of diagnosis and patient management, the more likely each will get at their goals, albeit in a different manner. Hospitals continue to find that running physician offices is very difficult and physicians who purchase hospitals and run them like a small country practice continue to have problems with cash flow and staffing turnover. Normal conflicts are dealt with in the normal course of business by understanding (Figure 10.2).

Abnormal or irrational conflict can arise when a person is threatened by change or so overly entrenched in the world he has made for himself that those around him are afraid to communicate with him for fear that he will go on a tirade and doom the strategy. Or it comes from those who are so fed up with mismanagement of doctor–hospital relationships that to do nothing *is* a decision. In forming a health plan for a large multispecialty group practice, I held an all-hands meeting of 60 doctors, and in the middle of the presentation on health plan development, one doctor stood up and shouted, "I do not care what anyone else here thinks or does as long as I get mine!" He gathered his papers and stormed out. At a chance meting with him on the running path the next day he revealed that he felt the whole earth was shifting under his feet and he was angry and chose that moment and those words to vent his frustration that he really did not understand what was being done or why. And we were friends and colleagues from that point forward. When questions arose he called me, and when I did not hear from him for a while I called him so he knew that his input was important.

Constructive Conflict

> Nobody made a greater mistake than he who did nothing because he could only do a little.

Edmund Burke

The nature of conflict in most organizations is probably overblown and usually stems from one of the essential conflict patterns seen here. In moving toward a performance-based environment, everything eventually connects with another. The theory of team practice of medicine is based on connectivity between friends who share a mutual trust and respect. In Hebrew, the word *friends* comes from the word *connected* (HVR). This also stands for *love*, which in this case means having a friend who is so close that what happens to you happens to them and vice versa. To illustrate this point, let's look at the operating room as a laboratory. It usually contains the staff, the technicians, the nurses, and the doctor, who feels that he does his or her best work when they all participate. This is another way of stating a mutual trust and respect for these people that are connected so closely to the physician talent and patient outcome that to move this team elsewhere or break up this team, the outcome may be different.

You will note that many of these physicians and friends do not always agree on things, ranging from stock tips to who will win the World Series, but when it comes to medicine they are more than friends. They are colleagues and many times their mutual respect has started with something these colleagues taught one another. Several studies* point to the fact that the majority of physicians graduating from a particular medical school will see an opportunity to practice in that general vicinity even if their internship and residency were many miles away. Why? Because they want to be in contact with their professors, their colleagues, and, yes, friends, who choose to eventually move back to an area with which they are familiar and have a trusted relationship with someone who has taught them something.

So does performance-based medicine offer an opportunity to strengthen the collegiality of the medical staff through developing an open learning organization

---

* Green, Marianne MD; Jones, Paul MD; Thomas, John X. Jr., PhD, Selection Criteria for Residency: Results of a National Program Directors Survey, *Academic Medicine* March 2009 - Volume 84 - Issue 3 - pp 362–367.

within the performance environment? Of course it does. Many of these top specialty and primary care doctors have the same concerns deep down inside that are in all of us—"Will I make the grade?" "Are my pattern of practice, my recommended treatment, and my diagnostic skills as good as if not better than those of my colleagues and friends?" This describes the opportunity and the barrier. "A friend that is dear to me could be in trouble and need help. If they look too closely at the medical records and background of the past few years." "I myself want to be only with top-notch doctors and we have some real bad doctors on our medical staff." What really binds a hospital medical staff is not a common interest other than to use the facilities as a workshop for use in the daily practice.

Unless actions are taken that make this hospital privilege a unique learning opportunity, collegiality and friendships will not develop.

Finally, "I have been here many years and think the hospital really cannot manage its way out of a paper bag and now we are going to share performance data with them? Why?" This is just a sample of what is going through many doctors' heads when hospitals or health plans introduce performance-based contracting.

Gap Analysis as an Ongoing Operational Management Goal

We have discussed in detail the ongoing total quality management (TQM) circle to try to improve quality outcomes and the process to get to that outcome. In analysis of data there will be comparisons and large swings in the data. Figures 10.3a and 10.3b show report cards for PCPs and specialty doctors, respectively.

Noting that the doctors in these reports vary a bit in their outcomes, and therefore on a performance basis may not be eligible to participate in a savings bonus pool, the effort to migrate all performance to the mean will eventually make all physicians build a better practice because the leaders will want to stay as leaders and the followers will always play catch-up with the leaders. This is true for physician practices as well as hospitals.

> We look for medicine to be an orderly field of knowledge and procedure. But it is not. It is an imperfect science, an enterprise of constantly changing knowledge, uncertain information, fallible individuals, and at the same time lives on the line.*
>
> **Atul Gawande, M.D.**

---

* Gawandad, Atual, "The Cost Conundrums," reprinted in the *New Yorker Magazine*, June 1, 2009.

Population Profiling System PCP Practice Report

Specialty: Pediatrics

Episode Count	ETG Number	Description	Provider	Peer Group
66	0690	Minor skin trauma, except burn and open wound	$0.00	$985.07
33	0746	Minor orthopedic trauma	$496.00	$1,258.81
32	0794	Routine exam	$625.88	$1,136.15
15	0331	Tonsillitis, adenoiditis or pharyngistis w/o surgery	$41.87	$1,657.42
11	0329	Otitis media, w/o surgery	$148.55	$2,879.95
10	0689	Open wound, w/o surgery	$3,000.00	$1,266.12
9	0752	Orthopedic and rheumatological signs and symptoms	$0.00	$1,017.09
7	0354	Otolaryngology disease signs and symptoms	$0.00	$257.70
5	0007	Infectious disease signs and symptoms	$200.00	$395.88
5	0678	Minor inflammation of skin and subcutaneous tissue	$0.00	$3,127.89

■ Provider   ■ Peer Group

Figure 10.3a   Primary care practice report.

Population Profiling System Provider Case Load by Complexity Level

Specialty: Endocrinology

Provider Name: 2285 Robert Gregory

	Mild		Minor		Moderate		Severe	
20	Provider	Peer Group	Provider	Peer Group	Provider	Peer Group	Provider	Peer Group
	3	31	42	860	30	1,638	3	
15	1.3	1.1	4.4	2.1	5.9	2.7	3.3	
	3.0	1.7	11.4	5.1	16.0	7.3	6.0	

10

5

0

Visits   Services

Figure 10.3b   Caseload complexity.

Disease Grouping Connected to Delivery Systems

The problem has been that to truly measure the delivery system and its disease management capacity, we need to have a common linkage of outpatient and inpatient care steps, including pharmaceuticals and other therapy units for each care episode linked to a diagnosis. This introduces the fact that some delivery systems do extremely well with cardiac and cancer and others do a better job with maternity and orthopedic patients. This begins to introduce the reality that every hospital may not be selected by purchasers as the top hospital for everything, and that means there is a race to move toward centers of excellence, as was discussed in early integration talks.

This also means that product line management will come to health care and, just like retail, we may start looking for the best facility or best doctor's group with the best outcomes regardless of where in the United States that provider group or hospital may be. This is the "destination selling" concept behind the DeBakey Heart Institute and several other specialty centers that are used by regional and national reinsurance companies who reinsure the difficult and expensive patients on behalf of insurance companies and health maintenance organizations (HMOs) that must purchase this high-end, stop-loss insurance to survive excess liability claims. Reinsurance companies have reams of performance data that are used to credential product lines of specialty care. They then negotiate a bundled payment depending upon the severity level of the patient. For example, stage 1 cancer and stage 2 cancer and so on, recognizing age and other illnesses present, has a lot to do with the actual cost to get this patient to a plateau of healing that allows her to return to the local service area for ongoing treatment and follow-up.

Patient Health Status Improvement

Many physicians believe that as the performance-based contracting environment becomes saturated with more data and agencies from AHQR to state credentialing, databases on health issues and professional licensure are more useful.

The ultimate goal will be improving the health status of this group of people by making modifications to the evidence-based guidelines or inserting new performance grading based upon new clinical findings.

Organized medicine, meaning societies and universities, have the ability to reset measures to a closer clinical pathway that will allow the true outcome to be measured.

I envision this to be the measurement of health status of the patient not just in one town or city but literally across regions of the country and perhaps even globally, sharing technology and clinical data to a broadest of audiences that need this information to improve the health status. To a great extent this is being done with some chronic diseases that were a death sentence a few short years ago but that are now manageable due to drug therapies and other interventions. Now many cardiac problems, dementia diagnoses, some forms of brain cancer and many degenerative diseases are no longer death sentences; instead, patients have manageable health status improvements and, with lifestyle changes, have lived longer than ever predicted by earlier studies and practices.

Building the "Front End" and the "Back End" of the Patient-Coordinated System

We talk to clients about this regularly and try to explain the fact that many patients who enter the system sideways may also end up leaving the system the wrong way unless there are some common care coordination habits put in place. Bridges has established early recognition of electronic pharmacy to reduce error rates and early recognition of hospitalists as an efficient way to manage patients who are institutionalized. It still allows the primary care doctor to practice but eliminates most rounds in the hospitals. The electronic medical record has helped obtain a continuous flow of patient data. Except for a few vendors who still do not allow patient's lab tests and similar reports to be available for all the referral doctors responsible for the patient, new vendors are dealing with real time transactions in an open source environment.

As bundled payments become the norm we see this as an incentive for change by even the most recalcitrant doctors, but we know that hospitals also have the same problem in gathering clear individual patient data from hospital admit and discharge records to measure patient status and determine whether they made a difference in improving health status. In a future environment, providers may have to prove their answer to this question to be recertified by Joint Commission on Accreditation of Healthcare Organizations (JCAHO) and National Committee for Quality Assurance (NCQA) before displaying a triple a rating as a "go to" facility for payers, patients, and physicians. As an example, a large primary care group in Indianapolis is already using health grades to determine which specialists and which hospitals they will refer to. They believe that it is in their own self-interest and the interest of the patient to be connected to the very best rated delivery systems in the region and, so far, the payers have agreed.

Patient Health Records

We thought this technology was far off in the future until Microsoft launched into the development of Health Vault.* One of our failings as users of the delivery system is our own disorganized and illiterate understanding of what our own

---

* Health Vault is a personal medical recall product of Microsoft.

medical history and the medical history of our families are. Keeping all of this straight seemed to be the doctor's problem. In the old days when you chose your doctor and did not have to deal with network and insurer changes on an annual basis, old Doc Smith would keep good records on your history. Now many of us change doctors often. As we get older we look toward internists and cardiologists as primary care rather than the primary care practitioner (PCP). So keeping up to date on your pills and your latest injury or health status change is critical yet is increasingly harder to do.

With technology, an electronic medical record is available to be downloaded to your own workstation where you can open the encrypted file that only you and your doctor can have access to. You fill out the forms and templates on recent visits and past medical issues and then upload and encrypt it back to the physician. This electronic connection to your doctor's office also offers the opportunity to make appointments with the doctors by offering available times and having the computer select the next time schedule match and designating this on your computer. The Microsoft and QuickBooks application to help you track deductible medical expenses for your health savings account. This is an example of the next generation of dashboards and software connections that keep you in the loop with custom-designed health promotion plans that can, in many cases, tie to the insurance coverage you own personally through upcoming Health Exchanges. Personally designed benefit plans sound like a luxury until one considers the personal habits that lead to diabetes, which, in turn, leads to coronary heart disease. We all know this in some way but do we actually watch our weight and fat/sugar intake? Corn syrup is not sugar and is twice as deadly, but for the soda companies it is a low-cost substitute for real sugar. If you had a personal report card on your behavior for the week and it recalibrated to help balance protein and carbs just for your metabolism, what would that be worth to you? It's being developed as we speak.

We can take this challenge of self-reporting a step further: if your doctors and/or your insurance company said that if you lose the weight, quit smoking, and get some exercise a couple of days a week we will eliminate your copay or lower your deductible, what is that worth to you as a consumer? This is a savings that goes to the bottom line of our discretionary income. In addition, the insurance companies have linked up with credit card companies to come up with bonus points to your personal card for buying exercise equipment, purchasing wellness magazines, and traveling to meetings having to do with wellness, all of which may be used for purchases of appliances or travel. The money for these perks can come from savings in your medical plan and savings your doctor created for the insurance company by developing better treatment protocols.

Gain Sharing and Risk Management

Geisinger's first-year savings on the proven care cardiac program was several hundred thousand dollars. Health Partners Minnesota achieved nearly $1 million in savings in 2009 and expects to exceed that incoming year.*

Our accountable care organization (ACO) calculations regularly show $10 million in savings for 20,000 members using bundled payment and episodes of care. This amount split between 60 to 70 PCPs, in addition to regular payments from Medicare, does not even begin to detail the enormous opportunity for negotiating similar contracts with private payers and Medicaid.

We want to emphasize that the old 2% earnings for larger enterprises who participated in demo projects seems like a lot. But for the local physician's small specialty practice this seems like a waste of time. Primary care physicians offered $3,000.00 or more per year to participate in PQRI and convert a handful of codes to codes for billing to Medicare have turned their nose up at this as a pittance compared to seeing additional patients each week to make up for their income gap from discounted private pay and substandard Medicare payments. The opportunity to share the savings between hospital and physicians in a joint mission to eliminate waste is a powerful incentive and an opportunity for skill and innovation to be rewarded. This encourages delivery systems to compete on quality, not just price.

This was the original theory behind the classic HMOs of the early 1970s. Reorganize the delivery system and redeploy savings from efficiencies back into the health plan while researching best practices for effective care using these savings.

In their book *Redefining Health Care*,[†] authors Michael Porter and Elizabeth Teisberg emphasize a value-based approach to care reorganization, and this includes moving competition away from health plan against health plan to a competition between provider organizations that have a value-based system of care delivery. This means that unlike the Wall Street folks who have found a way to reengineer money that produces no consumer value, the health care delivery system must stop trying to reengineer care to raise prices, creating mergers that raise prices, and manipulating fee schedules and percentage of charges to maximize income. Instead, they must address the question of what value we are delivering. What is the real cost of care at a micro-economic level—not charges but real costs? Finally, what metric are we using to really measure whether what was done actually helped to improve the patient's health status?

---

* Geisinger's Annual Report 2009 and Health Partners Annual Report 2009.
† Porter, M; Teisberg, E, *Redefining Healthcare: Creating Value Based Competition on Results* (Harvard Business School Press, 2006).

These and similar questions cannot be answered by most insurance companies because they are merely financing care and have no real influence on quality and value except to try to deny payments for overvalued procedures and threaten rate increases to employers who do not manage their workforce better. These are also questions that most employers have never asked and most consumers have not been able to articulate because the data was not there.

Community-Based Analysis versus National Standards

We now have a multitude of state and federally financed databases to begin the important task of measuring the outcomes of a population against norms of what we think is "good care." I say *think* because there are many variables here.

A national standard or benchmark is available for virtually every procedure. Episode-based payment actually has care standards built into each episode. This has a multiple layer effect and expectation that care savings are often available but there are unique differences in delivery systems that cannot be overcome by meeting national benchmarks.

Rural facilities, especially those named as critical care hospitals under Medicare, may not have all the latest diagnostics and testing material, may be serving a rural population with limited insurance coverage, and may have physicians who are competent but not necessarily seeing the future and willing to present care findings. The statistical database from the patient population in a rural area may not yield enough quality data to actually measure one doctor's performance against another. It takes a significant level of data to attain a confidence level with the data being measured. A handful of ETGs per doctor will not generate the real opportunity to adjust to the market, in which case national norms may be a better way to adjust and determine a range of confidence levels using local and national data. Our company recommended in the construction of many of these enterprises that rural hospitals should reach out to the competitor next door and start building a network of hospitals and physicians who collectively have some of the same features but who eventually, through collaboration, can build a regional care system with centers of excellence and care guidelines that allow doctors and hospitals to collectively contract and share savings on a regional basis with purchasers using the accountable care organization formats.

Many hospitals have thought of this in terms of consolidation or joint ventures with local providers. This always runs into antitrust questions, unless there can be a true community benefit and there are some aspects of clinical and financial integration presented in the plan. Certainly bundled payment, as is the ACO method of payment, represents some upside financial risk, but the real incentive here is that the clinical integration will occur with regional players and the community of caregivers has a larger influence and more opportunity to remove waste from the region.

> It is almost inconceivable that, 20 years from now, we would be satisfied with a health care system that does not take full advantage of the power of electronic technologies.

> **David Blumenthal, M.D.**
> *Director, Institute for Health Policy at Massachusetts*
> *General Hospital/Partners HealthCare System*

Payment as a Meaningful Driver of Permanent Behavioral Change for Physician and Patient

Studies reported in publications such as *Health Affairs, American Hospital Association*, and the *Managed Care Journal* all summarize the critical aspect of payment as a key driver to encourage providers to participate in quality improvement plans. The Centers for Medicare & Medicaid Services (CMS) has discovered that when nursing home quality performance is measured and made transparent to the public, consumers do, in fact, favor the facility with the best scores and therefore select these four-star facilities over the one- or two-star facilities available for long-term care. The facilities not designated as four-star facilities were forced to reevaluate their efficiency and effectiveness and plan for the future in building a pathway to a four-star facility. When Medicare stirred the pot by offering financial incentives to nursing homes and home health care agencies to achieve better scores in such things as making sure the right medications are brought to the right patients and making sure slips and falls occurred less frequently, agencies and institutions began to focus attention on improved performance and improved payments. This experiment preceded the Premier Hospital demonstration project and the Physician Group demonstration projects.

In the report to Congress in 2006, a summary of the payment structure and the 32 quality measurement guidelines are presented for this Department of Quality (DOQ) project. In general they cover congestive heart failure (CHF), diabetes management (DM), coronary artery disease (CAD), hypertension (HTN), and preventive care (PC).

A percentage of savings was shared with medical groups using a formula described on page 15 of the report. Savings was shared over a period of 3 years; the first was at 70/30, year 2, 60/40, and year 3 at a 50/50 split. We bring this up as a starting point to begin a program using measures similar to these because most of the measures are Healthcare Effectiveness Data and Information Set (HEDIS) or HEDIS adjusted for Medicare. NCQA is already working on this for accountable care organizations (ACOs).

The end result was several million dollars in savings distributed to these groups. Their true reward is that they are now set in a perfect position to build their accountable care organization as the opportunity is presented in January 2012. This means more savings shared for Medicare, and we are aware of several Blue Cross plans interested in moving to a bundled payment platform for private pay and a sharing of savings with organized groups such as Independent Practice Associations (IPAs) and Physician Hospital Organizations (PHOs) as well.

Managed Care Opportunity to Share or Suppress Data

In the early days of HMOs we saw simple reports of utilization and frequency and volume that were taken mostly from claims data and simply reflected use by provider or benefit grouping. It became exceedingly clear by the late 1970s that

1. There needed to be a premium yield, that is, expense per premium charged, plus a margin in addition to expenses per premium charged on a group by group basis; otherwise, the HMO would be like a traditional insurance company with money in and money out but no retained earnings and no ability to fund sustainable growth.
2. This yield had to be calculated on a group basis as a community rate in a category of utilization, high, low and medium. And it needed to be calculated down to the member level so for each group there was a per member per month (PMPM) compared to the entire population of enrolled members in the plan. These were the first real calculations on a cost or care average and deviation from the mean had to be accounted for by looking at where utilization was higher and eventually why. This was hard to pick off a claim form, but provider-sponsored plans had a secret weapon; they controlled the means of production of services and could therefore pull the medical chart to see what was reported on the claim versus what really happened to the patient.

3. Velocity of member months was as important if not more important than PMPM because even if a high-quality health system did a good job of managing the front end and back end of care, the lack of cash flow from too few members signing up or a loss of a large employer contract or plant closing really had a devastating effect on the plans, which, at that time, were all less than 100,000 members.

In today's world we see this very differently. PMPM is still a driving benchmark that now even the government has become involved with, by stating that the medical loss ratio (MLR) payout to providers must be 85% with no more than 15% going for administration. This is not a difficult task for most larger plans but for smaller plans this cap on administrative costs is a hazard and potential threat to long-term sustainability as a community-based plan or not-for-profit enterprise as many of the original HMOs were.

The fact is that most plans have been investing in information technology and reporting mechanisms between providers and health plans to get the makeup of the PMPM and start finding ways to help the providers actually manage the care. This investment has favored the larger companies, but we are seeing smaller plans and hospitals outsourcing this data gathering and analysis function. In some cases a collective of hospitals is using a central data repository and sharing the startup and ongoing management cost of this process center.

Decision Tools and Artificial Intelligence

The idea of moving clinical information grouped by health status, age, gender, diagnosis, and geographic location offers a life science application of this data that can be used for pharmacy study and eventually be incorporated into the genome DNA and measurement area. Identifying patients or patient groupings with tendencies toward addiction, cancer, and other maladies can assist plans and providers to work together to look at new applications of intervention and therapy to manage or, in some cases, reprogram the DNA to eliminate or slow the onset of Alzheimer's, breast cancer, and other chronic care disease.

We see this predictive modeling to be useful to disease management companies, pharmaceutical companies, and other new industries that are emerging around the focus of large-scale data analysis and DNA testing that will have a profound effect on underwriting and potentially health policy.

Building a Collaborative Model

Many board members are uncertain or simply uninformed about the necessity around a collaborative model between physicians and hospitals. Part of this came from the recent health reform squabbling that will remain for years to come, but most of this is around the attitude that the hospital is the focal point of all health care in a community. Looking at the horizon, the large and ever expanding building called the hospital is an essential component of a delivery system, but physicians are in fact the reason the hospital receives admissions. With the exception of the emergency department, all admissions come from PCPs and specialty care doctors, yet there are few board members and many managers who believe that people will select a hospital based upon its surroundings and reputation. In many cases this was possible in the early 1960s but is no longer the case with restrictive panels and linkages born from managed care agreements that guide patients to select doctors who make the call on whether an admission is appropriate and then with which hospitals. As performance criteria are implemented we see more tiering of physician networks, making smaller high-performance panels the desirable partner for the health plans and insurance companies and increasing both rewards and bonuses to physicians who keep patients out of the hospital for unnecessary care and only admit based upon approval by the plan that the patient's health status improvement process can only be found in an institutional setting. Cultivating a collaborative arrangement with physicians to have as many of these high-performance physicians on staff as possible should be the goal of a collaborative relationship.

Other issues that require collaboration are discussed next.

Biologics and Genomics

Many breakthrough drugs and DNA testing for disease in advance of treatment will require privacy and security precautions as well as Food and Drug Administration (FDA) approvals to implement patent protection. Coding, coverage, and payment and privacy and security are all emerging areas of information and testing that will need to be resolved as health reform moves forward.

HIT (Health Information Technology)

In most settings performance-based contracting is enhanced through electronic transfer of transactional and clinical chart data. A laborious process to pull charts and verify treatment pathways and outcomes can now be replaced with electronic queries and a health information exchange between hospitals and physicians.

Consumer electronics companies seek to develop health care products for consumers, triggering health regulatory issues, government contracts, and FDA issues.

Globalization

We have worked with several foreign governments as well as several consulting firms and research companies in guiding the efforts toward medical tourism.

These are global collaborations between health systems, insurance companies, and employers to see to it that their employees are well taken care of. This has now launched a more intense interest in transporting patients with elective surgeries overseas to obtain professional care and hospital/rehab stays for less than here in the United States. We now see payers authorizing coverage for these trips and paying 100% if the patient goes overseas but limiting payment if the patient stays in the United States. This trend will affect U.S. hospitals as many procedures will be bid out regionally and globally by patients and insurance companies.

Medicare Advantage patients do have coverage for medical tourism as long as it is a Medicare-approved facility.

ERISA Reform

Many changes will be made to the Employee Retirement Income Security Act (ERISA) as states try to mandate coverage as part of their reform legislation. Right now many of the organizations covered under ERISA are exempt for state laws, so several new provisions may be enacted that enforce state rules on large unions and corporations covered under ERISA.

Medicare Enforcement

We envision that every hospital and provider will need to revisit the Medicare enforcement under FERA and begin preparing for heavy-duty fines and investigations to pursue Medicare fraud and false claims.*

---

* We envision every hospital and physician organization will need to revisit Medicare enforcement under fraud and abuse and prepare for Audits of both reimbursement and quality. Heavy fines plus denial of care payment will apply .

Deinstitutionalize the Institutional Services

As hospitals start to move to a more coordinated care platform, technology will offer more options for patients to be treated on an outpatient basis. This may not shrink the supply of current acute care beds but will certainly expand the opportunity for more rehab facilities and more home care and disease management services to replace some of the previous treatment protocols. We envision that this will offer a large boost to case managers, navigators, and health coaches who have clinical and insurance training to help move patients through their disease process quickly and at less cost than a hospital stay. This same concept applies to the hospital discharge process that today is unpredictable. The readmission rate for most hospitals exceeds 20%; we have seen 40% of patients readmitted within 90 days. The majority are being readmitted for the same or similar diagnosis. Without at-home care supervision of a navigator to guide the effort from the hospital discharge to a fully compliant patient at home the readmissions will continue. CMS will continue to penalize hospitals through denials of payment and fines to reduce abnormally high readmission rates.

Moving toward Life Sciences Approach to Managing Care

Of all the outcomes of the performance-based contracting environment, we believe that as data from insurance companies, hospitals, and physicians are aggregated at the local level we will begin to see life science applications for better treatments for broader populations and perhaps avoid adverse events for different patients based upon their cultural traditions or lifestyles. An example is the treatment for heart conditions for Puerto Rican patients who live in Puerto Rico versus the Puerto Rican populations in Texas and New York. The same drug regime was used for all patients but in studying physicians' feedback, many who lived in San Juan, Puerto Rico, complained to their primary care doctors and cardiologists of chest pains in the morning after taking their medication. It was discovered that the breakfast of bread and coffee in San Juan was different from the American breakfast in New York and Texas and when dosage was changed the heart pain went away. The same was true for the Lipitor studies that revealed that many people were affected by grapefruit juice after taking their pill.

This life science approach can alert public health officials of an uncommon rise in infectious diseases and can be used to develop comparative studies of economical means to better treat patients earlier for probable diseases based upon examination of patients who have experienced this disease.

These applications have sophisticated but useable statistical models to encourage more root cause analysis. This will reveal some very simple and useful tools and techniques doctors can use to instruct patients on self-care and prevention.

All of this requires effort and curiosity and building upon what we know and what we think we know. The redeployment of dollars to fund preventive and primary care as a first step can occur with a focus on performance instead of just production and an attitude of quality exploration.

Appendix A

Acute Myocardial Infarction
CMS/Premier Hospital Quality Incentive Demonstration Project—Year 4
Participants in Acute Myocardial Infarction (AMI)

State	City	Hospital	CMS Certification Number	Adult Smoking Cessation Advice/ Counseling, % Patients Received	Aspirin at Arrival, % Patients Received	Aspirin Prescribed at Discharge, % Patients Received	ACEI or ARB for LVSD, % Patients Received	Beta Blocker Prescribed at Discharge, % Patients Received	Beta Blocker at Arrival, % Patients Received	Fibrinolytic Therapy Received Within 30 Minutes of Hospital Arrival, % Patients Received	Primary PCI Received Within 90 Minutes of Hospital Arrival, % Patients Received	Survival Index Mortality Rate Expressed as Survival Index, Can Exceed 100%	Total Case Count
AL	Dothan	Southeast Alabama Medical Center[a]	010001	99.54	95.97	97.58	93.22	96.70	92.74		46.51	98.19	660
AL	Opelika	East Alabama Medical Center And Snf[a]	010029	100.00	99.53	99.38	95.06	98.46	98.09		58.70	98.73	397
AR	Pine Bluff	Jefferson Regional Medical Center–Ar[a]	040071	100.00	95.72	98.84	93.59	92.74	94.85	Low sample (10 or less)	Low sample (10 or less)	93.76	328
CA	Apple Valley	St. Mary Medical Center[ac]	050300	100.00	94.61	93.97	88.06	91.09	95.14		59.26	98.76	353
CA	Bakersfield	San Joaquin Community Hospital	050455	97.22	100.00	95.90	78.38	89.68	97.62		45.00	99.57	159

State	City	Name	ID										
CA	Escondido	Palomar Medical Center[a]	050115	100.00	100.00	99.38	100.00	99.68	100.00	Low sample (10 or less)	73.74	97.23	434
CA	Fullerton	St. Jude Medical Center[a]	050168	97.96	99.61	98.02	100.00	96.72	99.16	Low sample (10 or less)	87.80	102.18	356
CA	Gilroy	Saint Louise Regional Hospital	050688	Low sample (10 or less)	94.74	85.00	Low sample (10 or less)	85.00	83.33	Low sample (10 or less)		93.00	50
CA	Glendale	Glendale Adventist Medical Center[a]	050239	100.00	96.67	96.55	90.48	95.30	81.76		69.35	100.90	306
CA	Los Angeles	White Memorial Medical Center[a,c]	050103	100.00	97.35	98.00	88.37	96.90	94.12		94.74	98.43	229
CA	Los Angeles	Saint Vincent Medical Center	050502	92.00	94.32	94.70	89.66	93.50	87.50	Low sample (10 or less)	Low sample (10 or less)	104.86	158
CA	Lynwood	St. Francis Medical Center[a]	050104	100.00	96.75	95.08	97.06	96.88	95.45	81.82	Low sample (10 or less)	95.20	186

(continued)

Acute Myocardial Infarction (continued)
CMS/Premier Hospital Quality Incentive Demonstration Project—Year 4
Participants in Acute Myocardial Infarction (AMI)

State	City	Hospital	CMS Certification Number	Adult Smoking Cessation Advice/Counseling, % Patients Received	Aspirin at Arrival, % Patients Received	Aspirin Prescribed at Discharge, % Patients Received	ACEI or ARB for LVSD, % Patients Received	Beta Blocker Prescribed at Discharge, % Patients Received	Beta Blocker at Arrival, % Patients Received	Fibrinolytic Therapy Received Within 30 Minutes of Hospital Arrival, % Patients Received	Primary PCI Received Within 90 Minutes of Hospital Arrival, % Patients Received	Survival Index Mortality Rate Expressed as Survival Index, Can Exceed 100%	Total Case Count
CA	Orange	St. Joseph Hospital[a]	050069	100.00	98.15	98.59	100.00	98.15	93.38	Low sample (10 or less)	86.84	101.01	288
CA	Paradise	Feather River Hospital[ac]	050225	Low sample (10 or less)	94.12	96.77	Low sample (10 or less)	94.29	98.00			98.84	88
CA	Poway	Pomerado Hospital[a]	050636	Low sample (10 or less)	100.00	100.00	Low sample (10 or less)	95.24	100.00			87.76	75
CA	Saint Helena	St. Helena Hospital[ab]	050013	100.00	100.00	100.00	100.00	100.00	100.00		Low sample (10 or less)	100.05	93
CA	San Jose	O'Connor Hospital[a]	050153	100.00	98.36	98.26	69.23	97.32	96.00		56.76	98.12	149

CA	Simi Valley	Simi Valley Hospital & Health Care Service	050236	Low sample (10 or less)	92.86	85.00	Low sample (10 or less)	86.36	70.59	Low sample (10 or less)		95.07	74
CA	Sonora	Sonora Regional Medical Center	050335	Low sample (10 or less)	94.29	88.89	Low sample	94.74	93.10	Low sample (10 or less)		88.00	68
CO	Grand Junction	St. Mary's Hospital and Medical Center[a]	060023	100.00	100.00	99.71	91.49	100.00	98.46		65.22	102.47	398
FL	Clearwater	Morton Plant Hospital[a]	100127	99.64	97.98	97.31	91.88	96.97	94.44		54.02	100.49	1,001
FL	Dunedin	Mease Healthcare Dunedin	100043	Low sample (10 or less)	97.10	77.78	Low sample (10 or less)	92.68	93.88			96.83	113
FL	Hollywood	Memorial Regional Hospital[ab]	100038	100.00	99.55	99.86	98.86	99.72	98.91		85.29	97.68	863
FL	Homestead	Homestead Hospital[ab]	100125	Low sample (10 or less)	98.97	100.00	Low sample (10 or less)	100.00	97.96			99.49	135
FL	Jacksonville	Baptist Medical Center[ac]	100088	100.00	96.61	96.10	86.21	96.38	92.02		58.70	102.34	459

(continued)

Acute Myocardial Infarction (continued)
CMS/Premier Hospital Quality Incentive Demonstration Project—Year 4
Participants in Acute Myocardial Infarction (AMI)

State	City	Hospital	CMS Certification Number	Adult Smoking Cessation Advice/Counseling, % Patients Received	Aspirin at Arrival, % Patients Received	Aspirin Prescribed at Discharge, % Patients Received	ACEI or ARB for LVSD, % Patients Received	Beta Blocker Prescribed at Discharge, % Patients Received	Beta Blocker at Arrival, % Patients Received	Fibrinolytic Therapy Received Within 30 Minutes of Hospital Arrival, % Patients Received	Primary PCI Received Within 90 Minutes of Hospital Arrival, % Patients Received	Survival Index Mortality Rate Expressed as Survival Index, Can Exceed 100%	Total Case Count
FL	Miami	Baptist Hospital of Miami Inc[a]	100008	100.00	98.87	99.61	97.89	99.63	95.20		86.90	100.63	644
FL	Miami	South Miami Hospital[ab]	100154	100.00	99.40	99.27	94.87	100.00	95.92		88.46	100.08	338
FL	Miami Beach	Mount Sinai Medical Center	100034	98.60	97.44	91.43	86.29	90.41	95.01	Low sample (10 or less)	50.00	100.11	648
FL	Naples	Naples Community Hospital[a]	100018	100.00	96.40	97.07	90.20	95.45	92.04		55.42	102.67	747
FL	New Port Richey	Morton Plant North Bay Hospital[a]	100063	Low sample (10 or less)	96.77	83.33	81.82	94.87	92.75	Low sample (10 or less)		101.03	134
FL	Pembroke Pines	Memorial Hospital Pembroke[ab]	100230	Low sample (10 or less)	100.00	100.00	Low sample (10 or less)	100.00	100.00			105.54	104

FL	Pembroke Pines	Memorial Hospital West[ac]	100281	100.00	99.26	97.02	97.56	97.30	97.00		92.78	100.52	401
FL	Plant City	South Florida Baptist Hospital[ac]	100132	Low sample (10 or less)	100.00	100.00	Low sample (10 or less)	Low sample (10 or less)	100.00			82.43	88
FL	Safety Harbor	Morton Plant Mease Healthcare Countryside[a]	100265	100.00	97.49	89.47	89.29	96.75	97.73		Low sample (10 or less)	97.18	342
FL	Saint Petersburg	St. Anthony's Hospital	100067	100.00	94.78	91.21	64.71	93.33	92.38		50.00	97.28	159
FL	Tampa	St. Joseph's Hospital[a]	100075	99.25	96.90	94.70	93.30	94.12	92.10		82.86	99.27	764
FL	Winter Haven	Winter Haven Hospital	100052	97.41	95.12	96.85	78.30	95.76	89.69		64.29	95.20	483
GA	La Grange	West Georgia Health System, Inc.[ac]	110016	100.00	100.00	96.97	100.00	100.00	100.00	Low sample (10 or less)	73.08	92.95	177
GA	Savannah	Candler Hospital	110024	Low sample (10 or less)	94.29	90.48	Low sample (10 or less)	100.00	80.95			90.93	50

(continued)

Acute Myocardial Infarction (continued)
CMS/Premier Hospital Quality Incentive Demonstration Project—Year 4
Participants in Acute Myocardial Infarction (AMI)

State	City	Hospital	CMS Certification Number	Adult Smoking Cessation Advice/ Counseling, % Patients Received	Aspirin at Arrival, % Patients Received	Aspirin Prescribed at Discharge, % Patients Received	ACEI or ARB for LVSD, % Patients Received	Beta Blocker Prescribed at Discharge, % Patients Received	Beta Blocker at Arrival, % Patients Received	Fibrinolytic Therapy Received Within 30 Minutes of Hospital Arrival, % Patients Received	Primary PCI Received Within 90 Minutes of Hospital Arrival, % Patients Received	Survival Index Mortality Rate Expressed as Survival Index, Can Exceed 100%	Total Case Count
GA	Savannah	Memorial Health University Medical Center[a]	110036	99.12	100.00	98.45	95.35	98.86	97.32		78.38	98.61	308
GA	Savannah	St. Joseph's Hospital[a]	110043	96.76	96.81	98.68	97.83	98.15	93.94		65.22	99.58	404
IA	Council Bluffs	Alegent Health Mercy Hospital[ab]	160028	100.00	98.89	98.78	Low sample (10 or less)	100.00	100.00		96.77	99.40	114
IA	Mason City	Mercy Medical Center–North Iowa[a]	160064	98.70	96.74	99.59	94.03	100.00	98.68		64.00	98.67	300
ID	Coeur D'Alene	Kootenai Medical Center[a]	130049	98.97	98.22	98.69	91.43	99.52	97.71		94.12	100.44	279

State	City	Hospital	ID										
IL	Chicago	Mt. Sinai Hospital Medical Center	140018	98.04	91.18	89.83	87.10	92.52	91.75	Low sample (10 or less)	61.54	96.50	166
IL	Elmhurst	Elmhurst Memorial Hospital[a,b]	140200	100.00	98.91	99.00	97.62	99.48	98.87	Low sample (10 or less)	90.00	100.11	232
IL	Peoria	Methodist Medical Center of Illinois[a]	140209	100.00	99.09	100.00	97.30	100.00	97.33		69.44	97.61	296
IL	Springfield	Memorial Medical Center[a]	140148	100.00	97.89	99.14	92.68	98.00	94.07		98.44	101.65	583
KS	Kansas City	Providence Medical Center[a]	170146	100.00	96.95	96.86	89.66	98.98	97.62		43.75	99.51	240
KS	Topeka	St. Francis Health Center[a]	170016	97.70	97.10	93.95	94.23	97.82	94.12		72.73	100.85	258
KY	Ashland	Our Lady of Bellefonte Hospital	180036	Low sample (10 or less)	91.67	92.31	Low sample (10 or less)	96.30	84.38			98.53	71
KY	Bowling Green	The Medical Center[a]	180013	100.00	95.96	97.07	83.75	95.18	93.37	Low sample (10 or less)	45.83	99.51	373

(continued)

Acute Myocardial Infarction (continued)
CMS/Premier Hospital Quality Incentive Demonstration Project—Year 4
Participants in Acute Myocardial Infarction (AMI)

State	City	Hospital	CMS Certification Number	Adult Smoking Cessation Advice/ Counseling, % Patients Received	Aspirin at Arrival, % Patients Received	Aspirin Prescribed at Discharge, % Patients Received	ACEI or ARB for LVSD, % Patients Received	Beta Blocker Prescribed at Discharge, % Patients Received	Beta Blocker at Arrival, % Patients Received	Fibrinolytic Therapy Received Within 30 Minutes of Hospital Arrival, % Patients Received	Primary PCI Received Within 90 Minutes of Hospital Arrival, % Patients Received	Survival Index Mortality Rate Expressed as Survival Index, Can Exceed 100%	Total Case Count
KY	Lexington	Central Baptist Hospital[a]	180103	100.00	97.58	99.29	94.48	98.31	96.19		70.59	100.18	869
KY	Murray	Murray– Calloway County Hospital	180027	Low sample (10 or less)	95.24	76.92	Low sample (10 or less)	75.00	90.48	Low sample (10 or less)		105.16	43
KY	Paducah	Western Baptist Hospital[a]	180104	99.50	99.48	100.00	94.44	99.32	94.44	Low sample (10 or less)	68.75	101.32	488
MA	Fall River	Southcoast Hospital Group, Inc.[a]	220074	99.00	97.94	97.53	79.05	98.66	98.76	Low sample (10 or less)	62.00	98.84	891
MA	Pittsfield	Berkshire Medical Center Inc.[ab]	220046	Low sample (10 or less)	100.00	100.00	100.00	100.00	100.00	Low sample (10 or less)		102.91	139

MA	Springfield	Baystate Medical Center[a]	220077	98.81	99.01	99.26	82.53	99.31	95.52	Low sample (10 or less)	79.07	101.56	1,176
MD	Baltimore	Bon Secours Hospital	210013	Low sample (10 or less)	93.10	96.00	Low sample (10 or less)	86.36	92.31			92.91	35
MD	Frederick	Frederick Memorial Hospital[ac]	210005	Low sample (10 or less)	96.61	100.00	Low sample (10 or less)	100.00	97.37			98.67	147
MD	Salisbury	Peninsula Regional Medical Center[a]	210019	98.74	95.79	98.63	93.65	97.99	91.46		66.18	98.59	768
MI	Grosse Pointe	Bon Secours Cottage Health Services[a]	230089	Low sample (10 or less)	98.39	95.56	88.89	100.00	98.44			106.47	122
MI	Lapeer	Lapeer Regional Medical Center[ac]	230193	100.00	100.00	93.55	Low sample (10 or less)	94.44	98.25	Low sample (10 or less)		100.05	126
MN	Burnsville	Fairview Ridges Hospital[a]	240207	Low sample (10 or less)	92.50	96.77	Low sample (10 or less)	96.88	95.12			104.42	80

(continued)

Acute Myocardial Infarction (continued)
CMS/Premier Hospital Quality Incentive Demonstration Project—Year 4
Participants in Acute Myocardial Infarction (AMI)

State	City	Hospital	CMS Certification Number	Adult Smoking Cessation Advice/Counseling, % Patients Received	Aspirin at Arrival, % Patients Received	Aspirin Prescribed at Discharge, % Patients Received	ACEI or ARB for LVSD, % Patients Received	Beta Blocker Prescribed at Discharge, % Patients Received	Beta Blocker at Arrival, % Patients Received	Fibrinolytic Therapy Received Within 30 Minutes of Hospital Arrival, % Patients Received	Primary PCI Received Within 90 Minutes of Hospital Arrival, % Patients Received	Survival Index Mortality Rate Expressed as Survival Index, Can Exceed 100%	Total Case Count
MN	Edina	Fairview Southdale Hospital[ab]	240078	99.33	100.00	99.57	98.04	99.59	99.29		97.40	100.34	532
MN	Minneapolis	University of Minnesota Medical Center[a]	240080	100.00	96.63	100.00	88.00	98.60	95.18		83.33	99.06	162
MN	Princeton	Fairview Northland Regional Hospital[ab]	240141		Low sample (10 or less)	Low sample (10 or less)	Low sample (10 or less)	Low sample (10 or less)	Low sample (10 or less)			100.38	30
MN	Saint Louis Park	Methodist Hospital[ab]	240053	100.00	100.00	100.00	96.08	99.14	99.11		95.59	101.02	408
MN	Winona	Winona Community Memorial Hospital[a]	240044	Low sample (10 or less)	92.50	96.97	Low sample (10 or less)	97.37	97.14			110.92	52

State	City	Hospital	ID										
MO	Blue Springs	St. Mary's Medical Center[a]	260193	Low sample (10 or less)	92.11	90.48	Low sample (10 or less)	95.24	93.75		Low sample (10 or less)	101.67	76
MO	Bridgeton	SSM Depaul Health Center[a]	260104	100.00	98.59	98.99	91.78	99.29	90.26	Low sample (10 or less)	68.97	98.72	401
MO	Kansas City	St. Joseph Medical Center[a]	260085	100.00	99.49	99.38	95.51	99.00	98.61		65.00	100.11	353
MO	Saint Joseph	Heartland Regional Medical Center[ac]	260006	100.00	97.48	97.25	95.16	99.42	95.82	Low sample (10 or less)	91.49	99.09	473
MO	Saint Louis	SSM St. Mary's Health Center[a]	260091	100.00	97.48	98.56	100.00	99.00	97.00		69.44	101.16	287
MS	Meridian	Rush Foundation Hospital[a]	250069	96.15	98.94	99.23	100.00	100.00	98.73	Low sample (10 or less)	57.89	94.36	153
MT	Billings	St. Vincent Healthcare[a]	270049	100.00	97.50	97.69	87.76	94.62	92.86		55.56	99.84	316
MT	Butte	St. James Healthcare	270017	100.00	96.23	91.11	Low sample (10 or less)	85.00	97.37	Low sample (10 or less)	78.57	95.54	72

(continued)

Acute Myocardial Infarction (continued)
CMS/Premier Hospital Quality Incentive Demonstration Project—Year 4
Participants in Acute Myocardial Infarction (AMI)

State	City	Hospital	CMS Certification Number	Adult Smoking Cessation Advice/Counseling, % Patients Received	Aspirin at Arrival, % Patients Received	Aspirin Prescribed at Discharge, % Patients Received	ACEI or ARB for LVSD, % Patients Received	Beta Blocker Prescribed at Discharge, % Patients Received	Beta Blocker at Arrival, % Patients Received	Fibrinolytic Therapy Received Within 30 Minutes of Hospital Arrival, % Patients Received	Primary PCI Received Within 90 Minutes of Hospital Arrival, % Patients Received	Survival Index Mortality Rate Expressed as Survival Index, Can Exceed 100%	Total Case Count
MT	Missoula	St. Patrick Hospital and Health Sciences[ab]	270014	100.00	99.26	99.63	97.50	98.80	99.22		85.71	101.72	295
NC	Albemarle	Stanly Regional Medical Center[a]	340119	100.00	94.03	98.41	95.24	97.06	93.02	Low sample (10 or less)		102.45	132
NC	Asheboro	Randolph Hospital[a]	340123	Low sample (10 or less)	100.00	94.12	Low sample (10 or less)	93.94	89.74			101.16	92
NC	Asheville	Mission Hospitals, Inc.[ab]	340002	100.00	99.81	99.71	97.19	99.92	98.83	Low sample (10 or less)	91.03	98.90	1,435
NC	Boone	Watauga Medical Center[a]	340051	Low sample (10 or less)	96.97	100.00	Low sample (10 or less)	100.00	92.31			104.49	66

NC	Burlington	Alamance Regional Medical Center[a]	340070	100.00	96.90	95.83	86.67	97.75	96.67	Low sample (10 or less)		93.09	172
NC	Clyde	Haywood Regional Medical Center	340025	Low sample (10 or less)	93.55	100.00	Low sample (10 or less)	100.00	93.75	Low sample (10 or less)		86.46	52
NC	Durham	Duke University Hospital[ab]	340030	99.69	99.63	99.22	94.42	99.30	100.00		85.11	99.50	937
NC	Durham	Durham Regional Hospital[a]	340155	94.52	98.31	99.38	85.37	97.45	90.35		37.14	102.69	244
NC	Fayetteville	Cape Fear Valley Medical Center[a]	340028	99.19	98.32	97.35	84.09	94.77	96.66	Low sample (10 or less)	59.46	96.20	438
NC	Gastonia	Gaston Memorial Hospital[a]	340032	100.00	99.26	99.73	96.30	98.97	98.53	Low sample (10 or less)	80.00	97.74	516
NC	Goldsboro	Wayne Memorial Hospital[a]	340010	100.00	100.00	91.30	Low sample (10 or less)	93.55	92.11	Low sample (10 or less)		94.63	106
NC	Hickory	Catawba Valley Medical Center[ac]	340143	100.00	98.00	96.00	84.62	98.65	94.95	Low sample (10 or less)	Low sample (10 or less)	96.80	140

(continued)

Acute Myocardial Infarction (continued)
CMS/Premier Hospital Quality Incentive Demonstration Project—Year 4
Participants in Acute Myocardial Infarction (AMI)

State	City	Hospital	CMS Certification Number	Adult Smoking Cessation Advice/ Counseling, % Patients Received	Aspirin at Arrival, % Patients Received	Aspirin Prescribed at Discharge, % Patients Received	ACEI or ARB for LVSD, % Patients Received	Beta Blocker Prescribed at Discharge, % Patients Received	Beta Blocker at Arrival, % Patients Received	Fibrinolytic Therapy Received Within 30 Minutes of Hospital Arrival, % Patients Received	Primary PCI Received Within 90 Minutes of Hospital Arrival, % Patients Received	Survival Index Mortality Rate Expressed as Survival Index, Can Exceed 100%	Total Case Count
NC	Lumberton	Southeastern Regional Medical Center[a,c]	340050	100.00	97.50	93.67	Low sample (10 or less)	98.86	84.78	Low sample (10 or less)	Low sample (10 or less)	92.63	183
NC	Pinehurst	Firsthealth Moore Regional Hospital[a]	340115	99.50	97.62	98.59	86.32	96.07	93.39		76.19	100.12	643
NC	Raleigh	Duke Health Raleigh Hospital[a]	340073	Low sample (10 or less)	96.77	100.00	Low sample (10 or less)	86.96	96.43			91.56	50
NC	Shelby	Cleveland Regional Medical Center[a,b]	340021	100.00	100.00	100.00	100.00	100.00	100.00			104.88	116
NC	Sylva	Harris Regional Hospital, Inc.	340016	Low sample (10 or less)	81.82	82.35	Low sample (10 or less)	83.33	77.27			98.37	62

State	City	Hospital	ID										
NC	Wilmington	New Hanover Regional Medical Center[a]	340141	96.15	97.55	99.09	76.56	97.75	91.85		78.57	101.22	406
NC	Wilson	Wilson Medical Center[ac]	340126	Low sample (10 or less)	97.37	90.48	Low sample (10 or less)	100.00	97.67	Low sample (10 or less)		96.30	84
NE	Fremont	Fremont Area Medical Center[ab]	280077	Low sample (10 or less)	100.00	100.00	Low sample (10 or less)	100.00	93.33	Low sample (10 or less)	Low sample (10 or less)	103.35	41
NE	Omaha	Alegent Health–Bergan Mercy Medical Center[ab]	280060	100.00	98.62	100.00	95.45	100.00	98.11		97.37	101.53	187
NE	Omaha	Alegent Health Immanuel Medical Center[ab]	280081	100.00	99.15	99.43	100.00	99.46	100.00		88.00	99.35	233
NE	Papillion	Alegent Health–Midlands Community Hospital[ab]	280105	100.00	100.00	100.00	100.00	98.85	98.53	Low sample (10 or less)	90.00	100.59	115
NJ	Hackensack	Hackensack University Medical Center[ab]	310001	100.00	100.00	100.00	99.38	100.00	100.00		82.86	99.50	865

(continued)

Acute Myocardial Infarction (continued)
CMS/Premier Hospital Quality Incentive Demonstration Project—Year 4
Participants in Acute Myocardial Infarction (AMI)

State	City	Hospital	CMS Certification Number	Adult Smoking Cessation Advice/ Counseling, % Patients Received	Aspirin at Arrival, % Patients Received	Aspirin Prescribed at Discharge, % Patients Received	ACEI or ARB for LVSD, % Patients Received	Beta Blocker Prescribed at Discharge, % Patients Received	Beta Blocker at Arrival, % Patients Received	Fibrinolytic Therapy Received Within 30 Minutes of Hospital Arrival, % Patients Received	Primary PCI Received Within 90 Minutes of Hospital Arrival, % Patients Received	Survival Index Mortality Rate Expressed as Survival Index, Can Exceed 100%	Total Case Count
NY	Bay Shore	Southside Hospital[a]	330043	100.00	98.59	94.64	84.21	97.41	99.08		79.07	96.86	237
NY	Brockport	Lakeside Memorial Hospital	330037	Low sample (10 or less)	84.21	Low sample (10 or less)	Low sample (10 or less)	Low sample (10 or less)	95.24			80.76	40
NY	Bronx	St. Barnabas Hospital[ac]	330399	100.00	100.00	98.15	100.00	97.78	98.53	Low sample (10 or less)		93.72	136
NY	Elmira	Arnot Ogden Medical Center[a]	330090	100.00	97.39	99.20	98.57	99.62	98.23	Low sample (10 or less)	65.00	100.49	314
NY	Forest Hills	Ns-Lij Hs-North Shore University Hospital at Forest Hills[ac]	330353	Low sample (10 or less)	96.92	96.67	Low sample (10 or less)	100.00	94.74			91.77	134

NY	Glen Cove	Ns-Lij Hs-North Shore University Hospital at Glen Cove[a]	330181	Low sample (10 or less)	100.00	92.86	Low sample (10 or less)	100.00	100.00	Low sample (10 or less)		93.54	66
NY	Huntington	Huntington Hospital[a]	330045	100.00	100.00	100.00	90.91	96.61	100.00		66.67	100.65	190
NY	Manhasset	Ns-Lij Hs-North Shore University Hospital[ac]	330106	100.00	98.57	99.19	93.75	98.61	100.00		Low sample (10 or less)	97.81	312
NY	New Hyde Park	Long Island Jewish Medical Center[a]	330195	100.00	98.02	100.00	100.00	99.47	96.67	Low sample (10 or less)	62.50	101.19	312
NY	Plainview	Ns-Lij Hs-North Shore University Hospital at Plainview[ac]	330331	Low sample (10 or less)	98.94	93.55	Low sample (10 or less)	100.00	97.96			99.82	166
NY	Port Jervis	Bon Secours Community Hospital[a]	330135	Low sample (10 or less)	93.10	100.00	Low sample (10 or less)	100.00	92.00			96.04	44
NY	Rochester	Rochester General Hospitals[a]	330125	100.00	98.10	98.78	98.31	98.08	94.41		80.00	100.71	1,074

(continued)

Acute Myocardial Infarction (continued)
CMS/Premier Hospital Quality Incentive Demonstration Project—Year 4
Participants in Acute Myocardial Infarction (AMI)

State	City	Hospital	CMS Certification Number	Adult Smoking Cessation Advice/Counseling, % Patients Received	Aspirin at Arrival, % Patients Received	Aspirin Prescribed at Discharge, % Patients Received	ACEI or ARB for LVSD, % Patients Received	Beta Blocker Prescribed at Discharge, % Patients Received	Beta Blocker at Arrival, % Patients Received	Fibrinolytic Therapy Received Within 30 Minutes of Hospital Arrival, % Patients Received	Primary PCI Received Within 90 Minutes of Hospital Arrival, % Patients Received	Survival Index Mortality Rate Expressed as Survival Index, Can Exceed 100%	Total Case Count
NY	Schenectady	St. Clare's Hospital[ab]	330066	Low sample (10 or less)	100.00	100.00	100.00	100.00	98.21			100.83	94
NY	Staten Island	Staten Island University Hospital[ab]	330160	100.00	99.43	100.00	100.00	99.53	100.00		100.00	95.90	312
NY	Suffern	Good Samaritan Hospital of Suffern[a]	330158	98.11	94.64	95.58	91.89	95.38	92.65		66.67	96.95	490
NY	Valley Stream	Franklin Hospital Medical Center	330372	Low sample (10 or less)	95.52	90.91	Low sample (10 or less)	95.45	86.67	Low sample (10 or less)		96.21	128
NY	Warwick	St. Anthony Community Hospital[a]	330205	Low sample (10 or less)	100.00	Low sample (10 or less)	Low sample (10 or less)	Low sample (10 or less)	100.00			74.24	42

OH	Akron	Summa Health Systems Hospitals[a]	360020	94.71	99.66	99.06	100.00	98.71	98.87		82.86	100.22	540
OH	Dayton	Grandview Hospital & Medical Center[a]	360133	100.00	98.33	99.18	100.00	100.00	97.85		72.22	97.12	162
OH	Kettering	Kettering Medical Center[a]	360079	100.00	100.00	96.95	91.76	99.51	94.57		81.93	101.68	522
OH	Lorain	Community Health Partners of Oh-West[a]	360172	98.65	97.89	99.53	100.00	100.00	97.45	Low sample (10 or less)	68.42	100.36	251
OH	Miamisburg	Sycamore Hospital[ab]	360239	Low sample (10 or less)	100.00	100.00	100.00	100.00	100.00			103.98	64
OH	Springfield	Mercy Medical Center of Springfield[a]	360086	100.00	95.27	97.93	93.33	94.62	88.59		72.73	99.31	251
OH	Toledo	St. Vincent Mercy Medical Center[ab]	360112	100.00	100.00	99.86	97.07	100.00	99.18		68.29	99.59	826
OK	Oklahoma City	St. Anthony Hospital[ac]	370037	96.39	97.06	98.08	100.00	98.51	97.30		41.94	100.11	235

(continued)

Acute Myocardial Infarction (continued)
CMS/Premier Hospital Quality Incentive Demonstration Project—Year 4
Participants in Acute Myocardial Infarction (AMI)

State	City	Hospital	CMS Certification Number	Adult Smoking Cessation Advice/Counseling, % Patients Received	Aspirin at Arrival, % Patients Received	Aspirin Prescribed at Discharge, % Patients Received	ACEI or ARB for LVSD, % Patients Received	Beta Blocker Prescribed at Discharge, % Patients Received	Beta Blocker at Arrival, % Patients Received	Fibrinolytic Therapy Received Within 30 Minutes of Hospital Arrival, % Patients Received	Primary PCI Received Within 90 Minutes of Hospital Arrival, % Patients Received	Survival Index Mortality Rate Expressed as Survival Index, Can Exceed 100%	Total Case Count
OK	Tulsa	Saint Francis Hospital[a]	370091	99.65	97.07	98.40	97.30	68.66	93.96	Low sample (10 or less)	69.88	99.74	894
OR	Medford	Rogue Valley Medical Center[a]	380018	99.43	99.55	99.35	95.00	99.38	96.79		83.12	101.03	582
OR	Portland	Adventist Medical Center[a,c]	380060	97.67	97.14	98.13	91.67	98.98	100.00		79.17	96.11	164
PA	Bethlehem	St. Lukes Hospital Network[a]	390049	100.00	95.44	98.28	90.91	99.07	97.83	Low sample (10 or less)	73.61	100.03	744
PA	Bryn Mawr	Main Line Health–Bryn Mawr Hospital[a,b]	390139	100.00	100.00	100.00	91.67	100.00	98.43		96.15	102.15	260

PA	Erie	Saint Vincent Health Center[ab]	390009	99.42	98.62	100.00	100.00	100.00	100.00	99.50		91.49	98.74	542
PA	Meadville	Meadville Medical Center	390113	Low sample (10 or less)	92.86	85.71	Low sample (10 or less)	90.00	80.95				96.06	71
PA	Paoli	Main Line Hospitals–Paoli Memorial Hospital[a]	390153	100.00	97.22	100.00	94.74	99.36	94.23		73.68	99.78	228
PA	Philadelphia	Frankford Hospital[a]	390115	98.82	98.00	97.55	90.54	96.68	94.00	Low sample (10 or less)	4.00	97.73	615
PA	Philadelphia	Albert Einstein Medical Center[a]	390142	100.00	96.23	99.20	89.39	98.97	92.92	Low sample (10 or less)	50.00	98.43	370
PA	Philadelphia	Thomas Jefferson University Hospital[a]	390174	97.98	99.06	98.38	94.34	98.79	99.38		28.57	96.61	397
PA	Wynnewood	Main Line Health–Lankenau Hospital[a]	390195	99.02	100.00	99.61	88.52	98.91	100.00		77.14	100.74	389
SC	Anderson	Anmed Health[ab]	420027	100.00	100.00	100.00	100.00	100.00	100.00		86.67	99.19	377

(continued)

Acute Myocardial Infarction (continued)
CMS/Premier Hospital Quality Incentive Demonstration Project—Year 4
Participants in Acute Myocardial Infarction (AMI)

State	City	Hospital	CMS Certification Number	Adult Smoking Cessation Advice/Counseling, % Patients Received	Aspirin at Arrival, % Patients Received	Aspirin Prescribed at Discharge, % Patients Received	ACEI or ARB for LVSD, % Patients Received	Beta Blocker Prescribed at Discharge, % Patients Received	Beta Blocker at Arrival, % Patients Received	Fibrinolytic Therapy Received Within 30 Minutes of Hospital Arrival, % Patients Received	Primary PCI Received Within 90 Minutes of Hospital Arrival, % Patients Received	Survival Index Mortality Rate Expressed as Survival Index, Can Exceed 100%	Total Case Count
SC	Columbia	Palmetto Health Richland[a]	420018	100.00	98.93	99.42	95.51	99.12	96.10		72.73	96.66	440
SC	Columbia	Palmetto Health Baptist[a,c]	420086	Low sample (10 or less)	100.00	95.65	Low sample (10 or less)	100.00	97.14			89.99	56
SC	Conway	Conway Medical Center[a,c]	420049	Low sample (10 or less)	100.00	96.67	Low sample (10 or less)	93.55	100.00	68.75		93.80	109
SC	Easley	Palmetto Health Baptist Easley[a,c]	420015	100.00	100.00	100.00	Low sample (10 or less)	100.00	94.00			93.00	104
SC	Florence	Mcleod Regional Medical Center[a]	420051	99.60	98.68	98.30	92.00	99.09	94.62	Low sample (10 or less)	79.07	99.63	728

SC	Greenville	St. Francis Hospital[ab]	420023	100.00	99.32	100.00	100.00	100.00	100.00			76.92	102.00	275
SC	Greenville	Greenville Memorial Hospital[ac]	420078	99.76	97.94	99.34	95.71	99.12	98.56			61.17	101.12	1,114
SC	Greenwood	Self Regional Healthcare[a]	420071	100.00	97.87	96.39	94.74	95.24	94.87			42.86	100.19	245
SD	Aberdeen	Avera St. Luke's	430014	Low sample (10 or less)	93.94	100.00	Low sample (10 or less)	96.00	88.89	Low sample (10 or less)			93.92	66
SD	Mitchell	Avera Queen of Peace[a]	430013		100.00	Low sample (10 or less)	Low sample (10 or less)	100.00	Low sample (10 or less)	Low sample (10 or less)			107.67	32
SD	Rapid City	Rapid City Regional Hospital[ac]	430077	99.36	97.95	99.38	95.92	98.19	98.43	Low sample (10 or less)	74.00	99.57	454
SD	Sioux Falls	Avera Mckennan Hospital & University Health Center[a]	430016	100.00	98.39	92.68	Low sample (10 or less)	100.00	100.00	Low sample (10 or less)	79.17	102.93	113
SD	Yankton	Avera Sacred Heart Hospital[ab]	430012	Low sample (10 or less)	100.00	100.00	Low sample (10 or less)	100.00	100.00			94.03	51

(continued)

Acute Myocardial Infarction (continued)
CMS/Premier Hospital Quality Incentive Demonstration Project—Year 4
Participants in Acute Myocardial Infarction (AMI)

State	City	Hospital	CMS Certification Number	Adult Smoking Cessation Advice/ Counseling, % Patients Received	Aspirin at Arrival, % Patients Received	Aspirin Prescribed at Discharge, % Patients Received	ACEI or ARB for LVSD, % Patients Received	Beta Blocker Prescribed at Discharge, % Patients Received	Beta Blocker at Arrival, % Patients Received	Fibrinolytic Therapy Received Within 30 Minutes of Hospital Arrival, % Patients Received	Primary PCI Received Within 90 Minutes of Hospital Arrival, % Patients Received	Survival Index Mortality Rate Expressed as Survival Index, Can Exceed 100%	Total Case Count
TN	Elizabethton	Sycamore Shoals Hospital	440018	Low sample (10 or less)	88.89	100.00	Low sample (10 or less)	Low sample (10 or less)	Low sample (10 or less)			88.29	36
TN	Johnson City	Johnson City Medical Center[a]	440063	99.16	96.00	96.31	78.79	97.46	89.81	Low sample (10 or less)	51.85	97.07	312
TN	Kingsport	Indian Path Medical Center[a]	440176	100.00	92.73	94.12	71.43	100.00	89.19	Low sample (10 or less)		104.01	99
TN	Memphis	Methodist Healthcare Memphis Hospitals[a,c]	440049	99.72	96.45	98.13	88.08	97.37	93.32		53.97	98.45	941
TX	Arlington	Arlington Memorial Hospital[a,c]	450064	100.00	98.98	98.62	96.15	98.02	97.48	Low sample (10 or less)	75.00	98.34	248

	City	Hospital	ID										
TX	Azle	Harris Methodist Northwest	450419	Low sample (10 or less)	87.50	72.73	Low sample (10 or less)	100.00	100.00			98.67	32
TX	Bedford	Harris Methodist H E B Hospital[a]	450639	98.28	98.84	97.09	95.45	97.67	95.56	85.71		100.12	203
TX	Cleburne	Walls Regional Hospital[ab]	450148		100.00	100.00	Low sample (10 or less)	100.00	100.00			89.51	31
TX	Dallas	Methodist Dallas Medical Center[a]	450051	100.00	97.34	98.00	87.88	97.14	94.87	47.06		97.75	293
TX	Dallas	Presbyterian Hospital of Dallas[ac]	450462	100.00	99.46	97.88	84.21	98.95	98.31	76.92		95.64	342
TX	Dallas	Methodist Charlton Medical Center[a]	450723	100.00	98.60	98.32	97.56	98.30	93.66	69.39		93.04	304
TX	Denison	Texoma Medical Center[a]	450324	98.72	95.36	95.15	100.00	94.25	89.60	65.22		101.86	217
TX	Fort Worth	Harris Methodist Fort Worth[a]	450135	99.62	97.86	99.55	89.68	98.19	95.26	67.23	Low sample (10 or less)	98.54	845

(continued)

Acute Myocardial Infarction (continued)
CMS/Premier Hospital Quality Incentive Demonstration Project—Year 4
Participants in Acute Myocardial Infarction (AMI)

State	City	Hospital	CMS Certification Number	Adult Smoking Cessation Advice/Counseling, % Patients Received	Aspirin at Arrival, % Patients Received	Aspirin Prescribed at Discharge, % Patients Received	ACEI or ARB for LVSD, % Patients Received	Beta Blocker Prescribed at Discharge, % Patients Received	Beta Blocker at Arrival, % Patients Received	Fibrinolytic Therapy Received Within 30 Minutes of Hospital Arrival, % Patients Received	Primary PCI Received Within 90 Minutes of Hospital Arrival, % Patients Received	Survival Index Mortality Rate Expressed as Survival Index, Can Exceed 100%	Total Case Count
TX	Fort Worth	Harris Methodist Southwest[a]	450779	100.00	100.00	98.70	95.65	97.26	97.87	Low sample (10 or less)		97.06	134
TX	Harlingen	Valley Baptist Medical Center[a]	450033	100.00	100.00	99.61	100.00	99.22	99.05		58.33	96.76	315
TX	Kaufman	Presbyterian Hospital of Kaufman	450292	Low sample (10 or less)	84.38	100.00	Low sample (10 or less)	92.31	82.35			86.26	50
TX	Lufkin	Memorial Medical Center of East Texas	450211	100.00	92.38	95.00	83.33	93.84	89.36		29.63	94.78	183
TX	Plano	Presbyterian Hospital of Plano[a]	450771	100.00	98.46	98.20	96.15	98.80	97.44		71.88	97.31	195

TX	Stephenville	Harris Methodist Erath County	450351	Low sample (10 or less)	100.00	88.89	Low sample (10 or less)	88.89	95.00	Low sample (10 or less)		91.57	55
TX	Tomball	Tomball Regional Hospital[ac]	450670	100.00	99.47	100.00	100.00	98.26	97.35		66.67	96.76	247
TX	Victoria	Citizens Medical Center[ab]	450023	100.00	100.00	100.00	100.00	100.00	100.00	Low sample (10 or less)	92.31	95.92	201
VA	Chesapeake	Chesapeake General Hospital[a]	490120	100.00	96.28	98.79	97.22	98.88	97.32		65.12	100.46	244
VA	Galax	Twin County Regional Hospital[ac]	490115	Low sample (10 or less)	94.44	92.31	Low sample (10 or less)	100.00	92.86			93.92	41
VA	Gloucester	Riverside Walter Reed Hospital[ac]	490130	Low sample (10 or less)	91.67	95.83	Low sample (10 or less)	92.86	92.11			102.09	68
VA	Mechanicsville	Bon Secours–Memorial Regional Medical[ab]	490069	100.00	98.49	100.00	97.06	99.64	98.20		93.62	101.36	323

(continued)

Acute Myocardial Infarction (continued)
CMS/Premier Hospital Quality Incentive Demonstration Project—Year 4
Participants in Acute Myocardial Infarction (AMI)

State	City	Hospital	CMS Certification Number	Adult Smoking Cessation Advice/ Counseling, % Patients Received	Aspirin at Arrival, % Patients Received	Aspirin Prescribed at Discharge, % Patients Received	ACEI or ARB for LVSD, % Patients Received	Beta Blocker Prescribed at Discharge, % Patients Received	Beta Blocker at Arrival, % Patients Received	Fibrinolytic Therapy Received Within 30 Minutes of Hospital Arrival, % Patients Received	Primary PCI Received Within 90 Minutes of Hospital Arrival, % Patients Received	Survival Index Mortality Rate Expressed as Survival Index, Can Exceed 100%	Total Case Count
VA	Newport News	Bon Secours–Mary Immaculate Hospital[a]	490041	100.00	98.72	98.41	Low sample (10 or less)	98.46	98.31	Low sample (10 or less)	47.62	99.30	103
VA	Newport News	Riverside Regional Medical Center[a,c]	490052	100.00	98.32	99.69	91.67	99.09	95.93		74.14	100.38	426
VA	Norfolk	Bon Secours–Depaul Medical Center[a]	490011	100.00	94.12	94.37	100.00	100.00	100.00		41.18	96.17	121
VA	Portsmouth	Bon Secours Maryview Medical Center[a]	490017	100.00	92.59	95.60	77.27	96.34	93.88	Low sample (10 or less)	46.43	102.14	215
VA	Richmond	Bon Secour St. Mary's Hospital of Richmond[a,b]	490059	100.00	98.40	100.00	98.61	99.53	96.65		80.77	99.59	255

VA	South Hill	Community Memorial Healthcenter[ab]	490098	Low sample (10 or less)	100.00	100.00	100.00	100.00	100.00				102.46	105
VA	Tappahannock	Riverside Tappahannock Hosp Inc	490084	Low sample (10 or less)	92.31	86.67	Low sample (10 or less)	100.00	81.82				90.39	45
WA	Spokane	Sacred Heart Medical Center[ab]	500054	100.00	100.00	100.00	100.00	98.60	99.10			74.14	99.82	685
WA	Spokane	Holy Family Hospital[a]	500077	100.00	100.00	98.73	88.24	98.86	97.40			85.00	98.68	158
WA	Walla Walla	St. Mary Medical Center[a]	500002	Low sample (10 or less)	96.30	93.33	Low sample (10 or less)	95.45	95.83				83.95	59
WI	Burlington	Memorial Hospital of Burlington[ab]	520059	Low sample (10 or less)	100.00	91.67	Low sample (10 or less)	95.24	100.00				109.14	51
WI	Elkhorn	Aurora Lakeland Medical Center[ac]	520102	Low sample (10 or less)	100.00	Low sample (10 or less)	Low sample (10 or less)	Low sample (10 or less)	94.12				80.11	49

(continued)

Acute Myocardial Infarction (continued)
CMS/Premier Hospital Quality Incentive Demonstration Project—Year 4
Participants in Acute Myocardial Infarction (AMI)

State	City	Hospital	CMS Certification Number	Adult Smoking Cessation Advice/ Counseling, % Patients Received	Aspirin at Arrival, % Patients Received	Aspirin Prescribed at Discharge, % Patients Received	ACEI or ARB for LVSD, % Patients Received	Beta Blocker Prescribed at Discharge, % Patients Received	Beta Blocker at Arrival, % Patients Received	Fibrinolytic Therapy Received Within 30 Minutes of Hospital Arrival, % Patients Received	Primary PCI Received Within 90 Minutes of Hospital Arrival, % Patients Received	Survival Index Mortality Rate Expressed as Survival Index, Can Exceed 100%	Total Case Count
WI	Green Bay	Aurora Baycare Medical Center[ab]	520193	100.00	100.00	100.00	100.00	100.00	100.00		Low sample (10 or less)	101.68	140
WI	Hartford	Aurora Medical Center of Washington County[ab]	520038	Low sample (10 or less)	100.00	100.00	Low sample (10 or less)	Low sample (10 or less)	Low sample (10 or less)			103.11	32
WI	Kenosha	Aurora Medical Center Kenosha[a]	520189	Low sample (10 or less)	100.00	91.67	Low sample (10 or less)	100.00	83.33			95.37	33
WI	Madison	St. Mary's Hospital Medical Center[a]	520083	93.98	98.31	99.14	84.27	98.53	94.49		86.79	100.64	478
WI	Milwaukee	Aurora Sinai Medical Cender[a]	520064	100.00	98.08	96.75	100.00	100.00	98.39		80.95	99.50	169

WI	Milwaukee	St. Lukes Medical Center[a]	520138	99.72	97.96	97.35	93.10	98.13	91.23		84.96	100.98	1,315
WI	Sheboygan	Aurora Sheboygan Memorial Medical Center[ab]	520035	Low sample (10 or less)	100.00	100.00	Low sample (10 or less)	100.00	100.00			103.54	89
WI	Two Rivers	Aurora Medical Center Manitowoc County[ab]	520034	Low sample (10 or less)	100.00	100.00	Low sample (10 or less)	100.00	100.00			102.28	47
WI	West Allis	West Allis Memorial Hospital[ac]	520139	Low sample (10 or less)	94.29	97.96	100.00	100.00	93.75			107.56	114
WV	Bluefield	Bluefield Regional Medical Center	510071	Low sample (10 or less)	93.18	93.10	Low sample (10 or less)	100.00	86.49	Low sample (10 or less)		92.96	88
WV	Charleston	Charleston Area Medical Center[a]	510022	100.00	99.12	99.17	96.19	99.52	96.02	Low sample (10 or less)	57.53	98.97	1,584
WV	Clarksburg	United Hospital Center[ab]	510006	100.00	100.00	100.00	100.00	100.00	100.00		97.96	98.76	367

(continued)

Acute Myocardial Infarction (continued)
CMS/Premier Hospital Quality Incentive Demonstration Project—Year 4
Participants in Acute Myocardial Infarction (AMI)

State	City	Hospital	CMS Certification Number	Adult Smoking Cessation Advice/Counseling, % Patients Received	Aspirin at Arrival, % Patients Received	Aspirin Prescribed at Discharge, % Patients Received	ACEI or ARB for LVSD, % Patients Received	Beta Blocker Prescribed at Discharge, % Patients Received	Beta Blocker at Arrival, % Patients Received	Fibrinolytic Therapy Received Within 30 Minutes of Hospital Arrival, % Patients Received	Primary PCI Received Within 90 Minutes of Hospital Arrival, % Patients Received	Survival Index Mortality Rate Expressed as Survival Index, Can Exceed 100%	Total Case Count
WV	Huntington	St Mary's Medical Center[a]	510007	99.23	96.43	98.89	87.69	97.88	91.25		63.16	99.86	851
WV	Huntington	Cabell Huntington Hospital[ac]	510055	Low sample (10 or less)	94.83	96.67	Low sample (10 or less)	91.43	100.00			98.41	91
WV	Morgantown	West Virginia University Hospitals[ab]	510001	100.00	100.00	100.00	100.00	100.00	100.00		75.00	98.82	498
WV	Morgantown	Monongalia County General Hospital[a]	510024	100.00	97.10	96.50	89.02	97.89	92.31	Low sample (10 or less)	58.97	99.60	327
WV	Weirton	Weirton Medical Center	510023	100.00	98.11	80.85	72.73	87.76	93.75		46.67	101.36	75

Note: The Centers for Medicare & Medicaid Services' Office of Research, Development, and Information (ORDI) strives to make information available to all. Nevertheless, portions of our files including charts, tables, and graphics may be difficult to read using assistive technology.

[a] Hospital received attainment award.

[b] Hospital received top performer award.

[c] Hospital received improvement award.

Date range = acute care inpatient discharges from October 1, 2006 to September 30, 2007.

Low sample (10 or less) = hospital provided service but had 10 eligible patients or less during this date range.

Data sorted by state (ascending order) and then city (ascending order).

Appendix B

Pneumonia
CMS/Premier Hospital Quality Incentive Demonstration Project—Year 4 Participants in Pneumonia (PN)

State	City	Hospital	CMS Certification Number	Oxygenation Assessment, % Patients Received	Pneumococcal Vaccination, % Patients Received	Blood Cultures Performed in the ED Prior to Initial Abx Received in Hospital, % Patients Received	Adult Smoking Cessation Advice/ Counseling, % Patients Received	Influenza Vaccination, % Patients Received	Initial Antibiotic Received Within 4 Hours of Hospital Arrival, % Patients Received	Initial Antibiotic Selection for Immunocompetent ICU and Non-ICU Patients, % Patients Received	Total Case Count
AL	Dothan	Southeast Alabama Medical Center[a]	010001	100.00	78.46	95.08	97.53	68.09	81.52	92.31	406
AL	Opelika	East Alabama Medical Center and Snf[a]	010029	99.48	91.26	93.18	100.00	93.33	86.18	94.39	289
AR	Mountain View	Stone County Medical Center[a]	041310	100.00	80.21	93.33	88.89	77.27	88.39	75.78	196
AR	Pine Bluff	Jefferson Regional Medical Center–Ar[a]	040071	99.14	77.78	80.33	100.00	56.06	80.00	88.11	439
CA	Apple Valley	St. Mary Medical Center[ab]	050300	99.49	94.76	90.04	93.52	90.11	91.98	84.15	580

CA	Bakersfield	San Joaquin Community Hospital[ab]	050455	100.00	92.90	94.97	98.61	96.15	83.15	93.92	417
CA	Escondido	Palomar Medical Center[ab]	050115	100.00	91.48	95.07	95.83	93.33	92.47	98.20	609
CA	Fullerton	St. Jude Medical Center[ab]	050168	99.68	90.73	90.64	86.44	100.00	87.61	92.04	486
CA	Gilroy	Saint Louise Regional Hospital[ab]	050688	100.00	66.33	91.11	94.74	71.11	90.74	91.09	195
CA	Glendale	Glendale Adventist Medical Center[ab]	050239	100.00	91.46	95.43	100.00	95.31	84.13	82.91	484
CA	Los Angeles	White Memorial Medical Center[ab]	050103	100.00	83.76	94.50	100.00	86.27	77.14	96.05	458
CA	Los Angeles	Saint Vincent Medical Center[ab]	050502	100.00	83.08	86.10	96.00	59.26	89.45	86.44	408
CA	Lynwood	St. Francis Medical Center[ab]	050104	99.57	93.29	89.42	100.00	84.21	59.79	99.02	358

(continued)

Pneumonia (continued)

CMS/Premier Hospital Quality Incentive Demonstration Project—Year 4 Participants in Pneumonia (PN)

State	City	Hospital	CMS Certification Number	Oxygenation Assessment, % Patients Received	Pneumococcal Vaccination, % Patients Received	Blood Cultures Performed in the ED Prior to Initial Abx Received in Hospital, % Patients Received	Adult Smoking Cessation Advice/ Counseling, % Patients Received	Influenza Vaccination, % Patients Received	Initial Antibiotic Received Within 4 Hours of Hospital Arrival, % Patients Received	Initial Antibiotic Selection for Immunocompetent ICU and Non-ICU Patients, % Patients Received	Total Case Count
CA	Orange	St. Joseph Hospital[ab]	050069	99.54	87.68	96.60	97.83	85.56	94.58	92.06	445
CA	Paradise	Feather River Hospital[ab]	050225	100.00	91.52	96.26	94.23	91.07	91.93	81.20	283
CA	Poway	Pomerado Hospital[ab]	050636	100.00	92.26	88.68	77.50	98.41	90.79	94.48	292
CA	Saint Helena	St. Helena Hospital[ab]	050013	100.00	86.05	96.43	100.00	89.47	91.49	96.67	93
CA	San Jose	O'Connor Hospital[ab]	050153	100.00	97.79	94.17	100.00	100.00	90.78	94.71	382
CA	Simi Valley	Simi Valley Hospital & Health Care Services[a]	050236	100.00	73.86	88.10	86.36	59.18	78.15	86.90	274
CA	Sonora	Sonora Regional Medical Center[a]	050335	100.00	83.73	88.60	91.30	80.77	89.20	93.57	246

CO	Grand Junction	St. Mary's Hospital and Medical Center[a]	060023	100.00	92.31	94.44	97.53	83.87	84.08	91.46	336
FL	Clearwater	Morton Plant Hospital[a]	100127	100.00	84.42	90.91	98.13	83.44	76.86	91.18	649
FL	Dunedin	Mease Healthcare Dunedin[a]	100043	100.00	81.62	92.98	100.00	85.00	91.45	93.00	269
FL	Hollywood	Memorial Regional Hospital[ab]	100038	100.00	99.12	94.09	98.83	99.34	92.29	96.35	786
FL	Homestead	Homestead Hospital[a]	100125	100.00	96.04	96.04	100.00	93.10	77.35	97.36	483
FL	Jacksonville	Baptist Medical Center[a]	100088	99.23	81.51	85.75	85.38	78.71	59.71	87.81	745
FL	Miami	Baptist Hospital of Miami Inc.[a]	100008	100.00	93.36	90.61	100.00	90.28	79.22	94.59	847
FL	Miami	South Miami Hospital[ab]	100154	100.00	98.60	97.78	100.00	96.74	91.02	93.83	469
FL	Miami Beach	Mount Sinai Medical Center	100034	97.02	68.79	90.20	97.30	50.81	67.90	82.71	572

(continued)

Pneumonia (continued)
CMS/Premier Hospital Quality Incentive Demonstration Project—Year 4
Participants in Pneumonia (PN)

State	City	Hospital	CMS Certification Number	Oxygenation Assessment, % Patients Received	Pneumococcal Vaccination, % Patients Received	Blood Cultures Performed in the ED Prior to Initial Abx Received in Hospital, % Patients Received	Adult Smoking Cessation Advice/ Counseling, % Patients Received	Influenza Vaccination, % Patients Received	Initial Antibiotic Received Within 4 Hours of Hospital Arrival, % Patients Received	Initial Antibiotic Selection for Immunocompetent ICU and Non-ICU Patients, % Patients Received	Total Case Count
FL	Naples	Naples Community Hospital[ab]	100018	99.82	87.78	86.36	94.96	42.42	67.51	88.25	839
FL	New Port Richey	Morton Plant North Bay Hospital[a]	100063	100.00	80.00	90.98	100.00	74.07	83.81	89.77	239
FL	Pembroke Pines	Memorial Hospital Pembroke[ab]	100230	100.00	99.45	97.91	100.00	100.00	96.61	97.45	400
FL	Pembroke Pines	Memorial Hospital West[ab]	100281	100.00	99.69	97.75	100.00	97.79	90.35	97.66	682
FL	Plant City	South Florida Baptist Hospital[a]	100132	100.00	87.31	97.06	98.51	86.21	89.92	81.48	308
FL	Safety Harbor	Morton Plant Mease Healthcare Countryside[a]	100265	100.00	88.39	94.06	98.65	85.95	81.90	90.05	547

FL	Saint Petersburg	St. Anthony's Hospital[a]	100067	99.65	77.78	91.30	97.98	78.26	82.38	93.23	444
FL	Tampa	St. Joseph's Hospital[a]	100075	100.00	72.49	71.27	98.52	61.05	71.47	93.12	825
FL	Tavernier	Mariners Hospital[ab]	100160	100.00	100.00	100.00	100.00	100.00	95.92	92.00	75
FL	Winter Haven	Winter Haven Hospital[a]	100052	99.75	89.84	93.19	94.00	90.91	69.86	86.22	680
GA	Baxley	Appling Hospital	110071	100.00	43.14	86.21	88.00	48.15	65.82	73.77	159
GA	La Grange	West Georgia Health System, Inc.[a]	110016	100.00	75.00	92.86	100.00	74.39	90.99	90.51	384
GA	Savannah	St. Joseph's Hospital[a]	110043	100.00	72.67	92.81	98.70	69.35	73.37	88.07	349
GA	Savannah	Memorial Health University Medical Center[a]	110036	100.00	85.11	97.92	85.71	78.95	82.81	89.66	240
GA	Savannah	Candler Hospital[a]	110024	100.00	78.46	88.68	100.00	71.54	77.67	90.11	608
IA	Council Bluffs	Alegent Health Mercy Hospital[ab]	160028	100.00	100.00	99.36	100.00	100.00	99.35	98.98	261

(continued)

Pneumonia (continued)

CMS/Premier Hospital Quality Incentive Demonstration Project—Year 4

Participants in Pneumonia (PN)

State	City	Hospital	CMS Certification Number	Oxygenation Assessment, % Patients Received	Pneumococcal Vaccination, % Patients Received	Blood Cultures Performed in the ED Prior to Initial Abx Received in Hospital, % Patients Received	Adult Smoking Cessation Advice/ Counseling, % Patients Received	Influenza Vaccination, % Patients Received	Initial Antibiotic Received Within 4 Hours of Hospital Arrival, % Patients Received	Initial Antibiotic Selection for Immunocompetent ICU and Non-ICU Patients, % Patients Received	Total Case Count
IA	Mason City	Mercy Medical Center–North Iowa[a]	160064	100.00	90.39	92.57	95.65	92.68	90.96	92.97	377
ID	Coeur D'Alene	Kootenai Medical Center[a]	130049	100.00	82.35	97.22	89.19	84.06	92.37	93.06	371
IL	Chicago	Mt. Sinai Hospital Medical Center[a,c]	140018	98.61	52.78	84.38	94.67	46.67	74.80	94.44	256
IL	Elmhurst	Elmhurst Memorial Hospital	140200	100.00	45.19	96.13	86.73	50.85	88.68	85.27	625
IL	Lincoln	Abraham Lincoln Memorial Hospital[a]	141322	100.00	90.38	100.00	88.24	86.67	94.34	95.45	97

IL	Peoria	Methodist Medical Center of Illinois[a]	140209	100.00	96.31	95.20	92.45	98.23	88.04	87.40	460
IL	Springfield	Memorial Medical Center[a]	140148	99.83	80.63	88.75	100.00	80.86	88.42	93.33	901
IL	Taylorville	St. Vincent Memorial Hospital[a]	141339	100.00	98.13	92.05	93.10	84.62	95.74	76.92	212
KS	Kansas City	Providence Medical Center[a]	170146	100.00	90.36	98.95	95.69	90.11	87.63	95.61	417
KS	Leavenworth	Saint John Hospital[a]	170009	100.00	72.97	98.08	100.00	90.91	82.81	81.82	120
KS	Topeka	St. Francis Health Center[a]	170016	100.00	94.87	92.25	89.36	90.10	86.94	95.24	442
KY	Ashland	Our Lady of Bellefonte Hospital[a]	180036	100.00	94.66	92.74	91.97	93.22	79.87	86.79	635
KY	Bowling Green	The Medical Center[a]	180013	100.00	89.97	92.20	99.55	91.88	74.62	82.77	729
KY	Lexington	Central Baptist Hospital[a]	180103	100.00	93.71	95.83	98.65	93.42	86.39	91.28	378

(continued)

Pneumonia (continued)
CMS/Premier Hospital Quality Incentive Demonstration Project—Year 4
Participants in Pneumonia (PN)

State	City	Hospital	CMS Certification Number	Oxygenation Assessment, % Patients Received	Pneumococcal Vaccination, % Patients Received	Blood Cultures Performed in the ED Prior to Initial Abx Received in Hospital, % Patients Received	Adult Smoking Cessation Advice/ Counseling, % Patients Received	Influenza Vaccination, % Patients Received	Initial Antibiotic Received Within 4 Hours of Hospital Arrival, % Patients Received	Initial Antibiotic Selection for Immunocompetent ICU and Non-ICU Patients, % Patients Received	Total Case Count
KY	Murray	Murray–Calloway County Hospital[a]	180027	99.07	69.57	91.45	89.23	76.39	79.19	78.85	304
KY	Paducah	Western Baptist Hospital[a]	180104	99.73	94.74	98.23	99.46	96.48	84.09	93.58	626
MA	Fall River	Southcoast Hospital Group, Inc.[a]	220074	100.00	89.90	88.43	91.01	88.25	76.60	92.56	1,858
MA	Pittsfield	Berkshire Medical Center Inc.[a]	220046	100.00	90.56	95.02	100.00	81.72	91.95	95.38	441
MA	Springfield	Baystate Medical Center[a]	220077	100.00	90.17	84.43	95.62	91.43	81.84	93.08	862
MD	Baltimore	Bon Secours Hospital[a]	210013	99.60	89.13	94.69	96.69	88.24	76.86	83.02	336

MD	Frederick	Frederick Memorial Hospital[ac]	210005	100.00	85.30	91.60	99.20	89.23	87.61	89.62	662
MD	Salisbury	Peninsula Regional Medical Center[a]	210019	100.00	75.09	92.40	97.59	79.17	83.46	89.78	536
MI	Grosse Pointe	Bon Secours Cottage Health Services	230089	98.87	71.69	87.90	92.86	71.59	70.74	82.25	412
MI	Lapeer	Lapeer Regional Medical Center[ba]	230193	100.00	97.04	93.00	100.00	98.77	93.33	95.63	362
MN	Burnsville	Fairview Ridges Hospital[a]	240207	99.61	86.49	92.07	80.65	87.30	84.07	88.72	371
MN	Edina	Fairview Southdale Hospital[a]	240078	100.00	89.57	98.63	98.48	88.52	87.15	92.96	557
MN	Minneapolis	University of Minnesota Medical Center[a]	240080	100.00	75.00	96.39	85.19	87.50	80.79	89.13	467
MN	Princeton	Fairview Northland Regional Hospital[ab]	240141	100.00	94.74	96.63	100.00	96.77	91.36	93.22	135

(continued)

Pneumonia (continued)
CMS/Premier Hospital Quality Incentive Demonstration Project—Year 4
Participants in Pneumonia (PN)

State	City	Hospital	CMS Certification Number	Oxygenation Assessment, % Patients Received	Pneumococcal Vaccination, % Patients Received	Blood Cultures Performed in the ED Prior to Initial Abx Received in Hospital, % Patients Received	Adult Smoking Cessation Advice/ Counseling, % Patients Received	Influenza Vaccination, % Patients Received	Initial Antibiotic Received Within 4 Hours of Hospital Arrival, % Patients Received	Initial Antibiotic Selection for Immunocompetent ICU and Non-ICU Patients, % Patients Received	Total Case Count
MN	Saint Louis Park	Methodist Hospital[a]	240053	100.00	83.40	96.48	100.00	78.07	84.26	95.27	832
MN	Winona	Winona Community Memorial Hospital[ab]	240044	100.00	98.08	94.29	92.59	100.00	92.98	95.65	156
MN	Wyoming	Fairview Lakes Regional Health Care[a]	240050	100.00	81.82	95.83	87.50	93.75	92.91	93.42	205
MO	Blue Springs	St. Mary's Medical Center[a]	260193	98.94	75.00	84.83	94.12	53.85	75.86	79.84	257
MO	Bridgeton	Ssm Depaul Health Center[a]	260104	100.00	90.37	96.31	98.18	92.36	80.70	92.34	782
MO	Kansas City	St. Joseph Medical Center[a]	260085	100.00	81.73	90.41	100.00	69.62	81.77	77.78	412

MO	Saint Joseph	Heartland Regional Medical Center[a]	260006	100.00	92.35	95.20	96.52	88.36	83.51	92.72	732
MO	Saint Louis	SSM St. Marys Health Center[a,c]	260091	100.00	90.22	92.74	92.00	84.93	72.64	96.68	619
MS	Meridian	Rush Foundation Hospital[a]	250069	100.00	75.41	91.55	89.58	81.48	78.82	90.14	161
MT	Billings	St. Vincent Healthcare[a,c]	270049	100.00	87.45	86.33	97.94	88.46	84.84	90.70	439
MT	Miles City	Holy Rosary Healthcare[a]	270002	100.00	86.90	92.31	80.00	87.10	94.00	88.07	149
MT	Missoula	St. Patrick Hospital and Health Sciences[a]	270014	100.00	96.05	93.02	94.00	94.20	88.19	87.06	276
NC	Albemarle	Stanly Regional Medical Center[a]	340119	100.00	92.21	99.32	86.21	93.33	82.01	87.38	310
NC	Asheboro	Randolph Hospital[a]	340123	100.00	90.00	94.69	89.66	87.88	85.44	87.80	240
NC	Asheville	Mission Hospitals, Inc.[a]	340002	100.00	78.84	93.73	98.49	79.34	80.80	90.76	1,132

(continued)

Pneumonia (continued)

CMS/Premier Hospital Quality Incentive Demonstration Project—Year 4

Participants in Pneumonia (PN)

State	City	Hospital	CMS Certification Number	Oxygenation Assessment, % Patients Received	Pneumococcal Vaccination, % Patients Received	Blood Cultures Performed in the ED Prior to Initial Abx Received in Hospital, % Patients Received	Adult Smoking Cessation Advice/ Counseling, % Patients Received	Influenza Vaccination, % Patients Received	Initial Antibiotic Received Within 4 Hours of Hospital Arrival, % Patients Received	Initial Antibiotic Selection for Immunocompetent ICU and Non-ICU Patients, % Patients Received	Total Case Count
NC	Boone	Watauga Medical Center[a]	340051	100.00	82.12	90.40	92.50	61.40	68.38	86.08	269
NC	Burlington	Alamance Regional Medical Center[a]	340070	99.63	93.00	97.66	95.40	92.41	81.30	90.36	388
NC	Clyde	Haywood Regional Medical Center	340025	99.45	60.34	77.59	94.21	70.00	67.38	83.41	485
NC	Durham	Duke University Hospital[a]	340030	100.00	100.00	95.83	100.00	100.00	79.01	95.70	515
NC	Durham	Durham Regional Hospital[a]	340155	100.00	82.97	97.47	91.94	84.76	87.08	96.55	494

NC	Fayetteville	Cape Fear Valley Medical Center[a]	340028	100.00	96.01	90.35	100.00	96.74	81.58	91.10	1,067
NC	Gastonia	Gaston Memorial Hospital[a,b]	340032	100.00	99.20	99.21	100.00	99.02	94.91	99.16	1,296
NC	Goldsboro	Wayne Memorial Hospital[a]	340010	100.00	77.04	97.66	100.00	75.95	70.83	95.54	414
NC	Hickory	Catawba Valley Medical Center[a]	340143	100.00	84.31	91.30	100.00	80.36	78.57	90.13	343
NC	Lumberton	Southeastern Regional Medical Center[a]	340050	100.00	87.22	92.93	100.00	71.82	54.85	91.81	604
NC	Pinehurst	Firsthealth Moore Regional Hospital[a,c]	340115	100.00	91.98	96.75	95.41	86.49	88.00	91.11	610
NC	Raleigh	Duke Health Raleigh Hospital[a]	340073	100.00	80.43	93.27	89.47	82.50	90.20	96.20	169
NC	Shelby	Cleveland Regional Medical Center[a]	340021	100.00	93.23	84.62	100.00	98.28	82.48	89.27	471

(continued)

Pneumonia (continued)
CMS/Premier Hospital Quality Incentive Demonstration Project—Year 4
Participants in Pneumonia (PN)

State	City	Hospital	CMS Certification Number	Oxygenation Assessment, % Patients Received	Pneumococcal Vaccination, % Patients Received	Blood Cultures Performed in the ED Prior to Initial Abx Received in Hospital, % Patients Received	Adult Smoking Cessation Advice/ Counseling, % Patients Received	Influenza Vaccination, % Patients Received	Initial Antibiotic Received Within 4 Hours of Hospital Arrival, % Patients Received	Initial Antibiotic Selection for Immunocompent ICU and Non-ICU Patients, % Patients Received	Total Case Count
NC	Sylva	Harris Regional Hospital, Inc[ac]	340016	100.00	85.33	95.90	98.68	68.85	93.92	82.58	397
NC	Wilmington	New Hanover Regional Medical Center[a]	340141	100.00	85.23	87.70	98.72	77.03	75.18	88.66	369
NC	Wilson	Wilson Medical Center	340126	99.61	58.96	86.16	98.77	69.23	75.73	91.89	424
NE	Fremont	Fremont Area Medical Center[ab]	280077	100.00	94.33	100.00	86.11	97.92	95.90	86.57	211
NE	Omaha	Alegent Health Immanuel Medical Center[ba]	280081	100.00	98.03	99.16	100.00	100.00	99.19	100.00	327

NE	Omaha	Alegent Health–Bergan Mercy Medical Center[ba]	280060	100.00	98.17	97.87	100.00	96.00	97.50	98.53	413
NE	Papillion	Alegent Health–Midlands Community Hospital[ab]	280105	100.00	100.00	98.00	100.00	100.00	96.27	100.00	232
NJ	Hackensack	Hackensack University Medical Center[ab]	310001	100.00	96.32	99.62	96.35	94.02	97.05	99.35	989
NY	Bay Shore	Southside Hospital[ab]	330043	100.00	94.57	94.01	100.00	93.88	93.15	96.58	240
NY	Brockport	Lakeside Memorial Hospital[ac]	330037	100.00	57.78	94.69	96.43	55.56	80.00	86.84	174
NY	Bronx	St. Barnabas Hospital[ab]	330399	100.00	93.48	93.91	100.00	96.61	94.49	99.16	458
NY	Elmira	Arnot Ogden Medical Center[a]	330090	100.00	91.73	94.14	97.10	90.24	83.04	91.89	420

(continued)

Pneumonia (continued)
CMS/Premier Hospital Quality Incentive Demonstration Project—Year 4 Participants in Pneumonia (PN)

State	City	Hospital	CMS Certification Number	Oxgenation Assessment, % Patients Received	Pneumococcal Vaccination, % Patients Received	Blood Cultures Performed in the ED Prior to Initial Abx Received in Hospital, % Patients Received	Adult Smoking Cessation Advice/ Counseling, % Patients Received	Influenza Vaccination, % Patients Received	Initial Antibiotic Received Within 4 Hours of Hospital Arrival, % Patients Received	Initial Antibiotic Selection for Immunocompetent ICU and Non-ICU Patients, % Patients Received	Total Case Count
NY	Forest Hills	Ns-Lij Hs-North Shore University Hospital at Forest Hills[a]	330353	100.00	90.23	94.41	93.75	80.85	93.70	92.39	240
NY	Glen Cove	Ns-Lij Hs-North Shore University Hospital at Glen Cove[a]	330181	99.39	84.11	98.05	100.00	95.65	93.23	82.22	240
NY	Huntington	Huntington Hospital[a]	330045	99.38	88.68	94.41	96.30	93.33	89.76	98.02	240
NY	Manhasset	Ns-Lij Hs-North Shore University Hospital[a]	330106	100.00	84.18	98.58	100.00	75.51	98.37	95.83	266

NY	New Hyde Park	Long Island Jewish Medical Center[ac]	330195	100.00	88.79	97.86	92.31	87.10	88.62	91.40	240
NY	Plainview	Ns-Lij Hs-North Shore University Hospital at Plainview[a]	330331	100.00	94.30	98.78	100.00	100.00	95.74	94.95	240
NY	Port Jervis	Bon Secours Community Hospital[ac]	330135	100.00	94.06	97.32	100.00	94.29	93.94	95.89	191
NY	Rochester	Rochester General Hospital[ac]	330125	100.00	87.21	95.45	99.31	94.57	73.27	94.21	782
NY	Schenectady	St Clare's Hospital[ac]	330066	100.00	87.43	98.12	85.94	88.24	90.00	96.85	325
NY	Staten Island	Staten Island University Hospital[ab]	330160	100.00	98.36	98.26	97.87	100.00	88.80	94.20	263
NY	Suffern	Good Samaritan Hospital of Suffern[a]	330158	99.77	76.90	88.47	96.92	81.29	70.91	80.56	735
NY	Valley Stream	Franklin Hospital Med Ctr[ab]	330372	100.00	89.29	99.27	96.00	89.74	95.08	97.78	240

(continued)

Pneumonia (continued)
CMS/Premier Hospital Quality Incentive Demonstration Project—Year 4
Participants in Pneumonia (PN)

State	City	Hospital	CMS Certification Number	Oxygenation Assessment, % Patients Received	Pneumococcal Vaccination, % Patients Received	Blood Cultures Performed in the ED Prior to Initial Abx Received in Hospital, % Patients Received	Adult Smoking Cessation Advice/Counseling, % Patients Received	Influenza Vaccination, % Patients Received	Initial Antibiotic Received Within 4 Hours of Hospital Arrival, % Patients Received	Initial Antibiotic Selection for Immunocompetent ICU and Non-ICU Patients, % Patients Received	Total Case Count
NY	Warwick	St. Anthony Community Hospital[a]	330205	100.00	81.82	92.42	95.65	63.64	89.74	91.53	164
OH	Akron	Summa Health Systems Hospitals[a]	360020	99.67	75.94	86.56	70.32	74.78	83.95	90.14	1,065
OH	Dayton	Grandview Hospital & Medical Center[a,c]	360133	100.00	80.25	96.36	98.51	79.81	91.18	90.54	506
OH	Kettering	Kettering Medical Center[a]	360079	100.00	93.22	98.33	100.00	94.66	77.86	96.15	665
OH	Lorain	Community Health Partners of Oh-West[a]	360172	100.00	91.46	95.77	86.71	93.55	86.71	96.65	665
OH	Miamisburg	Sycamore Hospital[a,b]	360239	100.00	96.02	98.74	100.00	95.77	89.16	99.12	346

OH	Springfield	Mercy Medical Center of Springfield[a]	360086	99.17	89.07	77.50	100.00	87.10	83.26	86.92	540
OH	Toledo	St. Vincent Mercy Medical Center[a]	360112	100.00	71.89	89.67	100.00	76.00	79.41	89.55	471
OK	Oklahoma City	St. Anthony Hospital[ac]	370037	100.00	91.14	92.34	99.38	95.60	89.78	97.33	558
OK	Tulsa	Saint Francis Hospital, Inc.[a]	370091	100.00	97.24	93.47	99.68	95.67	78.16	89.45	1,488
OK	Tulsa	St. Francis Hospital South[ab]	370218	100.00	100.00	96.72	100.00	94.74	93.75	91.76	197
OR	Medford	Rogue Valley Medical Center[a]	380018	100.00	77.25	95.17	88.31	75.31	85.58	91.55	391
OR	Portland	Adventist Medical Center[a]	380060	100.00	87.11	93.36	92.73	89.47	87.50	91.72	429
PA	Bethlehem	St. Lukes Hospital Network[a]	390049	100.00	77.88	93.75	100.00	81.71	87.00	85.38	804
PA	Bryn Mawr	Main Line Health–Bryn Mawr Hospital[a]	390139	100.00	88.24	96.51	100.00	84.09	91.04	96.15	410

(continued)

Pneumonia (continued)
CMS/Premier Hospital Quality Incentive Demonstration Project—Year 4
Participants in Pneumonia (PN)

State	City	Hospital	CMS Certification Number	Oxygenation Assessment, % Patients Received	Pneumococcal Vaccination, % Patients Received	Blood Cultures Performed in the ED Prior to Initial Abx Received in Hospital, % Patients Received	Adult Smoking Cessation Advice/ Counseling, % Patients Received	Influenza Vaccination, % Patients Received	Initial Antibiotic Received Within 4 Hours of Hospital Arrival, % Patients Received	Initial Antibiotic Selection for Immunocompetent ICU and Non-ICU Patients, % Patients Received	Total Case Count
PA	Erie	Saint Vincent Health Center[a]	390009	100.00	95.45	95.00	97.03	84.16	82.63	91.86	499
PA	Meadville	Meadville Medical Center[a]	390113	100.00	86.61	92.71	95.12	72.73	83.96	98.67	229
PA	Paoli	Main Line Hospitals– Paoli Memorial Hospital[a]	390153	100.00	92.23	96.34	100.00	96.30	88.46	96.48	298
PA	Philadelphia	Thomas Jefferson University Hospital[ac]	390174	99.82	68.31	84.57	96.36	70.90	72.05	87.38	859
PA	Philadelphia	Frankford Hospital[ac]	390115	99.87	99.23	93.25	96.88	92.78	83.67	93.66	1,126

PA	Philadelphia	Albert Einstein Medical Center[a]	390142	100.00	92.38	94.15	100.00	95.70	89.82	98.60	561
PA	Wynnewood	Main Line Health–Lankenau Hospital[a]	390195	100.00	89.35	97.07	100.00	78.26	82.70	92.40	463
SC	Anderson	Anmed Health[a]	420027	100.00	97.16	96.97	98.97	91.04	80.04	93.43	1,135
SC	Columbia	Palmetto Health Baptist[a,c]	420086	100.00	97.28	92.76	97.94	93.55	88.21	86.39	383
SC	Columbia	Palmetto Health Richland[a]	420018	99.52	90.91	88.73	97.83	93.85	81.76	88.68	403
SC	Conway	Conway Medical Center[a,c]	420049	99.58	93.66	93.18	100.00	90.48	88.14	92.67	333
SC	Easley	Palmetto Health Baptist Easley[a,b]	420015	100.00	100.00	99.45	98.89	98.61	95.21	92.24	330
SC	Florence	Mcleod Regional Medical Center[a]	420051	100.00	79.12	96.32	98.71	78.99	83.43	92.08	664

(continued)

Pneumonia (continued)
CMS/Premier Hospital Quality Incentive Demonstration Project—Year 4
Participants in Pneumonia (PN)

State	City	Hospital	CMS Certification Number	Oxygenation Assessment, % Patients Received	Pneumococcal Vaccination, % Patients Received	Blood Cultures Performed in the ED Prior to Initial Abx Received in Hospital, % Patients Received	Adult Smoking Cessation Advice/ Counseling, % Patients Received	Influenza Vaccination, % Patients Received	Initial Antibiotic Received Within 4 Hours of Hospital Arrival, % Patients Received	Initial Antibiotic Selection for Immunocompetent ICU and Non-ICU Patients, % Patients Received	Total Case Count
SC	Greenville	Greenville Memorial Hospital[ab]	420078	99.72	92.88	84.85	100.00	92.97	82.33	92.51	681
SC	Greenville	St. Francis Hospital[a]	420023	100.00	89.71	91.26	100.00	93.23	87.50	94.68	594
SC	Greenwood	Self Regional Healthcare[a]	420071	100.00	95.65	93.81	98.75	93.33	86.27	91.89	390
SC	Greer	Allen Bennett Memorial Hospital[a]	420033	100.00	94.07	90.53	100.00	95.45	92.38	95.50	211
SC	Simpsonville	Hillcrest Hospital[ab]	420037	100.00	92.13	90.83	100.00	100.00	95.74	100.00	178
SD	Aberdeen	Avera St. Luke's[a]	430014	100.00	93.60	98.89	100.00	85.71	92.45	95.31	221
SD	Mitchell	Avera Queen of Peace[ab]	430013	100.00	100.00	98.11	100.00	100.00	96.39	93.18	303

SD	Rapid City	Rapid City Regional Hospital[ac]	430077	100.00	97.00	83.97	100.00	92.59	90.94	93.03	511
SD	Sioux Falls	Avera Mckennan Hospital & University Health Center[ab]	430016	100.00	95.41	97.30	100.00	94.37	89.77	92.98	393
SD	Yankton	Avera Sacred Heart Hospital[ab]	430012	100.00	97.56	98.70	100.00	94.00	93.65	94.92	219
TN	Elizabethton	Sycamore Shoals Hospital[a]	440018	100.00	98.11	91.95	100.00	100.00	77.55	84.09	216
TN	Johnson City	Johnson City Medical Center[a]	440063	100.00	80.00	66.32	98.41	77.50	80.95	91.46	245
TN	Johnson City	Northside Hospital[a]	440184	100.00	90.28	92.31	100.00	96.43	79.78	79.31	173
TN	Kingsport	Indian Path Medical Center[a]	440176	100.00	96.43	95.12	96.67	95.65	88.18	91.76	240
TN	Memphis	Methodist Healthcare Memphis Hospitals[ac]	440049	99.80	86.87	93.33	99.27	84.97	81.02	90.20	1,677

(continued)

Pneumonia (continued)
CMS/Premier Hospital Quality Incentive Demonstration Project—Year 4
Participants in Pneumonia (PN)

State	City	Hospital	CMS Certification Number	Oxygenation Assessment, % Patients Received	Pneumococcal Vaccination, % Patients Received	Blood Cultures Performed in the ED Prior to Initial Abx Received in Hospital, % Patients Received	Adult Smoking Cessation Advice/Counseling, % Patients Received	Influenza Vaccination, % Patients Received	Initial Antibiotic Received Within 4 Hours of Hospital Arrival, % Patients Received	Initial Antibiotic Selection for Immunocompetent ICU and Non-ICU Patients, % Patients Received	Total Case Count
TN	Somerville	Methodist Healthcare Fayette Hospital[a]	440168	100.00	97.06	89.19	94.44	100.00	93.33	86.84	74
TX	Allen	Presbyterian Hospital of Allen[a]	450840	100.00	95.06	95.54	100.00	91.67	91.59	85.33	152
TX	Arlington	Arlington Memorial Hospital[a]	450064	100.00	85.55	97.45	82.58	71.60	88.11	87.36	743
TX	Azle	Harris Methodist Northwest[ab]	450419	100.00	97.92	95.08	96.81	95.16	98.93	93.70	253
TX	Bedford	Harris Methodist H E B Hospital[a]	450639	100.00	94.74	91.21	98.28	95.49	90.86	91.17	615
TX	Cleburne	Walls Regional Hospital[ab]	450148	100.00	96.89	97.71	100.00	97.18	91.26	92.90	315

TX	Dallas	Methodist Dallas Medical Center[ac]	450051	99.54	93.13	95.34	98.97	82.14	84.48	91.97	359
TX	Dallas	Presbyterian Hospital of Dallas[a]	450462	100.00	90.49	96.04	100.00	93.53	91.84	90.45	525
TX	Dallas	Methodist Charlton Medical Center[ac]	450723	99.49	87.50	88.68	100.00	95.24	88.27	95.37	330
TX	Denison	Texoma Medical Center[ab]	450324	100.00	96.71	95.39	97.80	94.44	92.13	98.35	368
TX	Fort Worth	Harris Methodist Fort Worth[a]	450135	100.00	90.39	94.41	95.54	90.55	88.63	83.63	1,238
TX	Fort Worth	Harris Methodist Southwest[a]	450779	100.00	90.30	93.71	100.00	92.59	90.60	89.87	455
TX	Harlingen	Valley Baptist Medical Center[a]	450033	99.77	80.95	90.40	97.59	71.09	83.24	86.45	818
TX	Kaufman	Presbyterian Hospital of Kaufman[a]	450292	100.00	90.82	95.05	86.36	97.30	92.23	74.67	174

(continued)

Pneumonia (continued)
CMS/Premier Hospital Quality Incentive Demonstration Project—Year 4
Participants in Pneumonia (PN)

State	City	Hospital	CMS Certification Number	Oxygenation Assessment, % Patients Received	Pneumococcal Vaccination, % Patients Received	Blood Cultures Performed in the ED Prior to Initial Abx Received in Hospital, % Patients Received	Adult Smoking Cessation Advice/ Counseling, % Patients Received	Influenza Vaccination, % Patients Received	Initial Antibiotic Received Within 4 Hours of Hospital Arrival, % Patients Received	Initial Antibiotic Selection for Immunocompetent ICU and Non-ICU Patients, % Patients Received	Total Case Count
TX	Livingston	Memorial Medical Center Livingston	450395	99.18	72.41	76.56	85.94	75.00	72.97	76.04	181
TX	Lufkin	Memorial Medical Center of East Texas[a]	450211	100.00	78.86	87.23	98.98	89.36	78.07	79.75	240
TX	Plano	Presbyterian Hospital of Plano[a]	450771	100.00	86.67	90.99	96.08	87.10	91.51	87.23	237
TX	Stephenville	Harris Methodist Erath County[a]	450351	98.83	88.33	96.30	94.83	78.95	92.68	81.32	215
TX	Tomball	Tomball Regional Hospital	450670	98.78	80.50	73.99	99.14	83.48	75.38	71.77	536

State	City	Hospital	ID								Count
TX	Victoria	Citizens Medical Center[a]	450023	100.00	86.34	93.39	80.52	94.92	80.00	92.25	358
TX	Winnsboro	Presbyterian Hospital of Winnsboro[a]	450224	100.00	95.24	97.62	92.31	86.67	88.10	87.10	60
VA	Chesapeake	Chesapeake General Hospital[ac]	490120	100.00	93.28	94.38	96.95	97.14	82.86	92.82	622
VA	Galax	Twin County Regional Hospital[ac]	490115	100.00	95.12	92.12	100.00	96.61	90.91	90.74	270
VA	Gloucester	Riverside Walter Reed Hospital[a]	490130	99.33	87.04	86.29	90.32	91.18	82.05	89.68	200
VA	Mechanicsville	Bon Secours–Memorial Regional Medical[ab]	490069	100.00	98.60	98.07	100.00	95.20	93.45	96.02	577
VA	Newport News	Bon Secours–Mary Immaculate Hospital[a]	490041	100.00	71.05	94.95	100.00	74.47	81.25	94.59	232
VA	Newport News	Riverside Regional Medical Center[a]	490052	100.00	89.91	87.68	98.67	62.35	74.75	95.52	455

(continued)

Pneumonia (continued)
CMS/Premier Hospital Quality Incentive Demonstration Project—Year 4
Participants in Pneumonia (PN)

State	City	Hospital	CMS Certification Number	Oxygenation Assessment, % Patients Received	Pneumococcal Vaccination, % Patients Received	Blood Cultures Performed in the ED Prior to Initial Abx Received in Hospital, % Patients Received	Adult Smoking Cessation Advice/ Counseling, % Patients Received	Influenza Vaccination, % Patients Received	Initial Antibiotic Received Within 4 Hours of Hospital Arrival, % Patients Received	Initial Antibiotic Selection for Immunocompetent ICU and Non-ICU Patients, % Patients Received	Total Case Count
VA	Norfolk	Bon Secours– Depaul Medical Center[a]	490011	100.00	93.23	90.91	100.00	88.10	81.63	91.09	293
VA	Portsmouth	Bon Secours Maryview Medical Center[a]	490017	100.00	90.78	89.56	100.00	95.60	67.61	89.21	420
VA	Richmond	Bon Secours– Richmond Community Hospital[ac]	490094	100.00	73.33	85.00	100.00	Low Sample (10 or less)	77.78	84.62	86
VA	Richmond	Bon Secours–St. Marys Hospital of Richm[ba]	490059	100.00	99.07	94.27	100.00	98.67	88.07	94.89	419

VA	South Hill	Community Mem Healthcenter[ac]	490098	100.00	97.27	87.91	100.00	95.24	87.25	89.39	224
VA	Tappahannock	Riverside Tappahannock Hosp Inc.[a]	490084	100.00	92.73	93.62	100.00	94.12	77.19	95.74	107
WA	Chewelah	St. Joseph's Hospital of Chewelah[ab]	501309	100.00	97.30	93.33	100.00	Low Sample (10 or less)	88.57	96.30	82
WA	Colville	Mount Carmel Hospital[a]	501326	100.00	93.42	97.96	88.46	95.00	87.10	90.00	142
WA	Spokane	Holy Family Hospital[ac]	500077	100.00	91.80	96.13	92.47	84.47	84.47	88.32	482
WA	Spokane	Sacred Heart Medical Center[a]	500054	100.00	81.01	93.60	99.22	79.07	80.38	88.73	642
WA	Walla Walla	St Mary Medical Center[ac]	500002	100.00	78.57	98.10	100.00	47.83	90.20	98.46	189
WI	Burlington	Memorial Hospital of Burlington[ab]	520059	100.00	96.88	98.90	100.00	100.00	97.80	95.77	170
WI	Elkhorn	Aurora Lakeland Medical Center[ab]	520102	100.00	98.61	98.51	100.00	100.00	96.50	98.91	219

(continued)

Pneumonia (continued)
CMS/Premier Hospital Quality Incentive Demonstration Project—Year 4
Participants in Pneumonia (PN)

State	City	Hospital	CMS Certification Number	Oxygenation Assessment, % Patients Received	Pneumococcal Vaccination, % Patients Received	Blood Cultures Performed in the ED Prior to Initial Abx Received in Hospital, % Patients Received	Adult Smoking Cessation Advice/ Counseling, % Patients Received	Influenza Vaccination, % Patients Received	Initial Antibiotic Received Within 4 Hours of Hospital Arrival, % Patients Received	Initial Antibiotic Selection for Immunocompetent ICU and Non-ICU Patients, % Patients Received	Total Case Count
WI	Green Bay	Aurora Baycare Medical Center[ab]	520193	100.00	92.16	98.11	100.00	100.00	96.08	94.74	138
WI	Hartford	Aurora Medical Center of Washington County[ab]	520038	100.00	92.96	100.00	100.00	96.30	98.75	95.74	116
WI	Kenosha	Aurora Medical Center Kenosha[ab]	520189	100.00	100.00	99.08	100.00	100.00	99.11	98.57	208
WI	Madison	St. Mary's Hospital Medical Center[a]	520083	100.00	63.61	90.73	87.23	72.50	77.18	90.05	584
WI	Milwaukee	St. Lukes Medical Center[a]	520138	99.65	81.57	96.11	100.00	86.33	92.01	94.98	1,526

WI	Milwaukee	Aurora Sinai Medical Center[ab]	520064	100.00	93.51	96.15	100.00	87.50	93.37	95.65	257
WI	Sheboygan	Aurora Sheboygan Memorial Medical Center[ab]	520035	100.00	94.57	95.29	100.00	97.30	93.48	95.65	169
WI	Two Rivers	Aurora Medical Center Manitowoc County[ab]	520034	100.00	97.06	96.83	100.00	100.00	94.52	93.75	119
WI	West Allis	West Allis Memorial Hospital[a]	520139	100.00	92.84	98.38	99.07	87.07	92.02	91.52	558
WV	Bluefield	Bluefield Regional Medical Center[a]	510071	97.84	67.03	94.48	90.20	25.00	76.44	86.62	322
WV	Charleston	Charleston Area Medical Center[a]	510022	99.66	83.61	91.74	98.54	80.98	73.88	88.86	1,056
WV	Clarksburg	United Hospital Center[ab]	510006	100.00	95.71	98.85	100.00	88.65	92.28	95.44	740
WV	Huntington	Cabell Huntington Hospital[ac]	510055	100.00	87.84	86.89	92.08	94.55	75.38	97.46	369

(continued)

Pneumonia (continued)
CMS/Premier Hospital Quality Incentive Demonstration Project—Year 4
Participants in Pneumonia (PN)

State	City	Hospital	CMS Certification Number	Oxygenation Assessment, % Patients Received	Pneumococcal Vaccination, % Patients Received	Blood Cultures Performed in the ED Prior to Initial Abx Received in Hospital, % Patients Received	Adult Smoking Cessation Advice/ Counseling, % Patients Received	Influenza Vaccination, % Patients Received	Initial Antibiotic Received Within 4 Hours of Hospital Arrival, % Patients Received	Initial Antibiotic Selection for Immunocompetent ICU and Non-ICU Patients, % Patients Received	Total Case Count
WV	Huntington	St. Mary's Medical Center[a]	510007	100.00	82.72	83.15	98.02	78.08	74.18	94.43	770
WV	Morgantown	Monongalia County General Hospital[a]	510024	100.00	94.00	96.85	93.75	94.00	90.91	95.58	291
WV	Morgantown	West Virginia University Hospitals[a]	510001	100.00	82.86	96.88	100.00	82.05	78.68	91.55	469
WV	Weirton	Weirton Medical Center[ab]	510023	99.41	93.43	97.97	100.00	97.37	91.20	94.97	514

Note: The Centers for Medicare & Medicaid Services' Office of Research, Development, and Information (ORDI) strives to make information available to all. Nevertheless, portions of our files including charts, tables, and graphics may be difficult to read using assistive technology.

a Hospital received attainment award.
b Hospital received top performer award.
c Hospital received improvement award.

Date range = acute care inpatient discharges from October 1, 2006 to September 30, 2007.

Low sample (10 or less) = hospital provided service, but had ten (10) eligible patients or less during this date range.

Data sorted by state (ascending order) and then city (ascending order).

Index